George H. Quester
NUCLEAR MONOPOLY

George H. Quester

NUCLEAR MONOPOLY

TRANSACTION PUBLISHERS
New Brunswick (U.S.A.) and London (U.K.)

Library of Congress Catalog Number: 00-030271
ISBN: 0-7658-0022-5
Printed in the United States of America

Library of Congress Cataloging-in-Publication Data

Questor, George H.
    Nuclear monopoly / George H. Questor.
        p. cm.
    Includes bibliographical references and index.
    ISBN 0-7658-0022-5 (alk. paper)
    1. Nuclear weapons—United States. 2. United States—Military policy.
3. Deterrence (Strategy)—History—20th century. 4. World politics—1945-
1955. I. Title.

UA23 .Q4723 2000
355.02'17'0973—dc21   00-030271

Contents

For Aline

Acknowledgements

For the ideas presented in this book, the author is indebted to a very large number of students and colleagues, over a long period of time, in particular to the students at Cornell University, UCLA, the National War College, the University of Maryland, and the United States Naval Academy (the students to whom this paradox of 1945 to 1949 has again and again been presented for discussion, as part of outlining the basic logic of today's nuclear deterrence), and to faculty seminar colleagues at all the same institutions and at the Institute for Defense Analyses.

It should be made clear at the outset that these audiences contributed particularly much to the array of "arguments against" preventive war, substantially expanding the list of such arguments (even perhaps to the point of logical fratricide, where such arguments could contradict and negate each other, leaving the non-use of the American nuclear monopoly as much of a puzzle as ever).

Even more than in what has become a standard disclaimer with other books, the portions of this book that readers find shocking and disagree with should thus be blamed on the author, rather than on all these students and colleagues.

As ever, special thanks have to be directed to my spouse, Aline, who never tires of her work, and hence leaves anyone around her incapable of tiring of a logical puzzle.

1

Introduction

The intention of this book is to sort the realities, and the "lessons" and myths, of a very peculiar period in the history of nuclear deterrence—the years from 1945 to 1949, when only the United States had nuclear weapons.

When strategic analysts discussed nuclear deterrence and mutual assured destruction from the 1950s to the 1990s, they stressed again and again how important it was for *each* side to have an assured ability to strike back at the cities of the other. Yet what then explains the lack of war, and lack of imminent expectation of nuclear war, in the years when the USSR had no such ability vis-à-vis the United States?

At the very least, there has been a fundamental gap between two of our intuitions here: first, the intuition by which mutual assured destruction must indeed be *mutual*, so that anything threatening the Soviet grip on American cities (whether this was to be some surprisingly successful version of SDI, or the hard-target, silo-busting accuracies of the MX) was to be cautioned against, and second our intuition about the years between 1945 and 1949, whereby the U.S. "of course" did not consider preventive war.

The goal is to explore the logic of these intuitions more fully, against the background of the facts of these years, and against the evidence we have on the thoughts entertained about choices at the time.

If most Americans remember these years as somehow proving something good about their own country, that is, that we are unusually peace loving or trustworthy, this may be an important part of the self-image and psychological baggage we carried into all the later rounds of arms confrontations and arms control discussions. But we, in the same memory, may then assume that Stalin's Soviet Union (or any Soviet Union) would have behaved very differently if the situation had been reversed, if Moscow alone had possessed such weapons.

For just one illustration of the later relevance of such memories, some versions of President Reagan's Strategic Defense Initiative (SDI)[1] would indeed have aspired to return the world to the situation of 1948, as U.S. cities would become safe against Soviet nuclear attack, while Soviet cities would not have such protection against American attack (this was often cited by Soviet critics of SDI as violating the basic assumptions of mutual deterrence.)[2] President Reagan then at times suggested that such protection would in turn be offered to Soviet cities as well, in effect returning the world to the nuclear situation of 1938; if anyone were to question American sincerity, suspecting that the U.S. would not let go of a monopoly of nuclear threats against its opponent, but might instead exploit this monopoly, Reagan and other Americans could have responded by noting the years from 1945 to 1949, the years we are discussing here.

For a very different illustration of a later relevance, we will also have to consider the possibility that the U.S. was deterred from an exploitation of the nuclear monopoly simply and definitively by the vulnerability of Western Europe to a Soviet conventional invasion. As will be discussed, this "Occam's Razor" explanation has many problems.

If such an explanation for American restraint were to be at all correct, however, then Moscow would already have been attributing to the United States a very strong and altruistic identification with Europe ever since 1945 (what we sometimes were later to label the "status of the fifty-first state"). When doubts were voiced on whether the U.S. willingness to defend Europe was credible to Moscow,[3] whether extended nuclear deterrence was workable, this history would have been quite relevant, for what was "an extension" of the U.S. for one purpose should be so for other purposes as well.

This book will thus focus on how we *should* remember these years of U.S. nuclear monopoly, but also on how we *do* remember this time. Relating these years to more general strategic discussions, this author remains convinced that the distinction between monopoly and anything else is the only crucial distinction here for comparisons of nuclear forces, with any later distinctions among "superiority" for the U.S., and "parity" and "superiority" for the Soviet Union, paling by comparison, or being basically indefinable and meaningless.

Even a few nuclear weapons in the hands of an adversary like Stalin's Russia, it will be argued here, are sufficient to deter, once one has had a look at the photographs of what happened at Hiroshima and Nagasaki.

This is indeed the viewpoint stressed by many of today's advocates of substantial nuclear disarmament, calling for "finite deterrence," for reductions in the United States nuclear arsenal well below the level of 3,000 or so projected by President Bush.[4] Yet this is always a double-edged message, for if the U.S. needs so few to deter, North Korea or Iran may similarly only need a few to deter. And Stalin only needed a few to deter. For most purposes, the period that is so crucially interesting thus lasts only four years, from August of 1945 to September of 1949.

Why exactly did the United States not then use this monopoly to force some major political concessions on the Soviet Union, perhaps even to force on Moscow what was imposed on Tokyo and Berlin, a surrender and disarmament and democratization? Or why was the monopoly not at least used to perpetuate itself, to retain and maintain whatever advantages stemmed from our being able to bomb Leningrad or Moscow with no fear of nuclear retaliation against Washington or New York? In retrospect, the monopoly could thus at least have been used to impose a *nuclear* disarmament on the Soviets, precluding the prospect of thermonuclear war between the superpowers, the prospect that afterward so plausibly threatened the survival of all mankind.

These were the years when Bertrand Russell was not the only person proposing that such a monopoly should be exploited while it was at hand, rather than being allowed to become a duopoly and nuclear confrontation. While Russell, as we shall discuss, was later to minimize the seriousness of his suggestions, with his role in the 1950s shifting to directing blame at U.S. foreign and defense policy, his advocacy of a preventive war immediately after 1945 was fully articulated, going well past the casual or "throwaway" remark.[5]

In retrospect, would the United States not have done a tremendous service for the peace and well-being of the world if it had been ready to threaten and execute a preventive nuclear war, in effect treating the Soviet Union as it had treated Japan and would have treated Germany, ready to destroy cities one after another, until such cities were given the benefits of a free-election system?

Atomic bombs are horrible, but one atomic bomb a week is far less horrible than the prospect of thousands of thermonuclear weapons being fired on the first day of a World War III. And the democratization and economic liberalization Russia experienced after 1991 could have been begun forty years earlier.

One must thus generally regard the years of the U.S. nuclear monopoly as insufficiently analyzed, with the explanations for what happened then, and for what has happened since, being underdeveloped and underdetermined. If we think that it is "easy" to explain Truman's failure to use his atomic bombs against Stalin, then it would not be "so easy to understand" Soviet concerns about SDI or about any American developments of counter-force weaponry. Conversely, if one finds it axiomatic that the Soviets had to oppose any U.S. development of counter-force weaponry, any and all threats to their nuclear retaliatory capabilities, the years from 1945 to 1949 again become more of a puzzle.

Each side has lived in the fear that the other would strive to accomplish a monopoly of nuclear strike force, if it could. This is in the tradition of military planning as presented by Clausewitz or Mahan or Douhet. Then why was the U.S. nuclear monopoly allowed to expire in just four years, as compared with the British naval monopoly after Trafalgar, which established Pax Britannica for almost a century, or with the Roman monopoly on effective military power, which established a Pax Romana for three or four centuries? The nuclear underpinnings of a Pax Americana were allowed to erode by 1949, at least as NSC-68 (and many other analyses at the beginning of the 1950s) viewed the realities; and a fuller assessment of the implications of this remains to be undertaken.

Three Views of American Foreign Policy

Always one of the most important factors here will be the inferences Americans and others would draw later from such assessments of the atomic monopoly, inferences about American national character and about the origins of the Cold War confrontation. The flattering self-estimate for why the monopoly was allowed to pass is consistent with equally flattering self-estimates on where the blame should be placed for the post-1945 emergence of the Cold War.

At the risk of major over-simplification, one could outline three major interpretations of United States foreign policy, not just for the short period of the American nuclear monopoly, from 1945 to 1949, but for all of the Cold War, and for the years before, and the years since.

One such interpretation would be that of scholars like Hans Morgenthau [6] and Kenneth Waltz,[7] and of many others studying international relations, a "realist" interpretation by which all countries basically behave the same in the anarchic international arena, seeking power for themselves, or at the minimum having to fear the accumulation of excessive power in the hands of other states. By such an interpretation, it makes little difference for foreign policy whether a state is democratic or Marxist or fascist, or traditional, in its domestic structure. The United States, by this kind of an analysis, is an "ordinary country," motivated by the same drives as other countries, no better and no worse in its impact on the welfare of other states.

Such a "realist" or "neo-realist" interpretation is popular, as noted, among scholars who specialize in international relations, and it is also popular with professional diplomats around the world. It is a view that many Europeans would have regarded as elementarily sensible.

A second interpretation is what could be called a Marxist or "radical" interpretation of American foreign policy, the view that was taught, to the exclusion of all others, in the universities of the Soviet Union and Eastern Europe before 1989, and is still taught in North Korea and Cuba. It is also a view which still draws a wide following, without any state dictation and pressure behind it, in the universities of Latin America and Western Europe, and also in Japan and much of the third world, and it is a view that captured a wide following among professors and students at universities within the United States itself, during and after the Vietnam War.

This is an interpretation that sees wars and aggressive foreign policy as being caused by the inherent defects of capitalism.[8] Since the United States is the most capitalist country in the world, by this kind of analysis, it is an unusually troublesome country, provoking other states by gunboat diplomacy and excessive military spending. International security problems, in this view, are indeed closely tied to the domestic nature of the societies involved, something the "realists" very much questioned. Domestic problems cause international problems, and the greatest domestic problems of all are those of capitalism.

A third interpretation is instead what most Americans would have found plausible, explicitly or at least implicitly, for most of the period until the Vietnam War, and then even afterward, a view by which the United States has not been an "ordinary" country (or an "unusually troublesome" country), but rather, because it has been a successful democracy at home, an "unusually good" country abroad. This is what most of the world would label a "liberal view," a trust in checks and balances on governments in domestic life, a trust in free elections and free press, and so on.[9]

The links between domestic and international politics in this view would be every bit as strong as in the Marxist analysis, since each ideological position sees good things as going together, and bad things going together. Liberals agree with Marxists that wars and arms races are evil, and that domestic evils are to blame for causing such wasteful international behavior. But the liberal has a very different view from the radical or Marxist on what is good and what is evil domestically, stressing the importance of free elections ahead of the desirability of economic leveling.

Each of these views would then deliver a different interpretation of the blame for the emergence of the Cold War, and each would at the end develop different theories of why the Cold War ended. The realist would lean toward a "no-fault" interpretation of events after 1945. The defeat of a common enemy had caused alliances to end often enough in the past, and the defeat of Hitler thus caused the forces commanded by Stalin and Truman now to confront each other.

The Marxists and other radicals, especially in the 1970s, tended to present a "revisionist" interpretation of the Cold War by which the West had been aggressive after 1945, and Stalin had mostly been on the defensive, that is, by which the "fault" for the Cold War mostly had to be assigned to the United States, rather than to the Soviet Union.

The much more typical interpretation for Americans was, of course, that Stalin and the Communists had been the violators of the post-1945 peace, the ones who broke their word and imposed Communist dictatorships on others, what would be consistent with a liberal general interpretation of the causes of international conflict.

In the analysis of the nuclear monopoly in this book, each of these three basic interpretations of American foreign policy may thus play some role.

After the Cold War

When the Cold War was still with us, Americans and many others expressed mixed feelings about the existence of nuclear weapons, noting that they had perhaps deterred the outbreak of conventional wars with the Soviet Union (and that they had spared the Western world the enormous economic burdens of preparing for such wars), but at the same time fearing that such weapons, if a total war ever broke out between the United States and the Soviet Union, might destroy all human life.

It would have taken a brave soul indeed to predict that the Cold War would come to an abrupt end as it did, with the tearing down of the Berlin Wall and the termination of the Warsaw Pact, and the end of the Soviet Union. The news of the collapse of Communism was surely good news for most Americans, and for most people around the world, with prospects of political freedom and economic improvement, and with the assumption that the risks were now substantially reduced of a major conventional or nuclear war in Europe, or elsewhere around what had been once called the "Iron Curtain."

Yet this news had been unpredicted, as most of us would have expected the Berlin Wall to remain in place for decades yet, and as most thought that the nuclear confrontation between Moscow and Washington assured each of these capitals against any total defeat in the ideological struggle between the Marxist and liberal worldviews.

By the logic of nuclear deterrence, it should have been impossible that Communist forces would take over the streets of Washington, or that anti-Communist forces would take over the streets of Moscow. Yet the latter did happen, producing joy, but also confounding deterrence theory, and leaving a list of unsolved problems with regard to the nuclear dimension.

To begin, what about all of our cautions that we should never push the opposing Communist leadership into a position of "use them or lose them" with regard to their enormous nuclear arsenal? Did not the defeat of Communism impose precisely such an outcome on some lifelong military supporters of Communism, like Marshall Akhramayov, for example, who after the failed coup attempt of 1991 took his own life, but fortunately did not try to take New York or Chicago with him?[10]

And was there any assured end of the trail with regard to the (politically very justified) seizure of independence by Belorus and Ukraine and Kazakhstan, if such newly independent states, former members of the Soviet Union, became inclined to seize also some of the Soviet nuclear weapons that had been stationed on their soil?[11]

And, if a termination was long overdue in the excessive central management of the Soviet Union, and of Communist China, there are some serious problems to be confronted if this "privatization" and "deregulation" shows up in the wrong places, in the central command and control and management of Soviet tactical nuclear weapons, for example (as rumors emerged of clandestine sales to Iran or Yugoslavia), or in sloppy central controls over the Chinese exports possibly supporting missile or nuclear warhead production abroad.[12]

Until we saw it actually happen, few would thus have predicted an end to the Cold War. Where such a prediction would ever have been ventured, it would have been linked to an assumption that the nuclear menace would be gone as part of peace breaking out. Surely such a dramatically happy and basically peaceful resolution of Western-Soviet conflict, by the dissolution of the Soviet Union, would have suggested that any drastic earlier action to head off thermonuclear war had not been needed. Thus, 1989 would have seemed the wrong year to publish a book on the great missed opportunity of 1946, the opportunity to head off thermonuclear confrontations by a preventive war.

Yet it is ironic and sad that the end of the Cold War has instead produced some heightened concerns about the damage that nuclear weapons can inflict, amid the prospect of more rapid nuclear proliferation, as Ukraine sought to hold on to the Soviet nuclear weapons on its soil, as North Korea no longer seemed amenable to any non-proliferation influences exerted from Moscow,[13] and as India and Pakistan detonated nuclear weapons in the spring of 1998.

How one can eliminate the nuclear menace from the world, so that cities are no longer threatened with such rapid and enormous destruction, indeed may seem a more difficult problem, rather than an easier one, as we leave the 1990s. This sad prognosis thus sets the stage all the more for the question to be addressed in this book, how the nuclear confrontation was ever allowed to happen.

Alternative Worlds

There are many people in the world who would wish that nuclear physics had never been discovered, that the counter-intuitive physics of Einstein could somehow have been wrong, so that weapons of mass destruction would not have come on to the scene. And there would be many, many, more such people if nuclear weapons were ever to come into use in anger again, for the first time since the bombing of Nagasaki in 1945. But physics is physics, and cannot be changed, and would certainly have been uncovered sooner or later.

The "might have been" in this book instead pertains to a different possibility, one more in the realm of social science analysis. Was it so impossible that nuclear weapons, once uncovered, could not have been retained as a monopoly of the first state to develop them, that is, the United States? If nuclear physics cannot be amended so that nuclear war could never happen, could nuclear weaponry not have been kept in the hands of a single power, so that nuclear war still could not happen?

By a certain logic, an aggressive maintenance of the American 1945 nuclear monopoly would simply have been the original non-proliferation effort. Compared to preventing an expansion of the nuclear-weapons club from five to six or seven, would the prevention of an expansion from one to two not have been a much greater accomplishment, for the maintenance of peace, for the prevention of the potential of the nuclear nightmare?

The task here will be to surface the degree to which such thinking drew any favorable or unfavorable attention at the time, to assemble a collection of important advocates of preventive war, the advocates who had any chance of being listened to, ranging from Bertrand Russell to Winston Churchill in Britain, and Navy Secretary Francis Matthews and General Orvil Anderson, commandant of the Air War College, in the United States.

This list will not be complete. The presumption is that additional persons advocating a use of the nuclear monopoly might yet be found, but also that there were not very many more, which may itself be the major paradox. Despite various forms of a "revisionist" account (e.g., Alperovitz, Herken)[14] by which the United States is argued to have made a very extensive use of its nuclear monopoly, Adam Ulam's summary judgment in his *Dangerous Relations* [15] remains the more plausible, that the U.S. made almost no use of this (certainly—here we return to our basic conceptual problem—as compared with what anyone today might claim to dread as the consequence of a breakdown of mutual nuclear deterrence).

Having collected persons advocating preventive war, the book then collects together lines of argument working *against* such action, that is, the lines of reasoning which the great majority of American decision makers would have found plausible. It would be impossible, and unnecessary, to catalog all the many officials in the U.S. who were *not* ready to try to use force to prevent a nuclear duopoly, *not* ready to apply the nuclear monopoly to preserve itself or to impose world peace and world government. Rather we will be sorting out the kinds of arguments that this great majority found persuasive; and in the process we will inquire somewhat more into whether these arguments should really have been quite so persuasive.

The intention of this book is thus to explore the logic of 1945 to 1949, against all the nuclear deterrence debate that has evolved and persisted since then. The years up to 1949 were hardly irrelevant, once this period of transition was behind us, since most Americans would assume that their failure to maintain the monopoly showed something about the national character of the United States.

The United States in 1945 was able to inflict nuclear destruction, and was free of fear of nuclear retaliation, and it had used this monopoly once, to end a war that Japan had initiated. But we were as free to initiate a war with the Soviet Union, so the retrospective American memory might have it, and had chosen not to do so. Would Stalin have been as generous and noble? Would any other power holding the advantage of such a monopoly have let it become a duopoly?

For as long as nuclear weapons are not again used to destroy a city, for as long as mutual deterrence persists, the retrospective case will seem to remain strong against any preventive war to head off nuclear duopoly, or against even the mere ultimata of a threat of preventive war for this objective.

If another way is found to "put the nuclear genie back into the bottle," if democracy settles into place in Russia and China and all the rest of the world, the case might then become absolute against a military venture between 1945 and 1949.

But what if we go decade after decade with continuing international tensions, and with great uncertainty as to where democracy will take hold? If one can not guarantee that such decades will see a perfect persistence of mutual deterrence, would the case for an earlier action then not have become much more arguable?

2

The Option Specified

It is hardly the case that Americans were indifferent, in the years between 1945 and 1949, to the possibility that the Soviet Union, or some other adversary, might acquire nuclear weapons. Some steps were indeed taken to preserve the American nuclear monopoly. The question before us instead is why more was not done, why the monopoly was allowed to be terminated in such a short time, rather than a greater effort being made to perpetuate it.

Efforts in the Preventive Direction

President Truman, when he announced the use of the atomic bomb on Hiroshima, had in the same statement declared that the United States, Britain, and Canada intended to hold the production secrets of this new weapon to themselves.[1] Within weeks, it was indeed clear that the United States would not share the bomb even with these English-speaking democracies.

Since the United States had of course very extensively shared other weapons and military technology with its allies during World War II, through the Lend-Lease programs directed to Great Britain and the Soviet Union ever since 1940 and 1941, Truman's 1945 policies were surely a signal that the nuclear weapon was to be seen as different, and/or that the termination of World War II, so near at hand after Hiroshima, would also be a termination of alliance sharing.

The Manhattan Project had been kept a closely guarded secret, to keep Nazi Germany and Japan from knowing about it before atomic bombs were ready for use, *and*, in the thinking of General Leslie Groves and others, to keep the Soviet Union from knowing about it.[2]

11

Yet it could have been more closely and effectively guarded. In the event, the Manhattan Project had indeed been penetrated by Soviet espionage agents, so that Stalin knew of the American efforts to produce nuclear weapons well before being told of this by President Truman at the 1945 Potsdam Conference, and so that the Soviets also were able to exploit some of the experience of the Manhattan Project in avoiding wrong turns and dead-ends on the way to bomb.[3]

The U.S. intention to hold back the secrets of the bomb was a particular affront to Britain, in light of the 1944 Hyde Park aide-memoire between Roosevelt and Churchill by which the weapon would be shared between these two English-speaking allies. Roosevelt had however held this agreement so closely that Truman simply did not know of it in 1945.[4]

More leftist analysts of the emergence of the Cold War would have seen this attempt to retain the nuclear monopoly as an affront or threat as well to Stalin's Soviet Union, but here at least there was no such explicit prior agreement to be violated. Countries do not normally share with other countries the weapons they have developed, except when they are allies in an active struggle against a common enemy.

Nuclear weapons were no ordinary weapon of course, so that some nuclear physicists indeed were to advocate that this weapon should have been shared from the very beginning, with the Soviet Union as well as with Britain. Other strategic analysts would have projected the uniqueness of nuclear weapons instead in the opposite direction being entertained here, that steps be taken to ensure that other states *never* acquired such weapons.

The attempt to restrain the spread of bomb-production knowledge was thus uneven, given the lapses in security in the Manhattan Project, and given the investment of Soviet intelligence resources in getting past such security. As another example of unevenness here, the U.S. government deferred somewhat to considerations of scientific openness by publishing the Smyth Report on the *Atomic Energy for Military Purpose*,[5] a report afterward criticized as being more helpful than it should have been, to *any* other country seeking to produce atomic bombs for itself, to the Soviet Union in the 1940s, or to some of the later nuclear proliferants of the 1960s and 1970s.

Many nuclear physicists are inclined to scoff at such criticisms of the Smyth Report, on the argument that scientific knowledge cannot be stifled, that the "secrets" here were already spreading even before 1945, and that attempts to limit science are a threat to many other things we all hold dear.

The United States Congress shared some of the basic American concern about keeping other countries from quickly acquiring nuclear weapons, but only some of it. The passage of the McMahon Act in 1946,[6] establishing a civilian Atomic Energy Commission to control all aspects of nuclear work in the United States, indeed stemmed from widespread fears that the U.S. military would be *too* cautious and constricting about nuclear technology, too afraid that someone else would acquire weapons, and would thus hinder the civilian applications of what the Manhattan Project had produced.

The irony of this showed up after the Indian nuclear detonation of 1974, when this dual-use nature of nuclear physics seemed to have become a major avenue to widespread nuclear proliferation, and when the Congress replaced the Atomic Energy Commission, on the precise argument that it had promoted the civilian uses of nuclear physics in a manner that created too many risks of weapons spread.[7]

Apart from trying to hold back "the secret," there was also an American effort to prevent Soviet or other nuclear weapons programs by preemptively acquiring uranium supplies wherever they could be found around the world. If the supply of such a crucial input material were not to be too great, the number of nuclear weapons that could be produced in the world would be small. If the United States could acquire what there was to be found of such material, in Canada, in the Belgian Congo, etc., nuclear proliferation might yet be headed off.[8]

Yet the supplies of uranium were to prove considerably greater than some preliminary estimates of 1944 and 1945 would have suggested, with enough of such material emerging in East Germany, and in the Soviet Union itself, and then in Czechoslovakia, so that the blockage of uranium supplies, just like the withholding of nuclear information, was to be a very imperfect barrier to a Soviet nuclear weapons program.

These very preliminary efforts to preserve the American nuclear monopoly thus show that the U.S. government was, at the minimum, aware of the generic question. But such attempts assuredly did not exhaust what could have been considered, if nuclear proliferation was to be headed off. Beyond the attempts to maintain secrecy, and the preemptive purchases, the United States could have considered using the nuclear weapons it, for the moment alone, possessed.

The Preventive Option

Let it be made clear what was at issue here. When the United States alone possessed nuclear weapons, it could at least have considered threatening such use, while no matching retaliation was possible. The threat of an attack with American nuclear weapons could have been used, in particular, to coerce the concessions from Moscow that would ensure that *no* Soviet atomic bombs would be produced. Whether there would have been other immediate demands, for example, for conventional disarmament and/or for democratization, is less central to the argument. What is central was what we today would call "non-proliferation."

Contemporary deterrence theory bases the non-use of nuclear weapons very heavily on the fact that they are not a monopoly. But the American nuclear force could thus have been used—as long as it persisted as a monopoly. Such a monopoly could at the least have been used to perpetuate itself, with the consequence that it could still have been used even later for other purposes.

Perhaps the mere threat would have sufficed, after Hiroshima and Nagasaki, so that nuclear war would never have had to be waged. Or perhaps cities would have had to be attacked, until Stalin or his successor gave in. There are those who would describe their opposition to such a policy as absolute and categorical. Yet can it ever be so absolute, if the alternative is the possibilities of thermonuclear destruction that we still have to dread and look forward to, in the world as it in fact developed?

Would it have sufficed to declare that the United States would launch a nuclear attack as soon as any acquisition of nuclear weapons had been detected in the USSR? This could almost surely *not* have been the policy, for the risks were too great that the first Soviet test detonation would have come when a number more of bombs had already been readied.

Rather what would have been involved here would have been more than deterrence, for it would have had to edge into what Thomas Schelling was perhaps the first to label "compellence,"[9] forcing a change in an adversary's current practice, as well as precluding certain new practices by that adversary. The United States would at the minimum have had to require that Soviet nuclear physicists and nuclear facilities be surrendered, and that other intrusive inspection steps be undertaken to insure that no bombs were ever to be produced.

Those familiar with the difficulties of imposing conditions on Iraq after Desert Storm, or on Germany after 1919, might conclude that such a post-1945 venture would have been hopeless. But the memory of the conditions imposed on Japan and Germany after 1945 would suggest the opposite, including a nuclear disarmament that has held (and a conventional disarmament that has not) and most importantly an installation of democracy that had held.

In any event, some of the frustrations of dealing with Saddam Hussein's Iraq only reflect the fact that the world has experienced nuclear proliferation since 1949. President Bush's hesitation about imposing the world's will more totally on Iraq stemmed importantly, if indirectly, from the fact that China, Russia, and India, were reluctant to see this, and that these states also now possessed nuclear weapons.[10]

What would have been demanded here is very much parallel to the Baruch Plan, with the important difference that it would have been imposed, rather than proposed.[11] The Baruch Plan, evolved from the Acheson-Lilienthal Plan, still draws some considerable controversy about whether it reflected some great missed opportunity for a *voluntary* commitment to an international management of nuclear energy, designed so as to make all future nuclear armament and proliferation, and nuclear wars, impossible. The central point for our discussion here is that Stalin was *allowed* to reject the Baruch Plan, was allowed to reject this barrier to joining the United States in the possession of nuclear weapons.

If the United States had moved to force such non-proliferation on Moscow, rather than merely advocating it, this would have come by the threat or use of nuclear weapons, and it would thus obviously have been less appropriate, at least for the short term, to speak of any matching American nuclear disarmament.

Indeed, at the end of the trail of any maintenance of a U.S. or other nuclear monopoly, the same question could have remained as with today's nuclear oligopoly, of how to get to "a world without nuclear weapons." Yet any advocate of peace and other humane considerations must at least face a very basic question. Would the urgency, and the difficulty, of getting rid of nuclear weapons not be much less today if there were only one possessor of such weapons, and if that possessor were, as in 1946, the United States of America?

Preventive War in the Abstract

Any reference to preventive war will draw the response that this is hardly such a new concept, and hardly so limited to nuclear weapons.[12] The assertion has been advanced that most of the wars of the nineteenth century, and then including World War I, were preventive wars, as a power that saw itself in decline would initiate warfare while it still had a chance of winning (rather than seeing its adversary initiate such war a decade or two later, when the advantage would have passed to the adversary).

Many of the Western ventures into discussing preventive war between 1945 and 1949 (and then indeed after 1949) are of this same generic form, as the idea of initiating warfare is presented in terms of the relative *power* of the sides, the ability to dictate politics through economic and military advantage. This is the kind of analysis that sticks closer to the *counter-force* impact of weapons, that is, whether an enemy can be defeated and disarmed in all the dimensions of military strength, and whether an enemy over time threatens to be able to do this to us.

A very different sense of preventive war was that presented by Bertrand Russell, however, where the issue is less whether one power or the other will gain in power, but rather whether a second state will gain the ability to inflict tremendous *counter-value* destruction. The case for preventing nuclear proliferation in 1946, for maintaining the nuclear monopoly, might thus not be so much a comparative power argument. The goal of making thermonuclear warfare impossible has a moral ring to it that is quite different from the simple self-interest of old-fashioned power politics.

If anyone were today to wish that the American nuclear monopoly had been used before 1949, because otherwise the Russians might conquer the world, he would be very rightly greeted with ridicule. The trends of conventional military power, and of nuclear weapons strength, still seemed very much in favor of the Soviet Union at the beginning of the 1980s; but by the end of that decade the superiority of the Western economic system had undercut all of this, as the Cold War was over, with a Western victory.

But if someone were today to wish that the American nuclear monopoly had been used to prevent *any* and all nuclear weapons from being aimed at New York and other American cities, he could not be so totally dismissed.

Advocates of a shift in U.S. defense planning in the 1960s and in the 1980s called for interpreting nuclear weapons not as a type of military power, but rather as weapons of such mass destruction that they should be used only to deter the use of similar weapons.[13] But this is in substantial agreement with the argument that nuclear weapons are unignorable in terms of their counter-value impact, which is the core of the very different kind of preventive war case being explored here.

The application of the nuclear monopoly could have been used to disband the Warsaw Pact and to introduce democracy to Russia much earlier, but at the cost of imposing a series of Hiroshimas on the Russians. Anyone seeing the changes since 1989 might be quick to reject this. But the application of the monopoly could also have prevented the nuclear war of 20??; and if this enormous nuclear war of the future remains at all possible, the arguments for earlier more radical action take on some life.

Elementary Action

Aside from issues of aggregate morality, or military feasibility, the idea of an artificial permanization of the American nuclear monopoly is rejected sometimes on the simple grounds that the details of this would have been unmanageable. It was naive in 1945, so it is often argued, to speak of "the secret" of the atomic bomb, since there were physicists all around the world after 1938 who understood that the chain-reactions of nuclear fission could indeed produce enormous explosions. Surely one could not burn all the physics textbooks of the world, even if the goal were heading off a nuclear holocaust.[14]

Yet all the major physicists of the world in 1938 indeed knew each other. A first step in crippling a Soviet nuclear weapons project, if Moscow's submission to this had been won, would thus have been to round up this inner circle of competent bomb-project leaders, the physicists and nuclear engineers whose pleasant incarceration somewhere in Colorado or California would certainly delay any nuclear proliferation. The confiscation or destruction of crucial physical inputs, as with the destruction of a cyclotron in Japan in 1946 (against the outcries of scientists in both Japan and the United States), would have been another part of the operation.[15]

Most important, after the initial period, would have been taking possession and control of all the sources of uranium in the USSR and anywhere it had occupied, for without uranium there could not be any nuclear weapons. This is indeed what the United States tried to do by market dealings, rather than by force, during and after World War II; but the hope was ill-founded that there would be relatively little uranium to buy.

It would have required military action, or at least military threats, to pry loose the uranium that was to be transformed into the Soviet nuclear arsenal.

The Moral Case Summarized

The *moral* case for preventive war before 1949, or for the threat of such war, could thus be summarized as follows: It would, at the immediate cost of repetitions of Hiroshima and Nagasaki, have eliminated the nuclear holocaust risk that loomed after 1949.

Since no thermonuclear exchanges erupted during the Cold War, someone might retrospectively claim that there would have been no gains to such an American initiative. But the majority of Americans (certainly those who would today be most predictably opposed to reconsidering preventive war) thought that the threat of a World War III was real, all too real. And if the possibility of a use of thermonuclear weapons is still to be real after 2000, action in 1946 or 1947 would also have headed this off.

What also could have been headed off were the enormous economic and human investments each side actually had to divert to Cold War preparations for conventional combat. American nuclear weapons were "used," even after the Soviets acquired them, *somewhat* to balance and counter Moscow's advantage in armored forces; but there always, after the 1950 example of the Korean War, had to be substantial investments in conventional forces as well, amid the concerns about whether the devices of "extended nuclear deterrence" would be credible. Had the American nuclear monopoly been maintained, the "limited wars" on the pattern of the Korean War would have been less plausible, and the resources assigned to preparations for such wars would have been saved.

At its most robust, the moral case for preventive action before 1949 would offer Russia democratic self-government and perhaps a market economy some thirty or forty years earlier than it was achieved; Russia today would lack the tens of thousands of tanks and the nuclear arsenal it inherited from the Soviet Union, but it would have the capital of the resources that were wasted on these military weapons.

An aggressive move to preserve the American nuclear monopoly would of course have had to maintain vigilance and energy thereafter into the future. It would do no good to preclude Stalin from acquiring nuclear weapons, and then to let another dictator, Russian or otherwise, do so some five years into the future.

As things actually happened, America had been energized to defeat and occupy Germany and Japan in 1945 (eliminating any possibility in the process of these Axis dictatorships acquiring nuclear weapons), but then had allowed Stalin to get the bomb. In the alternative being contemplated here, the Soviet Union would have had to be kept from such weapons, and so would any other state.

The on-going risks would have included a waning of American zeal and attentiveness, set against the emergence of foreign resentment of this American nuclear hegemony. The risks might thus have been of nuclear proliferation in 1959 or 1979, rather than 1949, and one can thus paint preventive war as indeed much less than the once-and-for-all solution to the problem of nuclear weapons of mass destruction.

Yet the comparison still has to be with history as it actually emerged, when the USSR was allowed to develop nuclear and thermonuclear weapons, with all the Cold War's risks of conventional and nuclear violence.

Such a comparison, it is being argued here, would hardly amount to an open-and-shut rejection of preventive war. Why such preventive action did not get more of a hearing will be the question to be examined throughout this book.

3

The Option in Perspective

Is the thought of maintaining a military monopoly so unthinkable? By some interpretations of the thrust of major writers on military strategy, this has been *the* goal of combat, to eliminate the opposing military force, and thus to establish the single potential source of violence from which law and order and civilization can stem.

Analogs to the Past

This was the thrust of the arguments of Hobbes,[1] in contrasting the state of nature which was so "nasty, brutish and short," with submission to a single sovereign. This is the thrust of the writings of Clausewitz[2] with regard to warfare in general, in the argument that unless the enemy's military forces are decisively defeated, in what we today would style the "counter-force" exchange, nothing permanent and substantial would have been accomplished.

Mahan's writings on the logic of naval warfare basically transpose this theme to the naval realm.[3] And Douhet's thinking on aerial warfare at points reads like little more than a transposition of Mahan, substituting "air" for "sea."[4]

The historical model for Clausewitz, and for many (but certainly not all) Europeans, was the Roman Empire, which indeed had achieved an effective monopoly of military power, reaching out in all directions until the population densities became so low that no contrary military threats remained. The Romans not only achieved a military monopoly, but they acted to maintain it, stamping out rebellions or secessions, doing battle to defeat threatening force constellations.

Those who would believe that no such monopoly of military force can survive will note the historical fact that the Roman Empire persisted for "only" four centuries. Yet these were centuries in which the level of civilization and culture under Rome's imperial sway rose to very high levels, and they were centuries in which "international relations" in effect had no meaning.[5]

A student of politics in the second century of the empire could hardly have been able to foresee a world of separate sovereignties threatening each other with war. In place of "international law" he would only have had to study Roman Law, that is, the domestic law of a civilized unified state. Indeed, the "international law" we try to apply to the "anarchic" international arena today gains a certain acceptance by still pretending to be an extension and continuation of Roman Law, on the logic that what makes something truly law is the backing of a sovereign.

The point has been made before that aspirants to a hegemonic domination of Europe such as Philip II and Napoleon were pulled forward by memories of what such a hegemony had accomplished.[6] "Pax Romana," "Roman Peace," was the phrase that captured much of what the issue was all about here. The Romans had not conquered all the world they knew, merely to let it lapse into quarreling and warring separate sovereignties again, at least not for another four hundred years, when the migrations of barbarian hordes from the East, or some other historical accident, brought this hegemony to an end.

Those opposed to any such hegemony thus might rejoice when they read the details of the final collapse of Roman rule, just as they heave sighs of relief when reviewing the history by which the Spanish Armada was defeated, and by which Napoleon confronted a disastrous winter in Moscow. But Europe suffered badly when the Roman Empire ended, declining by every measure of civilization.

If Spain had conquered Britain and all of the world, to renew the "Holy Roman Empire," we would all have been Catholics, and the Westphalian system of separate sovereignties would not have settled into place. If Napoleon had been similarly victorious, we would all be on the metric system, and the world would be using more French than English, again without the endemic possibility of war that so much characterizes the international system we know. For it is not so unreasonable to assume that Philip II or Napoleon would have striven to maintain their monopoly of force, once they had achieved it.

If some of the European analysis of military and political interactions reflects a nostalgia for the days of the Roman Empire, Mahan's writings about sea power reflected a parallel nostalgia for the period, just ending in 1890, where British naval power had dominated the seas. After the battle of Trafalgar, the British Navy was larger than *all* the other fleets of the world combined. If one indeed seeks a benchmark here for the salience of military hegemony required to achieve something politically meaningful, and/or something enduring, this certainly would seem to be it. In place of a Pax Romana, the world spoke of a Pax Britannica, in which British warships dominated every sea, able to move from ocean to ocean with little loss of fighting power.

These British warships stamped out piracy and the slave trade, and they facilitated a British policy of encouraging international trade and reducing tariffs and trade barriers. In short, they brought to the seas a greater order of civilization and human accomplishment than had existed before.

But Britain was not only intent on applying its naval predominance for good purposes, the purposes dictated by liberals or others in London[7] who sometimes felt morally uncertain about achieving humane purposes by threats of force; it also directed considerable attention to how such a predominance was to be maintained. It might have been prohibitively expensive to maintain a fleet larger than the total of all other ships in the world, but it certainly was the goal to maintain a fleet larger than any single fleet, and the declared British policy for decades was to have a "two-power standard," a fleet larger than any two other fleets *combined*.

Rome had dominated all the contiguous land up to empty space, and the contiguous seas as well. And Rome had maintained this for four hundred years or more. Within this contiguous area, it could take actions to preempt the development of any rival forces that could challenge the imperial hegemony. Except for some historical accidents, it was thinkable that this imperial hegemony could have lasted much longer into the future, perhaps forever. It is thinkable that the subject of international relations as we know it would never have emerged.

The British dominance of the seas was inherently less complete, because ships are designed and built on land, and it was not within the British energies or ambition to conquer all the land that fronted on the seas. Hostile forces could then work to assemble fleets inside deep harbors or up rivers and then bring them down for combat when the numbers were such as could challenge the British.

On shore, and even at some distance from the shore, new technologies could moreover be developed to undo the superiority of the warships currently deployed by the British, as the United States, France, Russia, Japan, and Germany all would be producing steel, and designing new modes of propulsion for ships, and sooner or later would be challenging the theme of "Rule Britannia."[8]

In the end, the British dominance of the seas lasted perhaps "only" some seventy years, as sailing ships were no longer to be the most effective vessel in combat, as new battleships propelled by steam would reopen the game for more competitors. The new mode of propulsion, now requiring coaling stations close at hand, would give more regional fighting strength to the Japanese in Japanese waters, and to the Americans in American waters, and so on.

Yet there is a phrase in the British discussions of naval matters, at the outset of the twentieth century, that still captures much of the logic that we have to debate here: "Copenhagening."[9]

The phrase referred back to two preemptive attacks that Nelson's Royal Navy had launched against the Danish Navy, when that fleet was about to be merged with the naval forces of Napoleon, preemptive attacks which were launched without warning to destroy the Danish naval vessels involved, in the process also inflicting a fair amount of damage on the city of Copenhagen.

"Copenhagen" then emerged as a *verb* in memos circulated within the British Admiralty at the very beginning of the twentieth century, contemplating a preventive attack on the German Imperial Navy, with a view to killing off this threat to British maritime hegemony before it matured. What precluded such a venture was not, so far as we can tell, any British feeling that preventive war would be immoral or counter to British traditions; indeed the British memory of Nelson was altogether positive, as Trafalgar was rightly remembered as the culmination of what effective naval combat is all about, putting the opposing navy out of business.

The objection to such preventive war against Germany, or against any of the other naval rivals emerging to challenge Britain, was rather the sad realization that opposing fleets could be sheltered while they were being built in estuaries and deep harbors, sheltered by coastal artillery, mine fields, submarines and other defensive barriers.

For the purposes of our analogy here with nuclear monopoly, the Roman and British traditions are thus hardly that a preventive maintenance of a dominance was immoral, but rather that, after four hundred years and seventy years respectively, it had become undoable. The U.S. nuclear monopoly, the third in this series, was to last a mere four years. And the central question of this book is "why?"

The goals of such an assertive maintenance of monopoly could always come in two forms, the extended and the basic. One could intend that such a recourse to warfare be harnessed to maximum benefits, imposing unification, law-and-order, and civilization on all of the world by means of a particular military technology. The "Pax Americana" about which we are speculating here could thus have entailed the extension of democratic government and market mechanisms not just to West Germany and Japan, but to Russia and every other corner of the globe, just as Rome had introduced Roman law wherever it could, just as Napoleon was intent on introducing the Code Napoleon and the metric system.

Or one could instead focus simply on the core of military monopoly, without seeking applications to justify the effort, and without getting into the possible political difficulties of all such applications. The inherent advantage of having the Roman Legion defeat and eliminate other armies is that one could thereafter not have land warfare. The inherent advantage of a British dominance of the seas was that it prevented naval warfare. The U.S. nuclear monopoly, had it been prolonged, would at least have made impossible the nuclear and thermonuclear wars we have feared so much ever since 1949.

One should repeat the central theme here, if only because this book will be seeking to determine why it was not more persuasive. Monopolies of violence, not just according to Hobbes, but actually in accord with our normal daily intuitions, are good in their own right, because they make it easier for one and all to know how to avoid being shot at. Monopolies can be applied to other purposes besides making wars impossible, to terminating slave trade or piracy, or to terminating dictatorships. But monopolies could, in any event, be applied to maintain themselves, while the holder of such a monopoly contemplates the uses to which they might additionally be put; our question in this book is why this was not done.

The Liberal Taboo on Violent Initiatives

If this book were to be summarized simply as a discussion of preventive war after 1945, it might be very quickly dismissed as an exercise in silly militarism. As noted above, such discussions of preventive war in the past have often come up in the context of comparative military power, as one or both of the sides to a confrontation become fearful that the other may be gaining in military strength over time, so that it is better to strike before it is too late.

This is how the outbreak of World War I on land is sometimes portrayed, amid charges that Imperial Germany saw the long-term power confrontation as worsening for itself, because Imperial Russia would solve its problems of internal cohesion, while the Austro-Hungarian Empire would be torn apart. By this version of history, Germany preferred war to peace in 1914, because it wanted to prevent a future weakness for itself, and it thus launched a preventive war.[10]

A diametrically alternative view, of course, is that France and Britain saw Germany growing too much in industrial prowess at this time, and that a decision for preventive war, a preference for war over peace, thus emerged in Paris rather than Berlin.[11]

Both of these interpretations are importantly different from another view that would depict World War I as the product of the perceived immediate advantage of the offensive on the ground, where neither side preferred war to peace in 1914, but where each preferred a war it had launched, over a war the other side had launched. This third view would blame neither side's grand intentions, as much as the immediate crisis instability of massive mobilization schemes, an instability that drew the opposing sides, once the Austrian archduke had been assassinated, into something close to the game-theoretic "prisoner's dilemma."[12]

Yet the possibility of either or both wanting a preventive war still has some important similarities to the logic of prisoner's dilemma, in that each side's military planners may be beset with prudential "worst case" analysis, wanting to be reassured about their own relative military power, and thus always watching for the threat of an opponent's power. Apprehensions about an enemy attack a decade later might thus be seen as nearly parallel to dreading an enemy attack tomorrow night, that is, the symptom of a "military mind," always expecting the worst of others, drawing all sides into fruitless and bloody self-confirming cycles of hostility.

Rather than even beginning to think in such terms of preventive war, in what can be an endless and fruitless pursuit of security and superiority, is it not better to endorse the liberal taboo on war-initiation (as Americans pride themselves as having done), ruling out fears as well as temptations? By the intuitions of most Americans, and of most citizens of any democracy, to be closed-minded about initiating war is a very helpful form of closed-mindedness.

Yet, to repeat a maxim that most liberals would endorse, nuclear weapons are not ordinary weapons. The comparison after 1945 was not with simple trends of relative power, but between a monopoly and a duopoly of what Bernard Brodie labeled "The Absolute Weapon."[13]

One can indeed press the liberal here, on whether there are no qualitative jumps that could ever justify preventive war. The Polish Marshall Pilsudski is reported to have proposed to Paris in 1933 that Poland and France launch a preventive war against Hitler.[14] In simple comparative terms, this would have been based on the calculations that Nazi Germany had not had a chance to rearm yet, so that the invasion of East Prussia and portions of the rest of Germany could still be handled more easily.

But the argument behind Pilsudski's proposal (which merits another "why not" book comparable to this one) was not limited to quantitative comparisons of troop totals. Hitler, and the Nazi Germany he would launch against the world, was to be something qualitatively different, something that it might have been very moral to head off by preventive threats and preventive action.

One would thus draw another analogy here, to the absolute ban most Americans favor on the assassination of foreign leaders, for example Fidel Castro.[15] The acid test, of course, is Hitler. If one could have done it over, would it not have been a tremendous moral accomplishment if the United States had dedicated some forerunner of the CIA to assassinating the Führer?

The analogy between assassination attempts (which the United States has sometimes engaged in) and preventive war (which the United States has not) is suggestive. The liberal will tend to want even the thought of either adventure avoided, lest one become engaged in a balancing of costs and gains which might tempt one to go ahead. The objection becomes a moral absolute, a taboo. To fortify such a moral absolute, various iron laws are introduced by which the forbidden venture, in addition to being immoral, could *never* work.

If Hitler had been assassinated, would not Himmler or someone even worse have naturally risen to power? If Castro or Saddam Hussein were to be killed, would we not then have to deal with someone even more radical and troublesome?

Similarly, if the Soviet nuclear program were to be shut down by threats and violent action from abroad, would this not simply whet the appetites of some other state for nuclear weapons, perhaps a state less deterrable that the Soviet Union proved to be, as "the secret" of the atomic bomb proved impossible to keep?

There is much to be said for thus maintaining the moral absolutes of a liberal democracy. It is regarded as absolutely out of the question, for example (and we should all be glad of this), to consider murdering the candidate of the opposing party. If one aspires (like most Americans, and perhaps like most people in the world) to transposing the domestic success of liberal democracy to the international arena, it will be important to transpose these moral constraints on the use of power as well.

Yet one does not have to be very much of a "realist" or believer in power politics to conclude that the world still has a substantial distance to go before international relations are replaced by any kind of world federalism. For the moment, as demonstrated by the continuing role of Saddam Hussein in Iraq, it only takes the presence of a dictator in a single country to generate substantial threats to international peace. And, as demonstrated by the special attention given to North Korea, it may only take a very small nuclear arsenal to impose serious constraints on what the rest of the world can do.

The U.S. has played with assassination attempts, without any real success to show for it, and with some substantial damage to its own self-esteem and image. But this author is of the opinion that an assassination of Adolf Hitler, whether undertaken by British agents or American, or whoever, would indeed have been a major accomplishment, by the hindsight of considering the millions of people who were murdered after 1933.

A preventive war is a much larger undertaking than an assassination. By the same hindsight, Pilsudski was right in favoring preventive war in 1933, and everyone else who was more peace-loving and less militant was wrong. (Yet, had such a venture been undertaken, and had it succeeded, we would then have an endless "revisionist" debate on whether the action had been unnecessary and premature, on whether Hitler had been misunderstood, with his "campaign rhetoric" being taken too seriously, on whether whoever was imposed in his place was not a greater long-term menace to France and Poland.)

Within an on-going international confrontation of powers, the normal option of preventive war was rightly to be disparaged, only in part because it was immoral, in larger part because it so typically did not offer any change in the fundamental structure of things, only making nations more ready to lunge at each other in preemptive strikes, in a power struggle that never ends. In an anarchic world of power competition, so the normal argument would go, a deposed Hitler would sooner or later be replaced by another German revanchist, with the added indignity of the Franco-Polish intervention to nourish his grievances. And if President Bush had sent his forces all the way to Baghdad in 1991, to depose Saddam Hussein, would there not have been a similar Iraqi grievance to nourish future anti-American feelings?

A preventive war to head off nuclear weapons in the Soviet Union, and anywhere else outside the United States, would have been a still bigger venture. But, most importantly, it could have had much more significant results, terminating international military conflict for an open-ended future, by the new threat of an "absolute weapon."

Perhaps people did not foresee that Hitler would be unlike other national leaders, and that World War II would be unlike all other wars, so that the preventive war proposed by Pilsudski would have a justification different from all others.

But a most important point here is that a great many people did indeed foresee the coming nuclear confrontation as something unlike all other military confrontations, with a World War III certainly being unlike all other wars (so awful that public opinion polls would draw the comment that most people would not want to survive the first day of it). If so, the preventive war proposed by Bertrand Russell had a very different justification from previous notions of such war. A preventive war to head off the possibility of a future World War III is not just "the same old logic of preventive war."

What Others Would Have Done

Apart from speculating about some great "missed opportunity," a review of the years from 1945 and 1949 can also be of value, as noted at the outset, for simply bringing to the surface the self-appraisal Americans extract from their non-use of the nuclear monopoly. As with many other portions of the American view of the U.S. world role, it is possible that much of this is subliminal and implicit, rather than clear and explicit.

Americans, at least until the gloom of the Vietnam War, tended to see their country not as an "ordinary country," selfishly engaged in power politics, but rather as an "unusually good country," doing service for others in World Wars I and II, and doing good for others in resisting the expansion of the Communist dictatorships.[16]

The fact that Stalin's USSR was detected as having tested a nuclear warhead in 1949 thus did not cause most Americans to gnash their teeth at a great missed opportunity, but rather simply produced regret that such a potentially evil force had acquired this weapon so rapidly. In the aftermath, many Americans would, at one level of consciousness or another, have been inclined to congratulate themselves on their restraint, to note that perhaps only the United States would have possessed such a monopoly and still not have used it.

What if Stalin's Soviet Union had possessed nuclear weapons in 1945 and the United States had not? Would he have allowed the United States to match this accomplishment in four years? Would he have allowed the United States to remain a liberal democracy?

The United States Manhattan Project had not been expedited in a race with the USSR, but because there were fears that a race was being run with Nazi Germany.[17] What if Hitler had possessed nuclear weapons in 1945, and the United States had not? Would Hitler have allowed the Americans to match his achievement? Would he have allowed the U.S. or any other power to remain able to challenge him, and would he have allowed anyone to remain a democracy?

The explicit premise behind the urgency of the Manhattan Project was indeed that Hitler would have used nuclear weapons as soon as he was the first to possess them, would have used such weapons to impose his will upon the world, including all the capitalization of a monopoly of power that is prerequisite to such dominance. Hitler would have used the bomb to kill millions, and to force the surrender of other millions. He would have used the bomb to prevent any rival from getting the bomb, and to force the conventional disarmament of others as well. He would have used the bomb to impose on one and all the Nazi vision of a proper world order.

Fortunately for the world, the German nuclear physicists who were Aryan enough and apolitical enough to stay behind in Nazi Germany, rather than going to America to become important parts of the Manhattan Project, had been either too unimaginative in their analysis of physics, or too politically uncommitted to Nazism, to get a serious Nazi atomic bomb project underway.[18] Since no one had ever convinced Hitler that nuclear weapons of mass destruction were imminently feasible, we do not have direct evidence in his "table talks," or other musings, of the use to which he would have put such weapons.

In light of the low level of Nazi German progress toward a bomb, some Americans would today question the urgency or appropriateness of the Manhattan Project, a project which had such horrible consequences for Hiroshima and Nagasaki. Yet almost all of such Americans, in light of Hitler's other decisions, would agree that the world would have been in peril if Hitler had beaten the United States to the nuclear monopoly.

What is the probable shape of our intuitive suppositions about Stalin, about what he, instead of Hitler, or instead of Truman, would have done with a monopoly of nuclear weapons? Whether Stalin was just as ruthless or just as cruel as Hitler was a staple of debates about the nature of the Cold War, about the logic of "containment" rather than "unconditional surrender," etc.

The premise of George Kennan[19] and of many others was that Stalin's Soviet Union was not as adventuristic as Hitler's Germany, that patience and the maintenance of firm lines of resistance would work to achieve a satisfactory outcome, where in the case of the Nazis the only solution had been to drive to Berlin. But Kennan was describing a Stalin who did *not* have nuclear weapons, facing an America that did.

Kennan had composed his advocacy of "containment" when the U.S. alone had the atomic bomb, and when it would have been used against Hitler, but when it was not to be used against Stalin. We are here inquiring about why, about what was the difference.

The American commitment to resisting fascism or communism stemmed from both what these regimes were doing in the territories they already controlled, and from the threat of further, perhaps unlimited, outward expansion of such territory.

If Hitler had merely been "contained," he would have killed millions more of people in the concentration camps. Stalin also had such concentration camps, where he imprisoned anyone suspected of potentially threatening his power, and where he killed some entire groups of people, e.g. Polish army officers; but his homicidal ambitions were not as great as those we know for the Nazi case.[20]

If Hitler had merely been contained, he would have nurtured dreams of yet breaking out of this somehow. But is there any evidence that the Communists so quickly lost faith in such an expansion? Kennan's predictions for the efficacy of containment, in shaking the ideological self-confidence of the Kremlin leadership, was that this would occur in a decade or two. In the event, the final collapse of Communism took more like four decades.

Finally and most importantly, as very highly placed Americans saw it in 1944, if Hitler had merely been contained, he might have developed nuclear weapons. But, this was of course the crux of the price of settling for containment with Stalin.

Our comparisons of the two dictatorial regimes, Hitler's and Stalin's, become most relevant when we return to the basic question above, what the typical American today, or even the typical Russian, would assume Stalin would have done with a nuclear monopoly.

Kennan's elaborated discussion of the arguments for containment, first in a series of February, 1946 cables back to Washington from the U.S. Embassy in Moscow, and then in the *Foreign Affairs* article, amounted very much to the alternative to preventive war. Unlike the situation in 1941, where President Roosevelt had found it urgently necessary to draw the United States into the war against Hitler, lest the Germans defeat the USSR and Britain, and dominate the world, Kennan saw the appropriate U.S. response to Stalin as a firm holding of the line.

Yet we must return here to the prior point. While Kennan was definitely not presenting an argument for a preventive war employing the U.S. nuclear monopoly, he did in 1946 express very clear opinions on what Stalin would have done with such a monopoly, namely that the Soviet dictator would have had no compunctions about using this weapon, just as he would exploit any other weapon. In the debate at the end of World War II about how much "sharing" of nuclear weapons or nuclear control or nuclear information there should be, Kennan was on the same side as Forrestal and others opposed to such sharing,[21] on the grounds that the Soviets would simply treat any such sharing as an accretion of their own power, that is, as a step toward a more rapid termination of the advantage of the American nuclear monopoly.

The dictator who had been so willing to kill millions of Ukrainian kulaks or thousands of Polish officers would most probably have been willing to inflict on American cities what had befallen Hiroshima and Nagasaki. The Americans, in the middle of an already-heated war, killed tens of thousands of Japanese with a view to forcing disarmament, and democratization, on Japan. Stalin, in the middle of an inevitable class struggle, would have been killing tens of thousands of Americans to force disarmament, and "socialism," on the United States.

By the way that the sequence of history evolved, Americans have had to think about a *Soviet* nuclear monopoly only as a counter-factual scenario. But all of the subsequent emphasis on assuring second-strike retaliatory capability against Stalin's successors suggested that we did not trust what *they* would have done with a nuclear monopoly, if a missile gap or bomber gap ever somehow conjured up such a monopoly.

In what is admittedly the most unscientific kind of opinion sampling, this author has occasionally asked Russian specialists on nuclear strategy to speculate on the same question: what Stalin would have done in 1945 if he alone had the atomic bomb. The answer has always come back: "He would have used it, to keep you from getting it."

One can indeed speculate, along the same lines, about what Winston Churchill would have done if his Britain had been the first to produce nuclear weapons.[22] In the great tradition of "Copenhagening," would Britain not have moved to keep the USSR from engaging in nuclear proliferation?

We do not normally spend much time, of course, comparing Churchill with Hitler or Stalin. The British share with Americans not just a language, but a commitment to democracy, and to the entire package of what can be characterized as a liberal world outlook. Yet one must also remember the power orientation that we are accustomed to attributing to the worldly-wise Europeans, as compared with the Wilsonian-American tradition of idealism and naivete; anyone dwelling on such a question might conclude that the British would at least have been *more* ready to think of exploiting a monopoly. As will be discussed, Winston Churchill indeed urged that the United States think about preventive war, in the time when Stalin had not yet gotten his bomb.

All of these counter-factual scenarios may be regarded by some scholars as an escapist distraction, as an attempt to enliven what had otherwise become a tedious and repetitive analysis of the basic Soviet-American nuclear rivalry.

Yet such counter-factuals have been at the center of the Cold War rivalry. What would Stalin or Khrushchev or Brezhnev do, if the United States were ever to lack the means for massive nuclear retaliation? This was the counter-factual question that continuously energized the American Strategic Air Command (SAC) to make certain such a situation never occurred.

And (merely a different form of the same question) what would Stalin have done, if he had acquired nuclear weapons *before* Truman?

Most Americans would today regard a preventive war in 1946 as an absolutely preposterous venture, and would be certain that no serious American leader at the time ever thought in such terms. Yet Americans have surely reflected on whether Stalin, if equipped with a similar monopoly in "the absolute weapon," would have used it. The "idea" of preventive war might be outlandish, but this hardly rules out speculation that an "outlandish" foreign regime, a dictatorial regime that had behaved ruthlessly enough already on the outskirts of Warsaw, etc., would entertain the idea.

We know, and the world knows, what the United States actually did with its nuclear monopoly. The United States used it to terminate a war already underway with Japan, and then did not use such weapons again in anger.

The logic of mutual deterrence is that no one can be trusted with a nuclear monopoly. But America surprisingly indeed then passed the test on such trust, while what any other state would have done remains in the realm of speculation, worrisome speculation.

The difference here is enough to reinforce American self-trust and self-esteem. One of the purposes of the explorations in this book might be to see whether this is so justified. If the intuitive American answer to "why didn't the United States use its nuclear monopoly to maintain itself, and to impose peace on the world?" is that "the United States is too democratic and peace-loving to launch a preventive war," will this in the end prove to be plausible as the actual answer, or will it not?

Issues of Sequence

The United States had nuclear weapons some four years before Stalin's Soviet Union acquired them. If the U.S. had not carried through its Manhattan Project, would the Kremlin have pushed ahead to acquire its own atomic bombs anyway, thus being the first, thus achieving its own nuclear monopoly?

It was not only the United States in the early 1940s that feared that Nazi Germany had to be beaten to the atomic bomb. Stalin's Soviet Union apparently worked on the same assumption, inferring a German lead in any race to such deadly weapons, based on the preeminent position that Germany had held in nuclear physics before the Nazis came to power.[23]

The surmise sometimes offered on the left, that Stalin would never have moved toward such weapons if there had not been a Manhattan Project, thus has to overcome some complicated issues of sequence. Given what we now often hear from physicists, that there was no real secret to the principles of nuclear fission, each of the powers would have had to fear that several other states, Germany, Britain, France, could be moving in this direction.

The espionage assets of the USSR were instructed to include nuclear programs in their list of what was to be monitored. After a time, such intelligence networks were indeed to detect the Manhattan Project, and at the same time had much less to report inside Nazi Germany. Yet, given that the United States was a much more open society than Hitler's Germany, Stalin could have been concerned almost to the last minute, just as the Americans and British were concerned, that the Nazis might be making progress toward the atomic bomb as well.

What is interestingly unique about the United States is that it alone could muster the resources, or have so much trust in its abstract science, that a nuclear weapons program was pursued even while all the burdens of the "conventional" World War II were also in place.

Hitler had brushed aside any suggestions that Germany actively pursue such weapons, perhaps because the relevant German scientists were dragging their feet and not making the option clear enough, but more directly because he only wanted weapons programs immediately relevant to winning the war underway. Stalin similarly postponed a Soviet nuclear effort because, until the German defeat at Stalingrad, the time horizon for a nuclear weapons project seemed too far ahead. And the British government's decision to merge its own nuclear research with the American Manhattan Project also stemmed from the burdens of the immediate war effort (as well as from assumptions that a joint American-British effort had the best chance of beating the Germans, if any race were really underway).

If the United States had not been able to free up the energy to seek after nuclear weapons, *as well as* pursuing victory by other means in World War II, there would have been less for Soviet espionage to detect, and less to copy. But, if Hitler had not invaded the Soviet Union in 1941, it is very possible that the Soviet nuclear program would have gotten going earlier.

4

Outright Advocates

This will now be an attempt to bring together some of the people who advocated the preventive use of the American nuclear monopoly being outlined here, people who, rather than simply being some kind of local "cracker-barrel philosopher," might have been influential enough to make some difference. The list of such people is not very long, which is, in itself, what this book is seeking to explain.

There may be some additional influential people who would belong on this list, people who advocated a similar preventive war, or threat of preventive war, against Stalin's Soviet Union, but who did so in so cautious and closely held a form as to elude the historical record; if so, the reticence of such people about publicizing their recommendations is similarly what needs to be explained.

For every one of such people who came out to favor an exploitation of the nuclear monopoly, there were dozens who would dismiss such an idea, and there will be no attempt to list all of them. Rather this book will turn a little later to listing the kinds of arguments that would have emerged rebutting such a preventive war, and to comparing the logics of such arguments.

Bertrand Russell

As noted, one of the earliest and clearest advocacies of a preventive war while the United States retained its nuclear monopoly (or at the very least an advocacy of an attempt to preclude Soviet nuclear weapons acquisition, by posing the threat of such a war) came from the world-famous British mathematician and logician, Bertrand Russell.[1]

Russell would after 1950 assert that he had never endorsed such a venture, as he was much better known for denouncing U.S. foreign and military policy, especially in Vietnam, and for advocating an accommodation with the Communist world.[2] He tended to brush off any earlier musings about preventive war as off-hand remarks, not intended to be circulated or published, or taken seriously.

Yet Russell in the years from 1945 to 1949 authored some very long letters, and newspaper and journal articles, lamenting the day of the future when more than one country would have atomic bombs, and applauding the fact that it had been the United States and not some other country that had first acquired them, and concluding that it would be a great service to humanity if the United States applied this monopoly to prevent any duopoly from emerging. Russell, in so many words, anticipated a problem in the particular liberal morality of American society, which would make preventive war difficult to launch. He made clear, moreover, his particular loathing for Stalin and the society he had imposed on the Russians and East Europeans, and his great fear of what could happen once Stalin got the bomb.

In Russell's own words, the argument for preventive war, while no one else had the atomic bomb, was crystal clear in its logic:

> If America were more imperialistic, there would be another possibility, less Utopian and less desirable, but still preferable to the total obliteration of civilized life. It would be possible for Americans to use their position of temporary superiority to insist upon disarmament, not only in Germany and Japan, but everywhere except the United States, or at any rate in every country not prepared to enter into a close military alliance with the United States, involving compulsory sharing of military secrets.
>
> During the next few years this policy could be enforced; if one or two were wars were necessary, they would be brief, and would soon end in decisive American victory. In this way a new League of Nations could be formed under American leadership, and the peace of the world could be securely established. But I fear that respect for international justice will prevent Washington from adopting this policy.[3]

Russell was among those who were impressed and repulsed by the simple counter-value damage that even a few nuclear attacks on cities could inflict, and he would thus exploit this to impose a ban on nuclear proliferation on the Soviet Union, and presumably on other countries as well.

Russell's attitudes on domestic social issues guarantee against any impression that an advocacy of preventive war would come only from the political "right." His disavowals of such advocacy in later years have struck several of his biographers as more deceitful than forgetful, given the extensive nature of his development of the idea before 1949.[4] It surely made him feel more acceptable among other critics of American foreign policy in the 1950s and 1960s to pretend that such advocacy had never occurred, with many of his admirers taking his word for it, but the written record is there.

Bertrand Russell's shift, from advocating a war with Stalin's USSR before it got nuclear weapons, to advocating much greater accommodation with the Communist world later, might indeed have been totally logical, rather than so morally inconsistent.

As Russell noted at the start, a nuclear monopoly was preferable to a nuclear confrontation. If the Americans, good people that they were, could be persuaded to preserve the monopoly, this would be the best solution, but this was unlikely. Once the monopoly was broken, it would then rather be appropriate to get the same Americans to make concessions and come to terms with Stalin's successors, for the most important goal would be to avoid a nuclear war, that is, a war where both sides were using such weapons.

Leo Szilard

Leo Szilard was a key player in persuading Franklin Roosevelt to launch the Manhattan Project in the first place, and is remembered then as a leader of the scientists who opposed the use of the atomic bomb against Japan, who after 1945 would argue long and hard for nuclear disarmament, and for an avoidance of a reliance on nuclear deterrence.[5]

But when the atomic bomb would still have been a monopoly, Szilard several times in 1944 and 1945, in conversations and correspondence, surfaced the logical argument for maintenance of the monopoly by exploiting it, that is, by the threat or actual execution of preventive war. Bernard Brodie indeed later commented that Szilard was the first person he had heard voice the logic of maintaining the nuclear monopoly by such means.[6]

When Szilard and a number of his colleagues had urged in the summer of 1945 that the atomic bomb not be used against Japan, several arguments were put forward, including the immorality of the act, and the shock that might be imposed on postwar expectations by the concrete example of such a destructive attack on a population center. Also included in the array was a slightly different argument, however, that not dropping the bomb on Japan might allow the United States to head off a postwar arms race, by keeping the entire Manhattan Project, perhaps the entire possibility of nuclear weapons, a secret.

In effect this amounted to another approach to maintaining the American monopoly, maintaining it by for the moment not using it at all, not even against Japan. Perhaps this was merely an effort by Szilard and his colleagues to exploit the fixations of other Americans, for example Leslie Groves, on the American secret of the bomb. This argument certainly went further than later devotees of "the secret," in suggesting that the Soviets could be kept from knowing not only *how* the bomb had been produced, but even *the fact that* it could be produced. In retrospect, we know that Soviet espionage had already passed one or several of these thresholds.

Leslie Groves

Bertrand Russell's attitudes are listed first above because they would today startle someone more left-of-center, with the initial response being to accept Russell's later attempt to deny or dismiss this round of argument. And the same holds for Leo Szilard, who did not expound on this theme as extensively, or for as long a time, as Russell.

Someone on the left of the spectrum would much more expect such arguments to come from senior American military commanders, and there are indeed some such advocacies of preventive war to be found.

Not so surprising, General Leslie Groves, continuing as director of nuclear activities into 1946 until the establishment of the civilian Atomic Energy Commission, was quite concerned that the Soviets not steal "the secret" of the atomic bomb[7]; and, after the Japanese surrender, he at times voiced the opinion that steps should be taken to head off Soviet development of nuclear weapons, even if they were doing it all on their own.[8]

Racing against "another nuclear program" was of course nothing new for Groves, since the Manhattan Project had been motivated by the assumption that Nazi Germany was working to acquire atomic bombs. Groves, as head of the Project, was indeed called upon to do more than move the American effort along as rapidly as possible; he was additionally given options of choosing targets within German-occupied Europe, to be attacked by the U.S. and British Air Forces, and by sabotage operations, with a view to crippling or slowing down German progress toward the bomb.[9]

As the laboratories where the remaining German nuclear physicists were working might be added as targets, and as even assassination attempts on someone like Heisenberg were entertained, it would be no great leap of imagination to think in terms of a similar targeting of the Soviet effort.

General Groves has sometimes been caricatured as a stereotypically narrow-minded Army officer, and/or professional engineer, unused to and intolerant of the academic needs of the theoretical physicists under his direction, excessively suspicious about the possibility of espionage, and thus slowing the accomplishment of the Manhattan Project by too much compartmentalizing the effort. The personality contrasts and conflicts between Groves and Oppenheimer have been much written about, and portrayed on the screen.

Much of this is indeed a caricature, with many of the physicists who worked under Groves showing great respect for the man and his administrative abilities, but it is indeed true that Groves, during World War II and after, displayed a serious concern that the United States beat not only Germany to possession of the atomic bomb, but also the Soviet Union, with his concerns about preventing espionage (concerns which were not to be matched with success) being directed at least as much at Communist espionage as at Nazi efforts.

When Groves was thus at times called upon to choose targets for the U.S. Eighth Air Force in its bombing of Germany, to slow whatever might be the Nazi German nuclear effort, he also at the very close of the war specifically directed an attack to preclude the advancing Red Army from capturing valuable German nuclear assets at Oranienburg, north of Berlin.[10]

Groves also was optimistic, and energetic, about the above-mentioned efforts to purchase uranium and other nuclear raw materials around the world, before and after the end of World War II, with a view to denying these to the Soviet Union.

Would Groves have been ready to advocate the next step, the initiation of war to prevent the USSR from acquiring atomic bombs? In various reports and speeches he delivered after 1945, Groves indeed suggested that this would make sense and be realistic, even though it would conflict with the idealism of American attitudes about the world, by which a good end should never be pursued by an evil means. To the extent that private conversations mattered, on an issue too sensitive to discuss publicly, Groves certainly did voice the logic of preventive war:

> If we were ruthlessly realistic, we would not permit any foreign power with which we are not firmly allied, and in which we do not have absolute confidence, to make or possess atomic weapons. If such a country started to make atomic weapons we would destroy its capacity to make them before it had progressed far enough to threaten us.[11]

Countering this somewhat (but only somewhat), Groves was also among those who belittled the quality of science and engineering in the USSR (and also underrated the efficiency of Soviet espionage) and thus tended to assume a longer interval until the USSR had mastered the production of atomic bombs. (These exaggerations of the "secret of the atomic bomb" are sometimes seized upon by liberal scientists to show that Groves was deficient in intellect or scientific training; but almost all the scientists connected with the Manhattan Project would have guessed the interval to the first Soviet bomb to be longer than the four years that actually remained.)[12]

And, for those who reject the very thought of preventive war, it will be noted further below how such suppositions of a longer interval played some role in holding back such a venture.

Orvil Anderson

Ultimately making much more of a public splash than General Groves was General Orvil Anderson, the commandant of the Air War College at Maxwell Air Force Base in Montgomery, Alabama, the most advanced school in political and strategic studies for mid-career Air Force officers.[13]

Anderson drew national attention in late August of 1950, months after the outbreak of the Korean War, by giving a Montgomery, Alabama newspaperman an interview advocating a preventive war attack on the Soviet Union. Anderson referred to "five nests" in which the Soviet nuclear weapons were stored, these to be the first priority of the American attack, an attack which would presumably restore the American nuclear monopoly, and head off further conventional or nuclear aggressions on the pattern just experienced on the Korean peninsula.

By the logic of this book, 1950 is too late, of course, since New York and other cities would already have presumably been vulnerable to a Soviet "second-strike" attack. In the ensuing uproar over the interview, General Anderson was removed from his post at the Air War College, but not otherwise particularly punished, and was indeed informally offered his choice of other commands around the Air Force, "any command except SAC."

What makes Anderson relevant is that he had already been advocating such a policy ever since Hiroshima, advocating preventive war, a preventive attack to preclude Stalin from possessing nuclear weapons. Anderson had come to the same conclusions as Bertrand Russell as early as the fall of 1945, that nuclear weapons were unique, and that their uniqueness should be exploited while the American monopoly could be maintained. Anderson apparently raised such possibilities quite regularly in these five years, in letters and conversations with other Air Force officers, and with important civilians.

Anderson is important in particular because of his fixation, unusual for Air Force officers, on the "absolute" nature of nuclear weapons. Rather than worrying whether a preventive war would require hundreds or thousands of bombers for a repetition of the air campaigns of World War II (campaigns premised on destroying the enemy's entire ability to wage war), Anderson's reasoning was that the mere threat of a devastation of single cities, the mere possibility of a single bomber getting through with an atomic bomb, would be sufficient to deter or compel an adversary, for as long as that adversary had no matching nuclear capability of its own.[14]

Before 1949, Anderson would have exploited this monopoly of nuclear weapons, against which, because only one bomb had to be delivered to a city, there would be no defense. After 1949, Anderson would have concentrated on catching whatever Soviet nuclear weapons had come into being, before they could do any damage to the U.S., and he would have thereafter applied the restored nuclear monopoly.

The premise of this book is that the post-1949 preventive war scenarios, if one accepted the awesome counter-value impact of even a few bombs delivered against a few cities, would have been burdened with insurmountable anxieties. In the uproar caused by his 1950 interview, Anderson was asked where he had gotten the number of five "nests" for the location of Soviet atomic bombs, and responded that he had pulled this number out of the air.[15] Whether or not he was being truthful here (rather than covering up for some inadvertent breach of security on what the United States knew in 1950 about the location and number of Stalin's accumulation of atomic bombs), the idea of trying to restore the American monopoly would always be qualitatively different from the idea of exploiting it before it had been broken.

Anderson's role at the Air War College made his views important in yet a different way, for there are reports of lectures on the theme of preventive war by other generals and officers visiting the institution, in the years before the monopoly was broken. Anyone looking for thinking about a preventive use of the atomic bomb, coupled to an ultimatum to Stalin to surrender his nuclear ambitions, might thus find it in the continuing circulation of such ideas at Maxwell Air Force Base.

But someone more skeptical of whether the United States Air Force, or the rest of the United States government, ever came close to such a policy would point to the very nature of the War Colleges, which offer a sort of mid-career "sabbatical" to senior officers, a period where they can stand back from the day-to-day operational experiences of their career, and engage in more abstract and theoretical thinking.

At its best, such an experience is mind opening, getting officers, and senior civilian officials of the foreign policy-related departments, to interact in exploring the interface of military force and politics. But much of such thinking is then also soon written off as "academic" and "abstractly theoretical," the kind of idea that surfaces in a seminar or a war game simulation, but never gets seriously considered in real life.

In short, the same general who might present a preventive-war argument in the abstract, when he was a guest lecturer at the Air War College, might not propose such a policy at a real policy meeting.

General Anderson's arguments, and the tones of the discussion at the Air War College, are indeed important in many ways. Our larger task in this book will be sorting out why they never became more important, why the policies discussed at Maxwell Air Force Base, the highest academic activity of the new U.S. Air Force, never came close to being implemented.

William Golden

William Golden, President Truman's science adviser, wrote a letter to Lewis Strauss, then a member of the Atomic Energy Commission, on September 25 of 1949, immediately after the public disclosure of the detection of the Soviet atomic bomb test, a letter outlining very succinctly the preventive war reasoning that is being dissected here:

> In theory we should issue an ultimatum and use the bombs vs. Russia now.... For once Russia is in a position to put A-bombs on our cities, no matter how inefficient those bombs may be and how few in number, she is in a position to do us unspeakable injury.... Studies along this line, and in more dilute version, should and doubtless will be (or have been) made by the Joint Chiefs....However, we won't do it, of course; no matter what the alternative cost in the long run, the public would never support so far-seeing a bombardment.[16]

One can exaggerate the influence of a science adviser, as some were more listened to, and some less. Yet this statement, if nothing else, is evidence of how close to the presidency the arguments for preventive war could at least be voiced.

John Von Neuman

A refugee from Hungary just like Edward Teller, John Von Neuman was a brilliant mathematician and logician, on a par with Bertrand Russell, but with a much stronger aversion to Marxism in all its variants, a pioneer in the development of computers and game theory, and a major scholar from the outset at the RAND Corporation advising the new U.S. Air Force on strategic analysis.[17]

Von Neuman's logic about the monopoly of nuclear weapons was indeed to be very much like that of Bertrand Russell, that serious consideration ought to be given to applying this monopoly to perpetuate itself, to threatening Stalin with nuclear attack if he did not submit his nuclear assets to American and/or international control. Von Neuman voiced such ideas regularly to colleagues, and to the Air Force and government he was advising, in the period from 1947 to 1949, and he then continued to float such ideas even after the first 1949 detection of a Soviet atomic bomb test.

Unlike Russell, who in his logic apparently based everything on the awesome destructive power of atomic bombs when directed against cities, and hence relied crucially on a nuclear *monopoly*, Von Neuman leaned somewhat more in the direction of the normal Air Force counterforce reasoning, where preventive war would have to be planned and executed with a view to defeating the enemy, rather than simply holding its cities at risk, that is, where such a war could still make sense even if the adversary had a few atomic bombs and might be able to devastate several American cities before the exchange was over.[18]

Von Neuman was brilliant enough, and influential enough, so that he would have to be cited on this list even if he were working all by himself. But the style of the RAND Corporation was to stress interaction and exchange of ideas. Von Neuman was not alone at RAND in feeling that the logic of a preventive operation should be entertained, that the value of the American monopoly should be appreciated, lest it be allowed to slip away. Among the others variously reported to have sympathy for such ideas were the game theorist John D. Williams and the political scientist Nathan Leites.[19]

Lauris Norstad

Lauris Norstad would rise to the rank of four-star general in the U.S. Air Force in the early 1950s, and would become the first Air Force general to command all the military forces, ground, naval, and air, of NATO. Already a major general in September of 1945, he authored a study of the Air Force's requirements for nuclear weapons which identified the USSR as the enemy, couched in the logic of the need to destroy all of Soviet industry, thus reaching relatively larger numbers for bombs required, some 466 of the size used against Nagasaki, than would have emerged from an emphasis only on the destruction of cities.[20]

When Norstad's study was referred to General Groves for comment, Groves responded that the U.S. did not have the ability to produce this many bombs in the near-term future, but that fewer bombs would suffice to destroy the bulk of Soviet cities.[21]

One cites Norstad's name here because he was to rise to such prominent positions within a relatively short time, and hence already had to be someone whose views were taken seriously. He is important also because he represents the much larger slice of Air Force and other military planners who were at least ready to *consider* preventive war, once the nuclear option had become real.

Norstad's detailed study of targets and numbers of bombs required was related to a JCS Joint Intelligence Committee analysis of the proper role for nuclear weapons in the postwar world, a study which concluded that the United States might well have to initiate a nuclear air war against the USSR, in either of two scenarios: where the Soviet had initiated a conventional aggression on the ground, *or* where the Soviets were about to become capable of attacking the United States or repelling an American air attack.[22]

Winston Churchill

We have already posed the abstract question of what Winston Churchill would have done if Britain had achieved a nuclear monopoly rather than the United States, very nearly parallel to asking what Stalin would have done with such a monopoly.

In real life, the British had to deal with the United States having held this monopoly to itself despite the Hyde Park memorandum; and Winston Churchill had been voted out of office after the German surrender in Europe in 1945, before the Japanese were forced to surrender (before the nuclear attacks on Hiroshima and Nagasaki), to remain a private citizen until his Conservative Party won a majority again in Parliament in 1951.

Churchill offered comments on the nuclear question publicly and privately at various stages over the years of the monopoly. He is remembered very widely for his speech at Fulton, Missouri in March of 1946 when he referred to an "iron curtain" descending across Europe.[23] The speech minted the phrase, and was seen in retrospect as one of the defining formulations of the Cold War. Much less remembered is that the same speech specifically discussed the American nuclear monopoly, cautioning the United States against handing over this weapons monopoly to an untried United Nations, expressing the view of Britishers (and probably others) that the world should be thankful that the United States held this monopoly, and not some other country.

Churchill is also importantly remembered for a later speech in Parliament in March of 1949 when he opined that, but for American nuclear weapons, the Red Army would by then have conquered all of continental Europe and advanced to the English Channel.[24] And still later, after becoming prime minister again, after the USSR and Britain had also acquired nuclear weapons, Churchill minted another phrase when he addressed Parliament in 1955 about the "balance of terror."[25]

The public statements thus show that Churchill was hardly likely to underrate the importance of whether there was still an American monopoly of nuclear weapons. In his public speeches and private comments of 1948, moreover, he several times broached the idea of a preventive war then, while the American monopoly still existed, or at least of an ultimatum to Stalin backed by the threat of such a war. For example, a Churchill speech to the House of Commons on January 23, 1948:

> I believe that the best chance of preventing a war is to bring matters to a head and come to a settlement with the Soviet government before it is too late. This would imply that the Western democracies, who should, of course, seek unity among themselves at the earliest moment, would take the initiative in asking the Soviet for a settlement.

> It is idle to reason or argue with the Communists. It is, however, possible to deal with them on a fair, realist basis, and in my experience, they will keep their bargains as long as it is in their interest to do so, which might, in this grave matter, be a long time, once things were settled. When this Parliament first assembled, I said that the possession of the atomic bomb would give three or four years' breathing space. Perhaps it may be more than that. But more than two of those years have already gone. I cannot think that any serious discussion which it may be necessary to have with the Soviet government would be more likely to reach a favourable conclusion if we wait till they have got it too.[26]

And, for another version, a Conservative Party annual conference speech in Wales in October of 1948:

> The question is asked: What will happen when they get the atomic bomb themselves and have accumulated a large store? You can judge yourselves what will happen then by what is happening now. If these things are done in the green wood, what will be done in the dry?...What do you suppose would be the position this afternoon if it had been Communist Russia instead of free enterprise America which had created the atomic weapons?...The Western nations will be far more likely to reach a lasting settlement, without bloodshed, if they formulate their just demands while they have the atomic power and before the Russian Communists have got it too.[27]

Statesmen out of power can sometimes indulge themselves with speculations that would be regarded as impossibly irresponsible when they held power. We thus have no evidence of what Churchill would have advocated about the use of the American nuclear monopoly while he himself was in a responsible position. Yet the idea of preventive war was surely something that Churchill, given all his experiences, would not simply grasp on to as a casual will-of-the-wisp.

Curtis LeMay

General Curtis LeMay, like General Leslie Groves, lends himself to caricature by liberals outside the military. Gruff in manner, talking off-handedly about bombing Vietnam or another enemy country "into the stone age," running as a vice presidential candidate with segregationist George Wallace after retirement from the Air Force, LeMay cannot be an appealing figure on the campuses of America.[28]

LeMay had commanded the 20th Air Force in the bombing of Japan in 1945, and had innovated the American reversion to night-time area bombing instead of daylight precision bombing, with the first such attack being the devastating fire-bomb raid on Tokyo of March 9, 1945, a raid in which more than 100,000 Japanese were killed, more than at either Hiroshima or Nagasaki.

LeMay was to draw other assignments around the U.S. Air Force before assuming command of the Strategic Air Command in 1948. Even his strongest critics would give him credit for enhancing the readiness of SAC after he took over, a readiness on which the deterrence of Soviet aggression, including nuclear aggression after 1949, would depend.[29]

Drawing the greatest disapproval, it has been reported that LeMay repeatedly toyed with the idea of preemptive attack, or even preventive war, after the Soviets had developed nuclear forces of their own. Accepting the counter-force logic that most professional Air Force officers tended to endorse, LeMay saw it as urgent to attack the Soviet Air Force before it could attack his own SAC, and before it could do too much damage to American cities and industry. To enhance this reliability of his own target plans, LeMay apparently took chances with violations of Soviet air space with reconnaissance flights.[30] And, as the ultimate failing, LeMay was sometimes off-handedly heard voicing disrespect for whoever was the president, his civilian commanders-in-chief, and disregarding their cautions about how nuclear weapons would be targeted, and when a war would be launched.[31]

The premise of this book is that many of such attitudes and postures were indeed dangerous after 1949, that any American leanings toward counter-force strike plans, and "launch-on-warning" initiations of attack, were likely to produce the same on the Soviet side, in a circle that very much threatened crisis stability. A "nuclear war that nobody wanted" could have been the result, one of the important scenarios for how the world could destroy itself, once nuclear or thermonuclear weapons were deployed on *both* sides.

For the purposes of the analysis here, LeMay's plans *after* 1949 are thus mostly an example of what should have been headed off. More relevant would be instances of this very important veteran of World War II, soon to rise to even more important assignments, speculating about preventive war *before* 1949, when the Soviets could still not hit back with any atomic bombs of their own.

William B. Borden

William Borden plays an interesting role at several stages of the American nuclear debate. A student at Yale after serving as a bomber pilot in World War II, working physically very near to where Bernard Brodie was writing his *The Absolute Weapon*,[32] Borden published a parallel book in the spring of 1946 entitled *There Will Be No Time*,[33] stressing the counter-force impact of nuclear weapons rather than the counter-value impact highlighted by Brodie. Borden's book suggested preventive war by its stress on how much danger the United States would be in once some other state acquired means for a nuclear attack; but it brushed off the possibility in a few sentences, noting that American morality made such a preventive war impossible.[34]

Moving from one professional position to another, Borden joined two other analysts in composing a memorandum, addressed in 1948 to Senator Brian McMahon, the author of the act establishing the Atomic Energy Commission, and the first Chairman of the Joint Committee on Atomic Energy, a memorandum outrightly proposing an ultimatum requiring Stalin to surrender his nuclear assets, an ultimatum which, if rejected, would have been followed by the American initiation of nuclear war.

McMahon responded by declining the policy advice proffered in this memorandum, but by hiring Borden to become one of his principal staff advisers on nuclear matters. Borden would then play a major role in 1954, after the Soviets had acquired nuclear weapons, in accusing J. Robert Oppenheimer of being too unreliable in loyalties, or judgment, to retain his security clearances.[35]

Francis J. Matthews

The Korean War had, of course, convinced many more Americans that the confrontation with the Soviet bloc would now have military dimensions. U.S. defense spending had not been high, as compared to World War II, or as compared to all the years since 1950, before the Korean War broke out.

The logic by which the Soviets would feel free to exploit their advantages in conventional weapons, once they had nuclear weapons of their own, was central to NSC-68, the study that President Truman had asked Paul Nitze to undertake after the first detection of a Russian nuclear test in 1949. Nitze's study had advocated a very substantial expansion of American defense spending, now that Moscow had atomic bombs, but Truman shelved these recommendations, and they were not to be implemented until North Korean tanks crossed the 38th parallel in June of 1950.[36]

Those with a longer vision might have predicted the rolling of such Soviet-built tanks, in all directions, once Stalin had nuclear weapons of his own, once the United States could not so easily inflict nuclear retaliation for a conventional aggression. Hitting Moscow to punish a tank attack would be easier, just as hitting Hiroshima had been easier, when San Francisco or New York could not be destroyed in response. By the elementary logic of mutual assured destruction, it would be much more difficult thereafter.

Nonetheless, just as Orvil Anderson captured more attention for his preventive war views after the Korean War had broken out (i.e., after it may have been "too late" in terms of the simple nuclear confrontation), Secretary of the Navy Francis Matthews had drawn even greater attention several days earlier, on August 25th of 1950, with a Boston speech advocating preventive war, a speech which President Truman had to take pains to disown as not representing United States government policy.[37]

One can exaggerate the influence in policy formation of the secretary of the navy, now that the U.S. military had been unified. Yet his speech surely had to be taken as a sign that the idea of preventive war was not totally illegitimate in Washington after the Korean War had broken out. If it was more legitimate in 1950, however, it was less cost-free, now that the USSR, since 1949, was known to have nuclear weapons of its own.

"Liberal" vs. "Conservative"

A reader looking back on these suggestions for preventive war might have guessed that these had to come from the right end of the political spectrum on domestic and foreign policy questions, while assuming that what contemporary Americans call "liberals," or the left-of-center, would of course be aligned against any such ideas. Yet, as has already been shown, the alignment is more complicated than this, with at least four possibilities to be matrixed out here:

	liberal	conservative	
favor	!	!	!
	!	!	!
	!	!	!
prev. war			
oppose	!	!	!
	!	!	!
	!	!	!

The gut reactions of those who are more traditional conservatives (in the European sense) might indeed lead them to be more ready to consider the use of force and the initiation of war. By comparison, the classical "liberal" in the European or global sense (by which almost all Americans are "liberal," including especially Goldwater and Reagan) is more distrustful of governmental power in general, and of power politics or the use of force. The average Americans has been a "liberal" in such an unquestioning and unchallenged sense that the very phrase has come to mean something different within the United States, applied to the subset of voters who lean somewhat toward democratic socialism, toward a greater role for the state (always as long as the state is still held in check against tyranny, still guaranteed as government by periodic elections, facing an opposition).

The classical liberal is thus distrustful of militarism, and of military preparations that might lead to militarism. Foreign dictatorships are a threat to one's liberty at home, but so at the same time are one's own military preparations against such foreign dictatorships, because they introduce a need for discipline and secrecy, and for readiness to use violence, so antithetical to government by consent of the governed.

By this elementary dichotomy, one would paint traditional conservatives or "realists" as *more* ready to consider a violent imposition of the Baruch Plan, and liberals as less ready to do so. Yet there is a re-

verse side to this dichotomy that might produce just the opposite alignment, filling out the remaining two boxes in our matrix above.

The liberal, reluctant to get drawn into continuing military preparations and their compromises of democratic freedom, sometimes favors
isolationism, and a foreign policy of doing nothing more than setting a
good example. But, if forced to conclude that this will not be enough to
prevent a hegemony by a repressive foreign regime, such a liberal will
want to get the resulting war over with as quickly as possible, thus
producing a commitment to "unconditional surrender" and total victory, commitments which a traditional practitioner of the game of balance of power might find ill-conceived. Such liberals will also be tempted
to reach for weapons which have a special impact abroad without requiring extensive mobilizations, or excessive military discipline, at
home.

British liberals in the nineteenth century thus tended to welcome the
Royal Navy as an alternative to maintaining large standing armies, since
armies would always be more of a threat than navies to liberties back
home.[38] And someone of similar instincts might thus have welcomed
nuclear weapons after 1945, perhaps as the tool to establish world law
and order once and for all, or later (as was actually to happen, once the
Soviets had nuclear weapons as well) as an alternative to the massive
spending and extended periods of compulsory military service required
to defend against the conventional forces of the Warsaw Pact.

An American liberal can thus be thankful to nuclear weapons for
dispensing with the draft, and generally for having lowered the total
amount of time young Americans had to spend in uniform. Thanks can
similarly be given that nuclear weapons allowed for the Western European economic boom after 1948, amid rates of economic growth that
the world had never seen before. The steel that otherwise would have
had to go into NATO tanks, to match the tanks on the Soviet side, could
instead go into additional steel mills, and into the production of auto-
mobiles.

Nuclear weapons *might* have been used before 1949 to head off all
the military burden of the Cold War that was to follow 1950. That is the
theme of this book, and it is a theme that a liberal can not so automatically reject. Nuclear weapons *were* used after 1952, by Eisenhower,
and indeed by all the U.S. administrations thereafter, to reduce the military burden of the Cold War. This always left concerns about whether
the deterring threats of nuclear escalation might not one day have to be

fulfilled, with horrible consequences for the world. Yet the alternative, of a totally conventional Western defense against the Warsaw Pact, had major drawbacks as well, from any humane standpoint.

One can thus find strands of liberal or other anti-militarist reasoning that might attach a unique significance to weapons of mass destruction, and to the prevention of their proliferation—and perhaps therefore to their use to preempt such proliferation.

Turning then to the fourth box of our matrix, there is also a logic by which more traditional or conservative intuitions would lean *against* any attempt to apply the nuclear monopoly. This is a viewpoint by which "absolute weapons" have emerged in the past, only to be proven as not so "absolute." This is a perspective by which every weapon and every strategy induces counter-weapons and counter-strategies. Rather than trusting in the unique ability of nuclear weapons to coerce an enemy into surrender, there would be generals and admirals here (and civilian analysts) who would contend that the enemy must still be defeated and disarmed in the end, that his territory must be occupied, that traditional standards of a military victory would still have to be satisfied.

As noted above, very different notions of preventive war are in play here, including those still stressing battlefield victory rather than deterring punishment. There are thus some very critical interpretations of the professional military outlook in the United States, or in any other country, that would make such officers *less* ready to consider preventive war, and *less* ready to attach any great significance to maintaining the nuclear monopoly.

Rather than estimating the value of a nuclear arsenal by comparing the number of our warheads with the number of cities on the other side, this more traditional "counter-force" view would tend to see nuclear weapons as "just another weapon," with the crucial question being whether the arsenal is big enough to *disarm* the other side.[39]

The discussion of any possible heading off of Soviet nuclear weapons thus becomes a debate about *how much* military preparation, how many nuclear warheads, are needed to carry off such an operation, with most of the professional military being inclined to raise the estimates of the prerequisites, and thus to argue against any early preventive initiative. By comparison, someone as left-of-center as Bertrand Russell was arguing more for the use than for the accumulation of weapons, that is, for earlier action before the adversary indeed "accumulated" *any* of such weapons.

To be really averse to nuclear weapons and the destructive potential they demonstrated at Hiroshima is logically equivalent to emphasizing how powerful a deterrent or *compellent* they can be. And the latter-day advocates of "finite deterrence" or "minimum deterrence" (of "no-first-use") belong in exactly the same box, stressing how even a few nuclear weapons are enough, thus suggesting that preventing "even a few" on the other side would have been the crucial accomplishment.

The "mutual assured destruction" position is typically seen to be a "liberal" posture in the 1980s, while the "war-fighting" position was labeled the "conservative" posture. "Mutual assured destruction" determined the number of bombs required not by how many bombs the other side had, but by how many *cities* they had. Where the other side had no bombs at all yet, however, there is no "mutual" here, and the number of American bombs could easily have matched the number of Soviet cities.

5

Arguments Against: Practical Considerations

It is time now to try to list the arguments that would have been arrayed against any preventive war to preserve the nuclear monopoly. The array offered here will not be exhaustive, and some of the arguments may overlap, but each of these were most probably in play. We will begin with what many analysts would regard as "perfectly sensible" objections to such a policy, arguments presumably based on objective and practical reality.

Arguments of Simple Inability: "Shortage of Bombs"

One of the explanations offered most often for the absence of preventive war between 1945 and 1949 is simply that the United States lacked enough nuclear weapons to carry out such a campaign. While the world was led to believe that the United States had a sizable stockpile of nuclear weapons, perhaps extrapolating from the fact that the attacks on Hiroshima and Nagasaki had come with a separation of only three days, one of the best kept secrets of the postwar years was that the total of nuclear weapons in the U.S. arsenal was indeed quite small.[1]

Had the Japanese not surrendered after the Nagasaki attack, it would have been several weeks before another atomic bomb would be ready for use; the American campaign to end the war with Japan was thus in a way a colossal bluff,[2] and so may have been the entire pattern of "nuclear deterrence" for the years after 1945.

By some accounts, moreover, even the few bombs for which components had been assembled in 1946 and 1947 were no longer functional or usable. Nuclear weapons have always been much more complicated than ordinary high-explosive bombs, requiring more constant maintenance and care to keep them ready for detonation. If the personnel for such maintenance were not in place in 1947, the total of nuclear weapons in the U.S. arsenal may indeed have amounted to zero.[3]

While the rest of U.S. disarmament after 1945 was wide open for all to see, however, this was not; the American people, and very possibly the Soviet leaders as well, might thus have had to assume that an American nuclear arsenal existed, even while the key U.S. decision makers, the people about whom we are speculating in this book, would have known better.[4]

If the United States did not have enough nuclear weapons in these years to impose a permanence of the nuclear monopoly, this would settle the question for many readers, and there would be no need to go any further with the arguments and inquiries of this book. Yet the shortage of nuclear weapons here obviously begs another question, for one has to ask *why* the United States, under President Truman, did not take the steps to keep nuclear weapons production and nuclear weapons maintenance going at maximum capacity, that is, why the physicists and engineers required for the Manhattan Project were allowed to return to their universities, or to their other employers, rather than being required or induced to stay in Los Alamos.

The "disarming" of the U.S. nuclear force after 1945 is nearly parallel to the disarming of conventional forces, to be discussed below. In each case, personal decisions were allowed to disrupt teams, in the nuclear case, the teams needed to make sure that an atomic bomb would be kept usable or that additional weapons could be produced, in the conventional case, the teams needed to keep tanks functional.

In addition to allowing "bombs on the shelf" to become unready, disassembled into components, with some of these components having to be renewed regularly because of short half-lives, but not being renewed, etc., there was continual anxiety about the availability of uranium to increase the total of such bombs (with any such limits to the known supply of uranium, as noted earlier, seemingly also offering some more positive assurances, about how difficult it might be for *other* countries to acquire a nuclear arsenal).[5]

Yet, regardless of the wrong predictions about long-term inherent limits to supply, the immediate quantities of uranium available were more straightforwardly a function of how much the United States was ready to pay for the stuff, and the urgency with which it saw the need.[6]

The urgency was low enough so that much less than a maximum effort was made to acquire uranium, unlike the case with the Soviets who put the acquisition of such materials in East Germany, and then Czechoslovakia, at the top of their list.

Once again, the "explanation" of American decisions thus requires a deeper explanation. The shortfall in effort can be traced partially to bureaucratic contests and failures of coordination; but it also has to be traced to what we are discussing here, the absence of any intention to employ the monopoly.

The lapsing of an active U.S. bomb production program, to be revived only really late in 1947, with results then appearing in 1948, would be analogous to Britain allowing its naval forces to be totally demobilized after the defeat of Napoleon. Peace always brings some demobilization, of course, as naval officers are released and the press gangs are terminated, and as nuclear physicists return to their civilian university positions. But why was so total a demobilization allowed in 1945, a demobilization, an absence of usable nuclear weapons, which had to be a matter of choice rather than necessity?

The actual totals of nuclear weapons possessed by the United States, counting components as if they were assembled into bombs, rather than badly maintained, is something like the following: perhaps three or four at the end of 1945, and nine by the middle of 1946 (but perhaps none if one takes issues of readiness into account), and perhaps thirteen by the middle of 1947.[7] By the middle of 1948, amid some serious concern about the Soviet behavior in blockading Berlin, the total had climbed to perhaps fifty. (Even this might have struck some analysts as enough to carry off a preventive war, if one were convinced that the adversary, Stalin's Russia, did not yet have *any* nuclear warheads.)

What the public was guessing about these American totals (what the Soviets also probably had to be guessing) would have been considerably larger, projecting out from the pace achieved by the Manhattan Project at the end of World War II.

We know that the step-up of nuclear weapons production and readiness maintenance by 1948 and 1949 produced totals of several hundred bombs. If we then have to guess at what the Truman administration could have achieved with even a moderate program of incentives to engineers and physicists, we might deduce a considerably more robust level of 1946 and 1947 weapons, perhaps fifty for 1946 and one hundred for 1947. And if Truman had elected to exploit the Soviet cheating on the Yalta promises, to stoke up American willingness to challenge Stalin on the over-arching nuclear issue, it presumably would have been possible to enlist a still larger effort, and to achieve several hundred bombs ready for use.

In summary, the "shortage of bombs" is thus more the puzzle we are trying to explain, and less an explanation for the puzzle. The same considerations, whether they be American natural peacefulness, or something else, would explain the decision not to use the atomic bombs against Stalin, and then the prior decision not even to build or maintain enough of them. These considerations remain to be identified.

We must dwell a little longer on the question of whether Stalin could have known of the American bomb shortage. The extent of Soviet espionage in the Cold War, most of which has only been disclosed now since the collapse of Communism, is quite truly amazing. Thousands upon thousands of pages of American classified documents were transmitted to Moscow, to speed the day when the first Soviet atomic bomb was ready, some transmitted by agents who were detected and arrested after a few years, others transmitted by agents whose identity is still not known today.[8] Indeed sometimes there had been more than one Soviet spy attending a key meeting discussing American weapons prospects, with each of the spies not being aware of the other's identity.

Given the extent of espionage on how the United States had produced nuclear weapons, and how it was planning to move ahead to advanced fission bomb design and then to thermonuclear fusion hydrogen bombs, it thus remains somewhat unclear how unaware the Soviet leadership was, from 1945 to 1949, about the actual size and status of the American "nuclear arsenal."

The U.S. government, under President Truman, went to extraordinary efforts to keep the numbers of ready bombs a secret, with documents never having such numbers typed in, and with briefers required to fill in the blanks from memory. The small size of this stockpile, perhaps with no bombs in ready state at all, was hardly known by Americans at large at the time, and was only to be disclosed several decades later.

But the same U.S. government had also gone to great lengths to hold back the technical details of how bombs were made, and had failed in maintaining security here. One must thus at least consider the possibility that Stalin had by 1946 heard reports that the American nuclear arsenal was in such a state of disrepair, and one must try to relate this to his other decisions.

Richard Rhodes makes the argument that Stalin's decision to expand his conventional military from some three million up to five million in 1947 showed that he feared American nuclear attack, and thus that the Soviet dictator did not know how few American bombs there were.[9] Yet one could certainly introduce other arguments for such an expansion, for example as a sign that the most urgent economic problems of Soviet recovery after the damage of World War II had been brought under control, or as a sign that Stalin intended to deploy conventional force for whatever it was worth, when he had no nuclear weapons yet and perhaps the Americans had only a few (just as he would continue to deploy such massive conventional forces after he had nuclear forces of his own).

Given the nature of Soviet society, Stalin and Beria did not trust all that their espionage agents were bringing in from the West, perhaps because the United States and Britain simply seemed too open to espionage to be believed. Some of the early details of technical approaches to the bomb were thus suspected of being disinformation, designed to lead the USSR into wasting its resources on wrong turns.[10] And Stalin surely would have had to distrust the "good news" that there were so few American nuclear weapons, all of them disassembled and requiring a substantial lead-time to be ready, all of them stored in a single location.

If Stalin had thus seen reports that the Americans had only a disassembled nuclear force, might he not have suspected a trap, an American trick to get him to aggress, thus to give President Truman whatever clear justification he might need for a war against the Soviet Union?

Simple Inability: "The Ineffectiveness of Bombing"

An alternative explanation for why the atomic monopoly was not used, and perhaps for why nuclear weapons were not even readied for possible use, was that the experiences of World War II had somehow proved that no country would give in to strategic bombardment. The British public and government had not collapsed with the 1940 bombing of London, and the German public and Hitler had not buckled in face of the much more extensive bombing of German cities through the rest of the war. The Japanese had similarly showed no signs of surrendering in face of extensive conventional bombing, including the massive fire raid on Tokyo.

The United States Strategic Bombing Survey in the years after 1945 was widely quoted as showing that strategic bombing had been a failure and a waste of resources.[11] It had failed, so some of the volumes suggested, at crippling the *ability* of the Germans or Japanese to fight, and it had also failed to eliminate the *willingness* of the enemy and its government to fight.

Yet different volumes of the USSBS were drafted by different authors, so that it is always misleading to claim that "the Strategic Bombing Survey indicated" something, without noting that the various volumes often contradict each other. The Japanese had indeed surrendered, moreover, after the nuclear bombings of Hiroshima and Nagasaki, at a time when most Americans would have expected Japanese resistance to continue at least into 1946, and very possibly to 1947.[12]

When criticized on moral grounds for having used nuclear weapons against Japan, President Truman repeatedly turned to the argument that the use of the bomb had shortened the war and had saved American lives, and that the bombings had even saved Japanese lives, those Japanese who would have fought so determinedly on the beaches of their home islands.[13]

Skeptics about the impact of strategic bombing would of course challenge the validity of Truman's logic. Yet the important question, for our analysis here, is what Truman and those around him believed in 1945. It is certainly plausible that Truman believed that the bombings had shortened the war.

Some of the analysts who have voiced such skepticism about the deterrent and compellent impacts of massive bombing (conventional or nuclear) were very possibly perpetrating a myth, a myth reinforcing their own moral feelings (if one is against the horror of aerial bombing, why not claim that such bombing also *never* works?). During the much lighter bombings of the Vietnam War, one heard, over and over again, the alleged lesson that such bombings always stiffened the will of those being punished,[14] rallying them to their leaders. Japanese spokesmen were similarly adept at nurturing a guilt felt among Americans for having made Japan the only victim ever of nuclear attack, while suggesting that Japan somehow would have surrendered very soon in any event.[15]

In the Japanese case, this claim has always begged the logical prior question of *what* would have produced such surrender, except for the comparable horror already being inflicted on Japanese civilian life by conventional bombing, and by the naval blockade of food. In the German case, the argument may hold that Hitler's resolve did not fail, but one has to remember that the German Army was emboldened to try to assassinate Hitler in 1944; are we to assume that the on-going destruction of German cities by British and American air attacks played *no* role in pushing Stauffenberg and his colleagues to this dangerous attempt?

Being bombed is decidedly unpleasant, and the most plausible conclusion is indeed that any nation facing a monopoly of the ability to inflict such destruction will have to consider surrendering in face of it, just as Japan surrendered in 1945. Doubts about the efficacy of counter-force-oriented strategic bombing campaigns (i.e., those campaigns which are in truth intended to disable an enemy, rather than to impose pain on that enemy) have been more readily extracted from the experiences of World War II. The U.S. Army Air Force had aimed for such "precision-bombing" (as contrasted with the Royal Air Force which had resigned itself to "area bombing" campaigns against Germany), and had failed to achieve a victory when ball-bearings and aircraft production facilities were the designated targets. A greater impact was achieved late in the war when the targets were instead railways and then petroleum facilities.[16]

The Royal Air Force Bomber Command had decided early in the war that daylight raids would entail excessively high losses of aircraft, and had engaged instead in nighttime "area bombing" raids, still *ostensibly* intended to cripple German war production by disrupting the life of the workers in German defense plants.[17] U.S. air planners sometimes quietly grumbled that the RAF was engaged in a less moral form of air warfare, because more German civilians were being killed,[18] but the distinction became somewhat moot when the two allied air forces cooperated in day-night-day attacks on the same city, as at Dresden in 1945.

In any event, the USAAF daylight attacks were less precise than described, so that these also had a substantial counter-value impact in worsening or ending the lives of German civilians, even while the official goals of both American and British air attacks were counter-force rather than counter-value, to disable the German war machine rather than to impose pain on the German population.

In the B-29 attacks on Japan, the USAAF had then shifted after a time to nighttime area attacks, deciding that these would be more effective than daylight "precision attacks," rationalizing this on the claim that the Japanese weapons industry had been dispersed across civilian neighborhoods in Japanese cities.[19] Over 100,000 people were thus killed in an early non-nuclear fire raid on Tokyo. And the nuclear attack on Hiroshima was also explained as being based on the fact that this city was the home-base for two Japanese army divisions.

In truth, the U.S. raids on Japan, just as the RAF raids on Germany, were intended to inflict suffering at least as much as disablement. Here, to repeat, it is much more difficult to claim that this was all ineffectual, since Japan indeed surrendered when this was administered by nuclear attacks. Those claiming that "Japan would have surrendered anyway" really then have to concede that this surrender would have been the result instead of *conventional* B-29 attacks, with 300 bombers having to fly the destructive mission, instead of just one.

An important source of confusion about effectiveness emerges here because, for reasons of *morality* and the traditional laws of war, it has always been essential to claim that *all* attacks are aimed at "military targets," that is, aimed to disarm an enemy and to render him unable to fight, with any damage to civilian targets being inadvertent "collateral damage," and with there being no intention to inflict such damage. This has made it very much easier for the critics of strategic bombing, pretending to take such statements of intention seriously, to announce then that the bombing campaigns in question, as for example the United States bombings of North Vietnam, had "failed."

If the perpetrators of the bombing are in truth intending to win their war by imposing pain, the war has then become an endurance contest, a contest of who will be the first to tire of the suffering. In such a contest, the side being bombed will of course pretend, for as long as it can, that it is not intimidated by the bombings, that its resolve to win is only being stiffened. Just as economic blockades and guerrilla attacks and battlefield carnage have in the past been the tools of such contests, the rounds of bombing amount to the same thing. The side that will surrender on Monday will most likely still be proclaiming its toughness and endurance on the previous Saturday.

Such pretenses of toughness aside, the assumption that bombing, conventional or nuclear, never induces concessions or surrenders is indeed a myth. To the extent that this myth was in circulation between 1945 and 1949 (and indeed has been in circulation ever since), it offers one possible explanation for what we are seeking to explain here, the failure of the United States to try to use its nuclear monopoly to perpetuate itself.

Yet, to repeat, the very recent surprise of a sudden Japanese surrender had to persuade many of the people around President Truman that bombing might indeed work, and in particular that *nuclear* bombing would work. Our search to explain the absence of preventive war has to continue.

Simple Inability: Totalitarian Toughness

Closely related to the above case against the effectiveness of strategic bombing would have been a special argument about Stalin's Russia, that this dictatorship in particular would have been callous enough to shrug off the damage being inflicted on Russian cities. Stalin would have been tougher than the Japanese leaders were in 1945, and at least as tough as Hitler had been when his cities were being leveled by conventional bombing.[20]

Despite many pleas by Goebbels that Hitler should visit cities like Hamburg, as Churchill had buoyed up British morale by visiting the bombed-out portions of London in 1940, Hitler refused to do so, perhaps because he was a moral weakling, unwilling to share the suffering of his German followers, perhaps because he wanted to gird himself to withstand any of the pressures the RAF and USAAF were applying toward a Nazi surrender.[21]

Could not Stalin, the same Stalin who had allowed millions of Ukrainian and Russian kulaks to die in the pursuit of a more collective approach to agriculture, not have similarly girded himself to ignore the leveling of one Russian city after another? Stalin's Soviet Union matched Hitler's Germany in how free it was of having to conduct election campaigns, or of having to worry very much about public opinion. Each had effective secret police systems, and concentration camps, to which would be sent anyone daring to protest the resistance to foreign pressure.

Such an assessment of Soviet invulnerability to counter-value attacks on cities was indeed to be a staple of the American debate that continued all through the Cold War, about what was required, once the USSR had massive nuclear forces of its own, to deter the Kremlin leadership from launching World War III. Believers in mutual assured destruction, stressing that nuclear weapons would be directed against cities, argued that this was more than enough to deter Khrushchev or Brezhnev. But other analysts argued that the United States needed much more extensive nuclear forces, to match those of the Soviet Union in size, and to attack a wide variety of counter-force military targets, because nothing else would be sufficient to deter the Kremlin.[22]

Brezhnev and his associates, it was argued at the beginning of the 1980s, would be relatively indifferent to American retaliatory attacks on Soviet cities, as long as key Communist cadres and key workers were sheltered against such attacks, and as long as Soviet conventional and nuclear forces were able to advance the Kremlin's political control across Western Europe and other parts of the world. To deter the Soviets from seeking a "victory" in a World War III, the only effective Western threat (by this American "war-fighting" view) would be to structure the force confrontation so that such a "victory" would go to the West instead. The Soviet leadership, under Brezhnev, and perhaps even under Gorbachev, was accused of being guided by considerations of power, and of being otherwise relatively indifferent to the transitory suffering undergone in the attainment of power.[23]

The analysts who thus advocated a "war-fighting" rather than "assured destruction" policy cautioned their fellow Americans never to forget that the USSR had suffered 25 million casualties in World War II. The presumption was that Moscow might well launch such a war if it could keep the costs under 25 million, and if it could conquer the world in the process.

It is very easy to project such arguments of the 1970s and 1980s back to the 1940s. The same Kremlin that might shrug off nuclear retaliation (once it had nuclear weapons of its own, as long as it was winning the war) might shrug off nuclear threats and retaliation even when it had no such weapons yet, and was being pressured to give up all attempts to acquire them. In either scenario, the Communist leadership would be guided by very different values and rules from the leadership of the democracies, not having to win elections, and perhaps not caring that much about the immediate suffering of the people, where the long-term future of the Marxist variety of "socialism" was at stake.

If we turn here to the actual Soviet pronouncements on this subject, it is easy enough to describe what Stalin and the rest of the Soviet leadership *said* about the significance of nuclear weapons. But it is harder to establish what they really *believed* about such weapons.[24]

The official pronouncements of the Soviet Union were what any strategist would recommend that one profess to believe, when one does not have such weapons of one's own yet, but has to face a United States which had demonstrated them. The most effective posture for bargaining purposes, for winning concessions rather than having to make concessions, would be to deny both the counter-force and the counter-value impact of such weapons, to pretend that atomic bombs did not make much difference (even if one actually realized that they could make a tremendous difference).

This is basically what the official posture of the Soviet Union was to be, for as long as Stalin was alive, and for a while longer, stressing that the "permanently operating factors" determined who won wars, rather than any marvelous new secret weapons, rather than campaigns of strategic bombardment, rather than atomic bombs, and suggesting that the damage inflicted on Hiroshima and Nagasaki, and the potential damage demonstrated at the 1946 Bikini test, was not all that great.[25]

The difficulty is that such pronouncements are fully consistent with either version of Stalin's real beliefs and attitudes. If he were truly indifferent to American nuclear attack, this is what he would say, simply speaking his mind. But if he were instead very fearful of American nuclear threats, and of a preventive war campaign launched on the basis of the American nuclear monopoly, this is *also* what he should have said, as part of a colossal bluff, a bluff intended to give him time to get his own atomic bombs.

Even what Stalin said privately might be interpreted either way. The best way to carry off the bluff, to pretend that one is not so fearful of a nuclear attack on Moscow or Minsk or Leningrad, is to voice such feelings in conversations with one's own associates, as part of psyching oneself up, as part of being convincing to the outside world.

To be introduced as counter-evidence, against Stalin's toughness in face of nuclear threats, is the strong support he gave the Soviet atomic bomb effort after Hiroshima, and even before, all of which suggests that Stalin's indifference expressed at Potsdam, when Truman informed him of the atomic bomb, was not so candid.[26] There is some evidence, in later reports of private conversations, that Stalin was genuinely shocked by the news of Hiroshima.[27] Perhaps this made the destructive power of the atomic bomb more real than reports of a test in the desert; or perhaps it was more shocking that the United States would actually use such a bomb in the anger of warfare, use it against a city.

Similarly to be cited, as evidence counter to the official Soviet skepticism about strategic bombing, was the effort applied to reverse-engineering the American B-29, to produce perhaps as many as 1,000 of the Tu-4 copies of the American bomber.

Yet one might also somehow explain Stalin's eagerness to acquire nuclear weapons and Tu-4 bombers without making the atomic bomb the absolute weapon. Some interpreters, after all the disclosures, would still be able to reconcile Stalin's pronouncements as being genuine, even while Soviet nuclear scientists and intelligence agents were being assigned such a high priority.

If Stalin saw the atomic bomb as an important weapon, but yet as just another weapon, he might have denied it all *military* importance in public statements until he had some bombs of his own, while he would in actuality be simply placing such weapons in a broader military context, before and after 1949.

Within this shadow-boxing game of possible pretense, the sub-question might be the one exercising American strategic planners so much, before 1949 and especially after, whether the counter-value impact of nuclear weapons would be decisive in itself, or whether these weapons were more important for what they offered to the grand (counter-force) effort to win a war, by the traditional measure of having disarmed one's enemy.

To repeat, if Stalin wished to be free of the threats being proposed by Bertrand Russell or Winston Churchill, he needed to brush off both the counter-force and the counter-value aspects of such weapons. But, of the two, until he had a reliable arsenal of his own to threaten enough American cities, it would be the most important to brush aside the counter-value impact.

There are those of us, *if* we had no nuclear weapons of our own, who would see twenty nuclear weapons in enemy hands an unignorable tool of blackmail, forcing us to surrender, just as we interpret the Japanese as having been forced to surrender. The part of Stalin's posture that he would most have wanted to be accepted in Washington or London was that no such blackmail was feasible, that no such surrender would be forthcoming, that the destruction of Soviet cities could be accepted.

Simple Inability: Difficulties of Targeting Intelligence?

A variant on the difficulties of applying strategic bombing to a toughened Stalinist Soviet Union is that the United States would have had difficulty in finding some of the targets it most urgently needed to hit, that is, the Soviet uranium-enrichment plants or plutonium-producing reactors generating the crucial fissionable material for the first Soviet atomic bombs.[28]

For a more grandly counter-force approach to a war with the USSR, the target would instead have been the entire steel and petroleum industries, and tank production lines, and so on, which were surely easier to find, but which would require larger numbers of American atomic bombs, and a larger bomber force getting past the Soviet air defense system to destroy such industries and keep them destroyed. This, as noted, was a view of a future World War III widely held by U.S. Air Force planners, perhaps too widely held.[29] Millions upon millions of Russians would have been killed in such attacks, but their deaths would in truth have been collateral damage, because the target planners in the United States had convinced themselves that Stalin had to be defeated in battle, rather than simply coerced.

Especially after General Curtis LeMay took command of the U.S. Strategic Air Command in 1948, extensive work was done on target planning for a nuclear air war against the USSR, most likely in response to a Soviet initiation of such a war, but perhaps even in a preventive anticipation of such a Soviet attack. This target planning would corral all the evidence available on how the Soviet economy and industrial system was interconnected, in a replay of the target planning that had been done for World War II against Germany and Japan, and after 1949 it would even include provocative overflights of the Soviet Union. This was not the kind of war for which American use of air power would be precluded simply for lack of targeting data.

But the more directly counter-value interpretation of a preventive war, that is, what is being outlined here, would have involved much less need to target steel or oil industries; the simple destruction of Soviet population centers, or even the mere threat of such destruction, would coerce Stalin into surrendering his nuclear potential, and perhaps all the military and political assets he controlled (just as the Japanese militarists had surrendered in 1945 after Hiroshima and Nagasaki had been bombed). There would have had to be a public pretense that military targets were being aimed at, just as has always been the case with aerial bombardment; but all the intelligence needed would have come with the longitude and latitude of the major city being destroyed.

At first glance, there would thus have been much less need for target intelligence in this kind of nuclear war. But an intelligence problem would then have emerged, for such an approach focusing entirely on the painful aspect of nuclear attack, once there were any real concerns that the Soviets were *close* to acquiring nuclear weapons, that is, close to being able to hit back to inflict similar damage on New York or San Francisco.

Here one would need to know not just the location of population centers or steel mills, but also the location in particular of nuclear laboratories and small reactors, exactly the problem one confronts later when Indians are contemplating a preventive war attack on the nuclear potential of Pakistan, or when the U.S. is conducting such attacks on Iraq during Desert Storm.

The Cold War was driven by a very major intelligence asymmetry. No matter how strenuously General Groves tried to keep secrets in the Manhattan Project, and no matter how closely secrets might have been held in the U.S. Atomic Energy Commission after 1946, the United States would inevitably be more open than Stalin's Soviet Union.

It would thus be difficult for Americans to determine how much effort the USSR was devoting to nuclear weapons production, and how soon such efforts would produce results, one of the inherent background factors in the entire puzzle we are sorting here. And it would be similarly difficult to determine the exact locations at which such an effort was underway, the chokepoints for any air attacks trying to keep such bombs from being produced.[30] The Soviet nuclear program would be an even more opaque target than the Nazi German "nuclear program" of World War II, where General Groves had knowledge of where Werner Heisenberg's research laboratory was located, so that it could be included in the targets for Allied air raids.[31]

Yet the Western intelligence task should still not have been hopeless. It is difficult to pin down how much of a problem such target information would have posed for an advocate of preventive war. It might have been more of a problem by 1948, when the chances were greater that Stalin already had his bomb, after Molotov had already claimed in a November, 1947 speech that the techniques of how to make a bomb had ceased to be a secret. But the time between 1946 and 1948, if nothing else, might also have been applied by Western intelligence agencies to identifying the locations of the Soviet nuclear effort.

Simple Inability: Indispensability of the H-Bomb?

A nearly parallel argument about the weakness of the atomic bomb as a compellent would see the thermonuclear (fusion) hydrogen bomb, rather than ordinary (fission) atomic bombs, as the necessary underpinning for any such attempt to monopolize nuclear weapons for the world. If the twenty kilotons of the Hiroshima bomb were not sufficient, surely the megaton-range bombs tested after 1952 would be.

The United States test-detonated several atomic bombs in July of 1946 at the Pacific atoll of Bikini, to see what such bomb could do against warships, and probably to reinforce the impression, in Russia or anywhere else in the world, that these were indeed powerful and meaningful weapons. The tests may have backfired, however, at least so far as could be tested by American public opinion polls, because a majority of respondents described themselves as generally underimpressed by the tests, and as surprised that the bomb was less destructive than had been expected.[32] The overall impact is perhaps captured best by the naming of a very skimpy women's swimsuit as the "bikini."

By contrast, the first H-bomb detonation, in 1954, at Eniwetok, did not impress anyone as a disappointment or dud, quite the opposite, after an island comparable to the size of Manhattan became a large crater in the ocean floor. There would be no swimsuits named "eniwetoks."[33]

Yet this would then generate a somewhat different explanation for the real-life failure to exploit a monopoly, since the race to acquire such thermonuclear weapons was much closer to a "dead heat." The United States indeed tested the first thermonuclear device in November of 1952, but the design was of a size comparable to a three-story building, hardly deliverable to a target in the Soviet Union. The Soviets tested their first H-device in 1954, already a smaller assembly, and may have been the first to test-detonate such a bomb in an actual drop from an aircraft in 1955. Since the United States did not detonate its own air-deliverable H-bomb until 1954 as well, there is hardly much of a period here in which one side could brazenly dictate terms of non-proliferation to the order.[34]

But there are again problems with this kind of explanation. It certainly is correct that the fusion thermonuclear H-bombs dwarf the fission atomic bomb in destructiveness, for the first time posing possibilities of the destruction of all mankind. Yet the world has not since then drawn the non-proliferation line on this fusion-fission distinction, but rather at the line crossed already in 1945, and then in 1949.

The atomic bombs demonstrated at Hiroshima and Nagasaki are indeed *already* weapons of mass destruction. Anyone seeing the results of the first Eniwetok detonation of a hydrogen device had to be impressed;

but anyone seeing the newsreels of the remains of the two Japanese cities hit with atomic bombs will also be repulsed and intimidated.

The United States could not have had an H-bomb before the Soviets got their first atomic bomb in 1949, but it could have had hundreds of atomic bombs if production had been pushed in 1946 and 1947, rather than being allowed to languish; it indeed did have over 100 warheads ready for use late in 1948, after production was stepped up in response to the Berlin blockade and other crises. The U.S. nuclear weapons labs had been run far less urgently than during World War II, but progress had also been made in making atomic bombs more destructive for the amount of fissionable material consumed, and also lighter and easier to deliver. Moreover, it has to be repeated that most Americans, and indeed most American political leaders, *assumed* that the total of U.S. nuclear weapons had gotten well into the hundreds, presumably ready for use. If the best-kept secret of these years was that this was not the case, it does not explain the general American failure to entertain thoughts of preventive war.

To close in this part of the argument, one could imagine a world of physics where fission bombs were possible, but where fusion weapons were not. In such a world, there would still be a tremendous threat to be headed off, the threat that hundreds of such cities on each side would be subjected, in a day or two, to the fate of Hiroshima and Nagasaki. The years from 1945 to 1949 could have seen a heroic effort to preclude this threat, but they did not.

The argument that the atomic bomb would not be sufficient to coerce other states, so that the thermonuclear H-bomb would be required, is thus not convincing to this author. The horror we feel about nuclear war is importantly derived from the real experiences of Hiroshima and Nagasaki, experiences imposed by "mere" atomic bombs, experiences sufficient to make Brodie's "absolute weapon" arguments of 1946 quite plausible.

Yet this leads us then into the debates about the American (and Soviet decision) to move ahead to H-bomb development, very soon after the American detection of the first Soviet atomic bomb test in 1949.[35]

Did the Soviet atomic bomb make an American hydrogen bomb somehow necessary, as a sort of trump card in a new layer of escalation? And/or was the real American fear that the Soviets would move right along to this next round of thermonuclear weapons, so that *their* H-bomb would be a trump card outweighing all of the American array of atomic bombs?

Two kinds of arguments get made by those who lament the development of the H-bomb, that the Soviets might not have developed theirs, *if* the United States had itself promised not to produce such a bomb, and that such thermonuclear weapons were not really relevant or necessary as any kind of topper for the atomic bomb.

The first argument seems wrong in retrospect, in light of the speed of the Soviet move toward H-bombs, such that some observers would actually see the United States and the USSR tied in the race for thermonuclear weapons. Just as we now know that Stalin would probably have sought atomic bombs even if there was no Manhattan Project, the evidence suggests that the Soviets would have sought thermonuclear weapons whether or not the Americans did.[36]

The second argument would seem more plausible, that a force consisting entirely of fission bombs might very effectively deter a force including fusion bombs; this is just another version of the mutual assured destruction premise, that even a smaller number of atomic bombs could deter a larger number, as long as the smaller number was sufficient to destroy the cities of the more powerful side.

But this revitalizes the case for exploiting the American monopoly of atomic bombs before 1949. If the atomic bomb was more than sufficient to deter Soviet atomic attack, such that U.S. hydrogen bombs were not needed *even if* the Soviets developed such hydrogen bombs, then the U.S. atomic bomb might also have been sufficient to compel a Soviet submission to the Baruch Plan in 1946 or 1947.

The argument introduced just above is that the American forbearance, the American failure to launch preventive war or to make nuclear threats, was not due to any American morality in these years, but due instead to the need for something bigger as a nuclear bludgeon, something as big as the H-bomb. But such an argument can not be voiced by those who claim that H-bombs were irrelevant and redundant as instruments of mutual deterrence and mutual assured destruction, that is, that there was never a need for Americans to move ahead from fission to fusion weapons.

Simple Inability: The Vulnerability of Western Europe

One could offer yet another, very different, kind of explanation for American restraint here, in some ways analogous to the incompleteness of the British naval monopoly. The United States indeed had a monopoly of nuclear power in 1946, such that it could have dropped atomic bombs on Soviet cities and would not have to fear any matching retaliation against American cities. But Stalin's Soviet forces could have retaliated in another way, by advancing to occupy and/or devastate the cities of Western Europe.[37]

As noted in the widely cited speech by Winston Churchill in 1949, it was perhaps only the power of U.S atomic bombs that had kept the Red Army from advancing to the Bay of Biscay. But if the prospect of American nuclear attacks were deterring the Soviets from seizing West Germany and France, might not, in reverse, the prospect of such a Soviet occupation of Western Europe have also deterred any actual use of American nuclear weapons?

Because Britain had dominated the seas, but not the land, the land was a base in the end from which its sea power could be challenged. Because the United States dominated the nuclear arena, but not the land, the Soviets would have the time and opportunity, already by 1949, to acquire nuclear forces of their own.

Yet, just as with the failure of the United States to maintain a meaningful or "adequate" stockpile of nuclear weapons after the Japanese surrender, the Western weakness here in conventional forces begs the question as much as answering it.

The demobilization of the United States conventional military forces after the German and Japanese surrenders was one of the most rapid (and most reliably verifiable for Soviet or other outside observers) in history.[38] Soldiers were released from service entirely on civilian and humane considerations, on the basis of who was going back to school or was needed on the farm, or of who had lost a brother in combat, all of this regardless of its impact on unit cohesion and military effectiveness. One unit would thus lack repairmen, and another would lack tank drivers, and so on, as what had been an American Army of 8 million men and close to 100 divisions was decomposed into a non-fighting force governing Japan and the American Zones of Germany and Austria, and otherwise waiting to go home.

The same haphazard processes of demobilization that so much disarmed American conventional forces had also disrupted the Army Air Force after the Japanese surrender, of course, thus reducing the number of crews that might be competent to fly heavy bombers on nuclear, as well as conventional, missions, and reducing the availability of mechanics, support personnel, and so on. In addition to having very few atomic bombs, the United States would thus have very few B-29 bomb-ers that had been retrofitted to carry them,[39] and very few crews trained for such a mission.

It would have been prohibitively expensive, in terms of U.S. overall priorities, to maintain the *entire* conventional fighting strength that had been the American contribution to the defeat of Nazi Germany and Ja-pan; but it would certainly have been possible to maintain much more of it than survived into 1946, if there had been any serious consider-ation for shielding Western Europe as part of precluding nuclear prolif-eration.

Revisionists and others looking at the outbreak of the Cold War have often scoffed at the Soviet threat to Western Europe, arguing that U.S. nuclear deterrence was not needed, that Stalin would never have wanted to send the Red Army forward to occupy Brussels and Frankfurt and Paris.[40] As support for their contention that Western fears were over-stated here (that it was perhaps Truman and Acheson that needlessly conjured up a Soviet threat), they argue that the pressing needs of re-building the Soviet Union, after the devastation inflicted by the Ger-man invasion, had required a substantial demobilization of Soviet con-ventional forces as well.

Rather than the "300 divisions" so often referred to in Western threat assessments ("divisions" which in any event were always smaller than a standard "division" of the U.S. Army), the force was probably much smaller in 1946 and 1947.

In later years, Secretary of Defense Robert McNamara, arguing against a need to rely on nuclear deterrence to hold back Soviet con-ventional forces, would similarly contend that these Soviet forces were being overrated in their mass and their fighting power, such that rela-tively manageable enhancements of Western *conventional* strength would have allowed NATO and the United States to put the nuclear deterrent on the shelf (so that nuclear weapons in the 1960s or the 1980s could be held in reserve, with no other function except to deter the use of Soviet nuclear weapons).[41]

But what if McNamara was correct for 1961 or for 1981, that the U.S. could protect its Western European allies without escalating to the nuclear level? The logical corollary would be that the United States before 1949, when Stalin still had no nuclear weapons, could also have applied its nuclear monopoly, without having to accept a Soviet occu-pation of West Germany and France as the price.

If the less worrisome assessments of Soviet conventional military forces in 1946 are thus correct, these forces are not all by themselves an airtight explanation for why the United States could not forbid Stalin from acquiring nuclear weapons.

The Truman administration, to pursue a monopoly-maintenance program, would thus have had to undertake two preliminary preparatory measures: keeping nuclear weapons in production and in readiness, and maintaining a conventional force (rather than a simple non-combat-ready occupation force) in Western Germany. Given the political tensions already at hand, such preparations and enhancements of readiness might well have been sold to the American public. Given the momentous consequences of tolerating a nuclear duopoly, it remains unclear why these moves were not undertaken.

Stalin's failure to maintain *all* the forces of 1945 (a much larger fraction of such forces was surely maintained than of Western conventional forces) might have reflected a lack of interest in spreading Communism by the power of arms. Yet it could just as easily, as the revisionist arguments acknowledge, have reflected the dire needs of rebuilding after the damage the USSR had suffered in World War II.

But, once that damage was addressed, would these forces not be augmented again? In the event, they were. And once the Soviets had nuclear weapons, would these conventional forces not be used? In retrospect, many were to see the Korean War as a realization of the latter fear.

There is yet another, very different, argument by which the vulnerability of the "hostage" in Western Europe might *not* have constituted such a powerful deterrent to an American use of nuclear weapons in 1946. Americans, to be sure, identified very much with the fate of the Frenchmen and Belgians and Dutch whom they had just liberated from Nazi occupation (and they also identified with the Poles who were now being subjected to Soviet dictation). But how much would Americans in 1946 have identified with the first layer of humans that would be exposed to an advance of Soviet tanks, that is, the Germans, still regarded as generally guilty of all that Nazism had inflicted on the world?

It is not clear that Americans would have so automatically flinched at the conventional damage Stalin could inflict between the Elbe and the Rhine, if the U.S. was meanwhile trying to win a contest of wills by inflicting nuclear air attacks.

For a not so totally far-fetched analogy, one should remember that Japanese ground forces had actually been *advancing* in China in 1944 and early 1945, as neither the Kuomintang nor the Chinese Communist forces were able to hold them back. The Soviet invasion of Manchuria, launched a day after the bombing of Hiroshima, supplied some counter to this; but anyone seeking a termination of Japanese war effort by the nuclear bombing of Hiroshima and Nagasaki nonetheless had to derive a link by which the Japanese conventional forces holding much of Southeast Asia, and growing portions of China, would have to be reined in, and still would have to be brought to surrender.

One would hardly argue, however, that Americans could be completely indifferent to a Soviet occupation and depredation of Paris, or that the recall and surrender of Soviet ground forces could be seen as so automatically achievable by imposing pain on cities back in Russia. *If* we see American nuclear weapons and extended nuclear deterrence as the crucial barrier to Soviet conventional attack, one might thus in reverse see the Soviet conventional grip on Western Europe as a necessary and sufficient counter to the American nuclear grip on Soviet cities.

After 1949, in the period when Soviet bombers did not yet perhaps have enough range to reach targets in the United State itself, this conventional hold on Western Europe would be augmented by a nuclear threat, since the first Soviet atomic bombs surely could be gotten to European targets. When missiles were to be introduced at the end of the 1950s, the American fear for a time was of a "missile gap" where the Soviets would have ICBMs and the United States would not.[42] In the event, Khrushchev's system was not to be able to produce ICBMs in quantity, so that the American responsive ICBM programs led to "a missile gap in reverse." While Soviet intercontinental missiles were thus late in coming on to the scene, the USSR did in the same period produce substantial numbers of intermediate-range SS-4 and SS-5 missiles, once again threatening Western European cities.[43]

Khrushchev's attempt to deploy such missiles forward to Cuba may have been an attempt to reinsure his deterrent posture by bringing American cities within firing range, if the vulnerability of West European cities was not thought sufficient for deterrence purposes, just as the earlier American deployment of medium-range missiles to Turkey and Italy had been an attempt to reinsure the U.S. nuclear deterrent grip on Soviet cities.

Once the Soviet Union had a more secure ability to destroy American cities (this evolved after Soviet ICBMs had been perfected and produced in quantity, and after Soviet submarine-based missiles had been reliably deployed), the strategic need, for purposes of deterring American nuclear forces, to be able to occupy (and/or to devastate) Western Europe, would have faded.

Nonetheless the Soviet Cold War experience included long periods where Moscow had to be counting upon the American identification with Western Europe as an important part of its own reassurance. Any of the arguments that explain American non-use of the monopoly by the vulnerability of Europe, when the U.S. was itself not vulnerable to either nuclear or conventional attack, thus cut across the broader interpretations of American motives in some strange ways.

Americans like to remember that they were too generous and humane to use nuclear weapons against Stalin's Russia. A "realistic" skeptic, seeking to disabuse Americans of such self-congratulatory feelings, would then charge them with being generous and humane toward West Europeans, and thus *deterred*, rather than morally dissuaded, from confronting Stalin.

But if Americans were *truly* as selfish as the realist sometimes describes (or prescribes), would they not have been able to shrug off whatever punishment the Red Army could inflict on Germans and other West Europeans, as long as no such punishment would befall Americans? A humane and altruistic concern for the welfare of Danes and Belgians might seem to reinforce the "realistic" interpretation of American restraint in 1947, but only if one substantially modifies the premises of this entire analytical perspective.

In any event, an explanation of American pre-1949 nuclear restraint, by concerns for the welfare of West Germans and West Europeans, still begs the question more than answering it. A sizable portion of the conventional military vulnerability of Western Europe had come about *by choice*, just as the American failure to build up a sizable nuclear weapons stockpile had come by choice. These choices for military weaknesses are the thing yet to be explained, rather than the ultimate explanation, as we trail the possibility of preventive war.

Simple Inability: The Requirement for Bases in Britain

If Soviet forces had overrun Western Europe, they would have done more than punish people for whom the Americans felt real affection. They would also have been intent on eliminating the bomber bases from which their homeland was being attacked. The United States had not yet begun quantity production of the B-36 bomber (which would have the range to strike at Soviet targets from bases in North America), but had to rely on the B-29, and then on an improved version of the B-29, the B-50, aircraft which needed forward bases to reach Soviet targets.[44]

The United States had based some B-29s occasionally in its occupation zone in West Germany after 1945, but there were no such American bases in Britain between the end of World War II and the Soviet imposition of a blockade on Berlin in 1948; B-29s were then brought to reopen U.S. Air Force bases in England, with some of these bases then remaining in use continuously to the present.[45] Japan's defeated-power status presumably meant that it did not have much of a veto on a U.S. air campaign against Siberian targets, but British agreement would be required for such a campaign, and this might pose greater problems.

To begin, while Winston Churchill, out of office, was suggesting preventive war to the United States, the Labour government of Clement Atlee was at least a trifle more ideologically sympathetic to the Soviet experiment, and was hardly thus to be counted upon for support in a grand American nuclear preemptive attack.

Would the United States thus have been more ready to protect its nuclear monopoly if it had not needed British bases and British cooperation? And, to turn to another question to be explored further in this book, would it have been just as ready to protect the monopoly against British proliferation as against Soviet proliferation?

The issues that actually emerged between Britain and the United States about the possession and control of nuclear weapons, over the years from 1941 indeed to the very present, have presented an interesting and complicated pattern. As noted earlier, Britain had reason, as part of the agreements between Churchill and Roosevelt at Quebec in 1943 and at Hyde Park in 1944, to assume that it would share equally in the possession and control of nuclear weapons, in exchange for having merged its efforts into the Manhattan Project, as part of insuring that Hitler's Germany would not win the race to get the atomic bomb.[46]

Churchill, in the 1944 secret executive agreement, had won Roosevelt's promise to share the technology for producing nuclear weapons after the war, but the document outlining this had literally been lost in the files in Washington. President Truman, knowing nothing of this Hyde Park agreement, had been made aware of the 1943 Quebec agreement (about which the Congress had also *not* been told), by which the

United States could not use nuclear weapons without getting British consent. Knowing that Congress might well balk at even this much sharing, by which Britain would have a safety-catch rather than a trigger, Truman was to inform the British that the United States could not be bound by it.

The McMahon Act would forbid the sharing of information about the production of nuclear weapons with *any* foreign country. While Senator McMahon was afterward to state that he had not known of the Roosevelt promises to Churchill, and that he would have drafted the legislation differently if he had been aware of the commitments made,[47] there is reason to suspect that such statements were simply intended to assuage British feelings, as the Congress in 1946 was much inclined to retain the American monopoly, at the least by not giving information away.

The United States had thus reneged on, or simply had forgotten having ever agreed to, both aspects of sharing the nuclear arsenal with Britain. In larger part, this may simply have been because of the power reality, since the bulk of the effort, and the physical location of all the result, had been American. One can ask here, if the situation had been reversed and the entire Manhattan Project had evolved on British soil and under British physical control (with American inputs simply having been merged into the common effort), whether Winston Churchill would have abided by a similar secret personal agreement with Franklin Roosevelt, or whether Clement Atlee, succeeding Churchill, would have felt bound to Truman succeeding Roosevelt.

The Hyde Park and Quebec agreements had been secret, and personal, and somewhat ad hoc. And they thus violated power-political realities, where possession is nine points of the law. They also violated the idea of treating the USSR no differently from other countries; if the bomb was to be shared with Britain, could it be denied to the other principal allies of the United States in the struggle against the Axis?

An Anglo-American shared possession of nuclear weapons could of course have taken a variety of forms. It could have meant that each country had nuclear weapons, free to use them whenever they felt the need. It could instead have meant a single nuclear force, to be used only when both nations approved. To translate this into the logic of later discussions of possible nuclear sharing, what was perhaps the most crucial was whether each country held the "trigger" ability to initiate nuclear war, or whether each country instead held a "safety catch" ability to veto and prevent such an initiation. And would such a veto have been a physical ability to prevent firing, as with some of the "permissive action links" (PAL) and "two-key" arrangements introduced in the 1960s, or would it have been simply of the form of a political promise and understanding?

The situation by 1945 was that Britain did not have nuclear weapons of its own, so as to be free to launch nuclear war on its own initiative, and that it also did not, except where its bases were required, have the physical ability to preclude such an American use of the bomb.

One aspect of the Quebec Agreement had indeed been adhered to, as the British had been consulted on the attacks on Japan and had given their go-ahead.[48] But even this much of a dilution of the American control over nuclear weapons would have struck many Congressmen and some of Truman's advisers as undesirable, on the right-wing by the fear that Atlee or another British leader might not be resolute enough in some future crisis with the Soviets, on the left by the argument that such a special British prerogative would be insulting to the USSR, not given the same veto. The British government was thus persuaded by 1947 to drop the Quebec agreement.[49]

Apart from the likelihood that a British government would oppose a preventive war with the Soviets, no matter how well the groundwork had been laid, there was also a question on whether British bases could physically continue to function, once Soviet forces had advanced to the channel, occupying France and the positions the Germans had held before the Blitz in 1940. Would the Russians not have directed massive conventional air attacks at any and all British bases from which U.S. nuclear missions were being flown? Might we not even have seen Soviet airborne forces landed, with the urgent mission of crippling such bases and the bombers on them?

Or the leverage could have been that London and other British cities would be threatened with as punishing a Soviet conventional air assault as could be mustered, as the retaliation for cooperating with the American nuclear assault, the retaliation which would cease as soon as the British government and military intervened to prevent further raids.

Regardless of whether the British government had a moral or legal veto on the more general use of U.S. nuclear weapons, it clearly could prevent such use where bases in the United Kingdom were involved. It would surely have been possible for the British Army to interfere with any raids about to be launched from such bases, much as the French

Army had prevented British bombers from taking off on air raids against Italy, when Mussolini had entered World War II just as the French resistance to the German advance was basically collapsing.[50]

Just as for the Americans, much would have depended, for the British people and government, on how the origins of a preventive war had been developed. Had Soviet tanks rolled westward in 1947 or 1948, it might have been fairly easy to get Americans and Britons to agree on an all-out attempt to eliminate any possibilities of Soviet nuclear weapons. But if Stalin held back his conventional threat to Western Europe, as in the actual event he did, a public approval for an imposition of the Baruch Plan might have been harder to obtain.

Some of this entire issue of a dependence on British bases would then relate to the broader question of how long anyone expected a preventive war to take. For Britain to be so physically threatened as in the scenarios just outlined, the war would have had to continue, without Stalin giving in or being deposed, for weeks and months as the Red Army advanced to within striking distance of Britain itself. A great number of nuclear strikes at Soviet cities would thus have already been conducted before Britain was within such easy range of Soviet paratroops or conventional bombers, all of such strikes without any decisive impact on Soviet choices. Under such a scenario, the very premises for the preventive war arguments of anyone like Bertrand Russell, that atomic bombing was something so uniquely painful that it had to be qualitatively different as a factor in international power politics, might have been proven null and void.

Fears of Soviet Air Defenses

We have above addressed the tension between two views of preventive war, one stressing an all-out war enlisting all the components of military power in a counter-force struggle for military victory, the other regarding the counter-value pain of nuclear attacks on Russian cities as sufficient to force Stalin to submit to a ban on Soviet nuclear proliferation.

Very much related to this would be the significance of concerns that developed after 1945, and even in the last year of World War II, about whether air defenses might become so improved that bombers would no longer be able to get through to inflict strategic bombardment campaigns. If Nazi Germany had produced jet fighters in sufficient quantity from the middle of 1944, it might have been able to impose such high losses on the B-17s and B-24s of the U.S. Army Air Force that air raids on Germany would have had to be curtailed.[51] Similarly, the U.S. Air Force in the Korean War was to become quite concerned with the high losses imposed on its B-29 missions by the jet fighters the Soviet Union had given the North Koreans and Chinese Communists.[52]

In the German case, the rewards for Hitler (if he had correctly applied his lead in jet fighter technology to the role of intercepting Allied bombers, rather than frittering away these aircraft as fighter-bombers) would have been to delay his defeat, *and* thus to become the first victim, rather than the Japanese, of nuclear attack. For it only would have taken a single aircraft, as at Hiroshima, and not a large and identifiable fleet of incoming bomber targets, to destroy an entire city.

Those analysts who would after 1945 worry about *Soviet* air defenses, and about the recovery of the bombers delivering nuclear weapons to Soviet targets, were thus again the strategists who still regarded it as essential to defeat the total of the Soviet military system in actual military engagement. Targets would have to be chosen seriously with the intention of crippling Soviet military potential, with an assumption that hundreds of nuclear weapons would be required; the calculation was that Moscow might win a victory, or at least stave off a defeat, if even half the U.S. bombers carrying nuclear weapons were intercepted before reaching their targets, or if any large fraction of such bombers could not get back to their bases to be readied for another attack in the next days or weeks.

But, if one accepted the interpretation presented quite early (if not then always consistently thereafter) by Bernard Brodie (the interpretation by which the real role of nuclear weapons was to intimidate an opponent by the prospect of pain, rather than to defeat that enemy by disablement), one would see very little accomplished if Soviet air defenses could stop half of an incoming attack. As was the case in the nuclear attacks on Japan,[53] the actual nuclear attacker would not look very different from randomly deployed reconnaissance aircraft, with only a single bomber needing to get through, and not necessarily thereafter needing to get back to its base. As was to be the case for a time later with missiles (before multiple-warheads led to "Mirving"), the incoming nuclear warheads would have been flanked by decoys, with the Soviet air defense system having great difficulty in spotting which U.S. aircraft was actually carrying the nuclear warhead.

While an air offensive directed "at military potential rather than at civilian targets" would have required at least 100 such attacks, and perhaps several hundred, the "more brutal" version of a preventive war scenario would thus have envisaged far fewer nuclear strikes. This more counter-value-oriented attack could then have used aircraft on one-way missions, with the crews afterward parachuting into the nearest sea to be picked up by submarine, or into the nearest neutral or friendly country. (A more counter-force-oriented strategy depended instead on recovering crews and aircraft for follow-on attacks, thus requiring aircraft like the B-36 with the range for round-trip missions, and thus raising a much greater concern again about the power of Soviet air defenses.)

For anyone who thus scoffs at the "war-fighting" aspect of nuclear attacks, counting instead on the frightful civilian destruction inflicted in even one or two such attacks as at Hiroshima and Nagasaki, such concerns about opposing air defenses would drop considerably in their relevance. As long as the air defenses could not be perfect or near-perfect, one could accept the losses of airplanes, for the disutility imposed on the opposing side in the destruction of cities was so much greater.

This kind of analysis had indeed sometimes been presented in the Air War College lectures of General Orvil Anderson. Anderson drew the contrast between German air defenses against massed B-17 raids, and the total ineffectiveness of the Luftwaffe against single C-47s flying agents in and out of occupied France or even Germany.[54]

The upsurge of air defense effectiveness at the end of World War II, or even then in the Korean War, came where the target was a large concentration of incoming bombers, which could be tracked on radar so that defensive fighters could be deployed. At the level of a single airplane trying to penetrate, the adage of Stanley Baldwin of 1932 still might be correct, that "the bomber will always get through."[55]

Being an Air Force general, Orvil Anderson would have wrapped even his own scenario, for a single aircraft dropping a single atomic bomb on a Soviet city, in counter-force terms. The devastation inflicted on the people of the city would remain inadvertent collateral damage, while the officially intended objective of the attack would be to cripple industry and to constrict that city's contribution to the enemy's overall military capacity. But Anderson, in favoring the issuance of an ultimatum to the Soviets, followed by, if there were no response, preventive war action to keep the Soviets from getting nuclear weapons, was definitely among those less prone to envisage a prolonged air war, and less inhibited by the prospect of Soviet air defenses.

In summation, the fear of Soviet air defenses becomes a barrier to preventive war thinking only for those who shared the counter-force interpretation of nuclear bombardment that tended to grip the U.S. Air Force. It should have been much less of barrier for those who did not see the atomic bomb as "just another weapon."

Simple Inability: The Burdens of Imperialism

A very different, much more political, interpretation of the American reluctance to exploit the atomic monopoly would stem from classic liberal fears of the burdens, and the domestic consequences, of imperialism.

If the project had to include not just the denuclearization of the Soviet Union, but also its general demilitarization, and democratization, perhaps this would be unmanageable, or the process of sending out American governors would in the end compromise democracy at home.[56]

Yet the experience of what was undertaken, not really so unsuccessfully, in the American zone of Germany, and in all of Japan, might have been a more encouraging model here.[57] Democracy indeed seems to have taken hold in both countries. Lucius Clay never posed much of a threat to democracy back home. While Douglas MacArthur may have posed a more plausible threat, few would today claim that American democracy was really in danger, even in 1950 when the great majority of Americans disapproved of Truman's decision to relieve the general; and MacArthur is indeed a complicated figure, proving surprisingly liberal, and nuanced, for anyone closely studying his command of the occupation of Japan.[58]

In short, the maximum effort here would have basically required a duplication of the training and language programs which had produced military governors for Germany and Japan, this time trained in Russian language and culture. Since Americans had not run away from the task against the defeated Axis powers, any congenital aversion to such tasks will not suffice as the explanation for America's failure to free Russia from Stalinist rule.

6

Arguments Against: Procedural Questions

Continuing with the arguments precluding any more serious advocacy of preventive war, we turn now to explanations that, rather than being "objective" barriers to such a policy, are focussed more on the American policy process, and on its particular subjectivity and possible failings.

Inherent Doubts about the Monopoly

Could the United States be certain that it would not be hit with a Japanese nuclear retaliatory attack, when the B-29 was dispatched toward Hiroshima from Tinian? This should be regarded as a "silly question"; if Japan already had nuclear weapons of its own, it of course would already have used them, when it thought that the United States could not retaliate.

The original race to build the U.S. atomic bomb was seen as a race against similar projects underway in Hitler's Germany. If the first U.S. atomic bomb had been ready in time, it most probably would have been dropped on a German city rather than a Japanese. Lest one worry about German *nuclear* retaliation for this, the logical assumption was again that any existing German nuclear weapon would already have been used, as Hitler would have exploited his nuclear monopoly against Britain just as the U.S. would exploit its against Japan.

Once the "secret" of nuclear weapons was out, however, once the U.S. had demonstrated its atomic bomb, an inherent epistemological question would then emerge on whether one could be sure that Stalin's Russia had not acquired nuclear weapons as well. The simple test that reassured one about Nazi Germany or about Japan in 1945 ("if they had the bomb, they would already have used it against us") could not work for Stalin's Russia, since the American bomb had been developed first.

We are in this book mostly debating the nature of U.S. policy up to 1949, up to September 23 of 1949 to be exact, the moment when President Truman disclosed to the world how radioactivity had been detected that could only have come from a Soviet nuclear weapons test. Yet Soviet Foreign Minister Molotov had already in 1947 given a speech claiming that the USSR had solved "the secret" of producing nuclear weapons.[1] What is the latest point in time that Truman and his advisers could have contemplated employing American nuclear forces without fearing Soviet *nuclear* retaliation? [2]

From explorations of all the data, including Soviet revelations several decades later, we can indeed now conclude that 1949, and not 1946, 1947, or 1948, was in fact the year that Stalin acquired nuclear weapons, just as it can be concluded that Stalin ordered the pursuit of such weapons to begin already in 1943.[3] But the more important question for this book is not the actual time the U.S. monopoly was broken, but what Americans could have known. An American considering preventive war scenarios after August of 1945 might still always have had to factor in the possibility of a most dreadful unpleasant surprise, that Soviet bombs already existed.

After the United States had introduced nuclear physics to all those who had been unaware of the possibilities of a fission chain-reaction, this inherent risk could never be totally written off. The discovery of Soviet nuclear espionage already in 1946 supplied evidence about Soviet intentions, *and* had to reinforce this inherent possibility of proliferation already having occurred.

It might be quite difficult to find such a nagging doubt articulated, a doubt about whether it would not already be "too late" to preserve the monopoly; but it had to be there, and would have to grow as the years passed. In form, it would be more than a little like the discussion, during the preparation for Desert Storm, on whether Iraq might already possess one or two nuclear warheads, or the 1994 discussion about whether Kim Il-Sung's regime in North Korea might already have such warheads.[4]

American Smugness

An exactly opposite explanation for 1945 to 1949 would base itself on a picture of Americans' arrogance and smugness, by which such

Americans blithely assumed that the Soviets would be incapable of matching the scientific breakthrough accomplished in the Manhattan Project, that is, assumed that the monopoly might perpetuate itself naturally far into the future.[5]

President Truman made statements that certainly lend themselves to his kind of interpretation. He at one stage apparently asked Robert Oppenheimer how long it would take the Russians to produce atomic bombs. When Oppenheimer responded that it was difficult to tell, Truman responded by offering his own answer to the question: "never."[6]

After the fogged photographic plates of 1949 offered evidence that someone had tested a nuclear weapon, Truman publicly announced that the United States believed that the USSR now had the bomb. Somewhat bizarrely, however, Truman in private conversations expressed continuing personal skepticism about whether any such Soviet nuclear weapons had been produced, and he then voiced these doubts publicly shortly after leaving the presidency in 1953.[7]

Many scientists in the decades since 1949 have been inclined to scoff at any such "secret" of the atomic bomb, noting how widespread the basic knowledge of nuclear physics had become already at the onset of World War II in 1939. Our current concerns about nuclear proliferation around the world stem from the dispersion of so much of the basic knowledge required for production of atomic bombs.

Yet the same scientists have often also scoffed at suggestions that the German failure to make progress toward atomic weapons was due to any German moral restraints, to any reluctance to equip Hitler's Nazi regime with such a deadly weapon. Dismissing such post-1945 German explanations as self-serving and hypocritical, the Americans who had worked in the Manhattan Project checked the German failure off to Aryan arrogance, to the incompetence of the German physicists who had remained, after the Jewish and other anti-Nazi physicists had been driven to leave Germany in the 1930s.[8]

If Germany, before 1933 regarded as the center of research on physics, had thus come nowhere near possession of nuclear weapons before 1945, it was not so difficult for an ordinary American, and even an American educated in science, to conclude that Russia, a less advanced place in technology, would also lag, and perhaps lag for a long time into the future.

As will be noted, some of the earliest strategic speculations about what kind of a nuclear challenge the United States might face, once the monopoly was broken, did not focus on the USSR as the likely nuclear adversary, but much more typically on something like a resurgent Germany. [9] This can be interpreted in retrospect as a kind of racism, by which the backward Slavs would never seem as competent as the "Western" Americans or Germans. (On the other had, it can also show a reluctance to lock on to Moscow as the adversary for confrontations of the future, a reluctance to initiate a Cold War with our wartime allies, the Russians.)

Even today, one can get very conflicting estimates from trained nuclear physicists as to how difficult, or easy, it will be for various countries around the world to divert plutonium from nuclear power reactors to produce atomic bombs, with some contending that this will be quite simple, and others arguing that it will be much more difficult. If this is the state of play some five decades after the introduction of nuclear weapons, it would hardly be so surprising that the American and Western scientific communities in 1945 had difficulty in predicting the rate of Soviet progress.

The suggestion that confidence in a naturally ongoing U.S. nuclear monopoly was based on a stupid smugness emerges most often from those critics who would not want to credit 1945 Americans with any absence of combativeness at this stage of Cold War history, who would not want the United States to be remembered as having passed some kind of moral test, as having proved itself as generous enough to be trusted with a monopoly of the absolute weapon.

Yet such a smugness is not per se the explanation for why Stalin was able to acquire nuclear weapons. It is hardly the case that the United States was busily scheduling a preventive war campaign for year eight, on the assumption that the USSR bomb otherwise would come along in year ten, only to have these hopes dashed when Stalin got his bomb in year four. When the Soviet nuclear test was detected in 1949, the idea of a preventive-war utilization of the American monopoly had not yet really gotten a serious hearing.

Assumptions About the Availability of Raw Materials

A portion of any optimism about the time left for decision stemmed from the one very definite attempt mentioned above to deny the Soviets the atomic bomb, the American effort, underway already during World War II, and continuing thereafter, to buy up all the world's uranium.

This operation, labeled "Operation Murray Hill" as a component of the Manhattan Project, worked from the premise, supported by some geologists and scoffed at by others, that there was only a very limited supply of uranium in the world.[10] An American effort to collect this up would thus be driven by the need to make more American bombs, as well as by the hope that Nazi Germany, and then Soviet Russia and perhaps all other states, would be unable to make many or any of their own.

Shortages of uranium have sometimes thus been introduced, as noted earlier, as the explanation of the small number of nuclear warheads in the U.S. arsenal in 1946 and 1947. While this clearly played some role, it was not so determining that there was nothing left to explain in terms of American decisions here. A greater emphasis in the Truman administration on having atomic bombs ready, and on having bombers ready to carry them, would indeed have produced a more awesome arsenal.

Yet any such difficulties in finding uranium around the world could have also been seen as good news, for those who did not want the world to move into the confrontation of mutual assured destruction. In light of the vast amounts of uranium that were ultimately to be found, coupled with much more efficient approaches to utilizing such fissionable material in nuclear weapons, the hopes expressed by General Groves and others have invited ridicule. Yet this was at the least a very benign and peaceful non-proliferation effort.

Perhaps the "secret" of how to produce nuclear weapons could never remain a secret very long. If some experts believed that there was little or no uranium in the Soviet Union, however, and if the United States felt assured that it was corralling in all of the limited supplies to be found in the Congo and in Canada, the hopes that were raised by these "experts" were certainly humane hopes.

One could imagine an extreme of such predictions (predictions about geology, rather than about nuclear physics) whereby the total of the uranium available in the world was somehow only enough for fifty bombs, and where the United States, having used up three bombs worth in a test and in the ending of World War II, retained the remaining forty-seven. Would this have been such a horrible world? (This is somewhat analogous to the hopes entertained during the Carter administration that INFCE would find a form of nuclear technology which could produce electric power without producing by-products of fissionable material. If nature had smiled on the world, the threat of mass destruction would be less.)[11]

As the geology of the world actually unfolded, however, the hopes for a uranium-shortage constraint faded, as the total of nuclear warheads produced since 1945 has come close to 100,000, and as thermonuclear weapons of the megaton range appeared in the American and Soviet arsenals. What we thus have is a "failed" attempt to maintain the nuclear monopoly, since uranium from Czechoslovakia, and from the Soviet Union itself, was more than enough to support a major Soviet nuclear force.

And what we also have is a portion of the explanation for the misprediction of the pace of the Soviet accomplishment here, a misprediction that caused much of Washington to be surprised in 1949, an excessive confidence in the "natural" duration of the monopoly, postponing any thoughts of military action to "artificially" prolong it.

The Shortness of the Actual Opportunity

Preventive war, utilizing the threat or actual practice of nuclear bombardment, would have been a world-shaking decision. If the implications of such an undertaking were so momentous, why not postpone it for deeper consideration? Why not take more of the time left to weigh the choices?

Whatever the inherent epistemological doubts introduced just above (by which it would always, after Hiroshima, be at least thinkable that the USSR had already *secretly* acquired nuclear weapons), Americans would at the same time be making guesses about the likely time until such nuclear proliferation would *definitely* appear.

In the event, this time was to be only four years, from 1945 until 1949. But, even apart from Truman's opinion, most of the American scientists expert on the subject had been inclined (based on how science in the Soviet system compared with that of the West, and based on how the Manhattan Project had been carried through) to guess a considerably longer interval, typically about ten years.[12] The decisions of 1946 might have been different if people in Washington had definitely *known* that the Soviets would have nuclear weapons by 1949.

Four years, when all is said and done, is a very short period of time. It is how long students in America typically take to earn a bachelor's degree, and it is less time than it typically takes to write a book like this one (although Bernard Brodie and William Borden were able to present important alternative analyses of the nuclear factor within *six months* of Hiroshima). It is exactly the term of a U.S. president, and less time than the term of a U.S. senator. It is less time than Hitler (who was certainly impatient and adventurous, and who had a definite view of history and the world) took to get World War II going. Perhaps even Stalin would not have been able to exploit such a short window of opportunity, the opportunity of a nuclear monopoly that would disappear naturally by imitation within just four years.

Four years, to make the comparison with contemporary proliferation problems, is about thirty years less than the time over which we have agonized about Israel perhaps getting atomic bombs, and twenty years less than our confronting of India's first "peaceful nuclear explosion." [13]

The non-proliferation effort intended to keep the world's number of separate nuclear powers from getting into double digits has often seemed more inclined to patience than to dramatic action. If no one (except perhaps Israel in its attack on Ossirak) has been ready for rash action to head off the more recent nuclear weapons programs (settling instead for an array of pressures on supplies and on motivations, intended at least to slow the rate of nuclear proliferation), how could anyone lament in retrospect the American failure to take action in a "window" of only four years?

Yet this argument against rapid action is also not so air-tight. To respond with a most central point, it can be argued that the "proliferation issue" between one and two nuclear powers, the issue of 1945 to 1949, was simply much more important, and thus should have produced more anxiety, than that between five and six, or between eight and nine.

The fear of each side, once there was a nuclear duopoly, was that the opposing side would not in the future be patient if any opportunity should reappear to bring back the nuclear monopoly. The concerns about the other side's "first-strike" forces, used in a counter-force attack to prevent our "second-strike" counter-value response, were what activated strategic planners on both sides, and produced substantial investments in nuclear strategic delivery systems. [14]

Would anyone have become so relaxed after 1950 about a missile gap or a bomber gap, or about a "window of vulnerability," if he were told that it would last "only four years"? The assumption of mutual deterrence theory was that no such window could be allowed to appear, lest the opposing side exploit this in a "splendid first strike" ("splendid" in the sense that it disarmed our nuclear forces, while the adversary retained a substantial portion of its nuclear forces, that is, establishing a new monopoly so that he could then threaten our cities while we could no longer threaten his).

If Brezhnev had been given such a four year opportunity in the 1970s, or Khrushchev in the 1950s, would we assume that he would not have used it? The premise of all American planning was just the opposite, so that maximum effort had to be devoted to assuring that no so such "window," even this short, could appear. And, if an American president, with the experience of the thermonuclear confrontation behind him, had seen such another four-year window, would he definitely not have exploited it? The Soviet reasoning certainly seems to be that no post-1949 American leader could be trusted with this.

Returning to our pre-1949 years, if Hitler had been able to use nuclear weapons even for four *months*, so as to prevent an enemy from getting them in that time, would he not have done so? And are we so sure that Stalin would not have done the same? But the United States had such a capability for four *years*, and did not use it.

The "shortness" of time here (with this shortness, as noted above, coming as a surprise) plays a role in accounting for the lack of action. But again, by the comparisons just noted, it is not satisfactory as a total explanation.

A More General Aversion to Gambling and Discontinuity

Launching a preventive war would have been a horrendously great undertaking. This will certainly be regarded as the most obvious thing to be said about the prospect being reexamined in this book.

Some would argue that it was so horrendous that *no* government could ever undertake such an act. To reinforce the view that a sensible and responsible government (i.e., a democratic government) could *not* be tempted by such an option, one can find a series of *retrospective* assessments of the nuclear preventive war option appearing among American strategic analysts, looking back at the years before 1949, and even at the years after 1949. In case after case, the opinion is that something like three years earlier might have been an acceptable time to launch a preventive war, a time when the damage to American cities would have been zero or minimal.[15] The *present* situation is again and again assessed as one of mutual assured destruction, but the past is remembered, even when the early 1950s are reflected upon from the later 1950s, and so on, as a possible avoidance of such unbearable Soviet retaliation.

The kind of caution, where past years are seen as years of opportunity, but present and future years are not, could then be a symptom of nothing more than an excessively responsible caution, where no grand venture will ever be undertaken, where nothing big ever gets gambled.

There are surely many Japanese who would wish that this had been the attitude of their own government at the time of Pearl Harbor. And many American readers might similarly be glad of this caution, as the barrier to preventive war thinking between 1945 and 1949. For the latter, of course, every part of any grand assessment still depends on how the generic problems of nuclear proliferation work themselves out, the problems for which a great gamble might have been required, to head them off before they began.

There has been more involved here than a reluctance to gamble, for preventive war would have been a leap across a discontinuity, a discontinuity to which any liberal democracy may be averse. Democracies regard peace as the normal state of affairs. When in that state of peace, they almost become incapable of even contemplating war, above all a war they themselves would have launched, but perhaps even wars other states have launched.

In the decades of the Cold War, the central question was, over and over again, whether NATO could hold its own in conventional warfare against a Warsaw Pact attack. Those arguing that it could, that no threat of nuclear escalation would be necessary, would compare the standing forces of NATO with those of the Warsaw Pact, and also compare the fully mobilized strength of NATO forces with those of the likely attacker, concluding that at *either* level the advantages of the defense might allow NATO to hold its own.

As argued very persuasively by Richard Betts,[16] however, these may have been the wrong comparisons, for it was uncertain that the NATO governments would mobilize in face of partial evidence of a Warsaw Pact mobilization, since such governments would be afraid of becoming part of a self-confirming spiral of crisis instability, the spiral that may have caused World War I. More broadly, the mere thought of war, when the world was still at peace, would be so discontinuously horrible for a democracy that it would be repressed. The unfortunate result, as argued by Betts and others who were pessimistic about NATO's chances, was that a non-mobilized NATO would be attacked by a fully mobilized Communist armored array, as the metaphor was that of a NATO "looking into the eyes of the cobra," a NATO paralyzed by its aversion to violence and war.

The same syndrome, perhaps showing up in all governments, but most probably affecting democracies in particular, would make it difficult to foresee what would happen when Stalin got his atomic bomb, and thus difficult to contemplate going to *war*, or even serious threats of war, to head this off.

The greatest problem for intelligence assessment, it would thus be argued here, comes on the borderline between peace and war, because it is so traumatic, so discontinuous. If nothing else, this would explain the American failures in interpreting the broken Japanese codes in the days before Pearl Harbor,[17] compared with the success at the same kind of intelligence before the crucial battle of Midway half a year later. Once a war was underway, the military and civilian leaders of a democracy could contemplate the threats and options more rationally. But considering the options of war, when one is at peace, may have been too difficult.

Perhaps the problem here is nothing more than a human tendency toward pragmatism and incrementalism, even apart from the humane nature of democracies, that is, the kind of explanation noted just above. If one did not know when Stalin would get his bomb, why not wait another month before thinking hard about whether to do something to head this off?

Dictators can override such incrementalism, in part because they do not have to consult with legislatures and opposition leaders. Perhaps the ideology of Marxism or fascism also had advantages in overriding the "one step at a time" style of pragmatism. But Truman and Acheson would have none of these resources of an ideological dictatorship.

Some would argue that states will generally not jump through "windows of opportunity,"[18] that the safe-and-sane pursuit of less adventurous paths will again and again veto something so major.

This is a plausible candidate for explaining the failure to maintain the nuclear monopoly, but it surely can also be challenged by considering some exploitations of opportunity windows in the past.

Japan's decision to attack the United States at Pearl Harbor,[19] and Hitler's decision to invade the Soviet Union,[20] are obvious examples of deviations from incrementalism, of decisions to plunge into the unknown, in quest of great gains, and/or to head off great dangers. We also have evidence that Stalin would have attacked Nazi Germany by 1942 or 1943, if Hitler had not invaded the Soviet Union earlier as he did.[21]

And, if one wishes to blame some of the Japanese decision in 1941 on the American economic and military pressures being assembled against Japan, then one would similarly have to credit President Roosevelt with a willingness to take risks and press the issue, rather than pragmatically simply pursuing the course of least immediate peril.[22]

Lest one conclude that the case against a preventive war policy is decisive for democracies, we must thus remember what Franklin Roosevelt was able to do when he was confronted by a similar menace in Nazi Germany. At the risk of making too much of the nuclear factor, we might introduce the argument that the American entry into World War II was already something of a preventive-war non-proliferation effort, because Roosevelt had been briefed of the risks that Nazi Germany might be capable of producing nuclear weapons.[23]

President Roosevelt, despite the more cautious and isolationist inclinations of his American voters, pushed policies intended to get the United States involved in World War II. Many other factors explain the American willingness to help Britain after 1940, and the Soviet Union after 1941, including all that was known about how the Nazis were governing and murdering the peoples they had conquered, and about the risks of Germany and Japan conquering all the world by conventional means. But the U.S. Manhattan Project was clearly driven forward by apprehensions of what a German nuclear project might be doing, and Roosevelt's willingness to work to draw the United States into the war against Hitler was also reinforced by these apprehensions.

Roosevelt also made the major non-incremental decision to invest resources in the Manhattan Project,[24] when the idea of atomic bombs was still entirely theoretical and untested, when the United States would find it crucial to augment its conventional military forces at the same time. Hitler did not have the same trust in the abstract science of nuclear physics, and did not thus gamble scarce resources on any first-priority search for nuclear weapons. And Stalin also did not make as early a commitment as had Roosevelt to such weapons.

The United States was, to be sure, not suffering a major invasion of its home territories as the USSR was in 1942, and not suffering substantial bombings of its cities as was Nazi Germany. But it would certainly have been able to find battlefield-related uses for the human and material resources that were assigned to the Manhattan Project. If World

War II had ended before the first atomic bombs were produced, such that no one could claim that these bombs helped win the war, the Project managers would have faced substantial Congressional investigations as to a possible waste of resources.

Once Stalin knew of the American nuclear effort, and once the German advance had been definitively halted at Stalingrad, his own commitment to achieving nuclear weapons begins (by all the accounts now emerging after the lifting of Cold War secrecy) to have matched the priority that had backed the U.S. effort.

The messages quoted from Stalin, and from Beria, about the urgency of acquiring atomic bombs for the USSR, do not suggest the patience, and confidence in ideological inevitabilities, that was sometimes imputed to the Kremlin at the outset of the Cold War. Stalin's urgency in seeking to acquire nuclear weapons, given all the difficulties of other economic rebuilding and recovery after 1945, suggests a less calm and incremental worldview.[25]

One returns then to the proposition that Stalin, or Hitler, or perhaps even some democratic political leaders, might have been ready to seize the opportunity of a nuclear monopoly, might have been ready to take a very grand and dangerous initiative.

Comparing Roosevelt's task facing Hitler with Truman's facing Stalin is what George Kennan's analysis of containment was all about, and what many analyses of the Cold War have addressed. Yet this comparison suggests, at the minimum, that there was nothing insuperable about an American incrementalism that so much discourages thoughts of war in times of peace.

Given all the provocations that Stalin had inflicted, in Poland and elsewhere, and assuming an astuteness in the American government about making such provocations more clear for the American Congress and public, it is not impossible to outline how the American nuclear monopoly might yet have been applied, by threats and then by execution of threats, to preserve itself.

The question remains of why nothing like this was done.

Military Aversions to War

It is not unusual for an antiwar protestor or peace advocate to accuse professional military officers of liking wars, of looking forward to what the rest of the world so much dreads, because of their "military mind" or inclination toward militarism, and/or because of the more rapid promotions that come with actual combat.

Yet anyone who has been close to a professional military establishment might regard this as an enormous slander, as we can find case after case where the professional military is reluctant to see a war launched, and has to be driven into such initiatives by the civilian leadership. Mrs. Gandhi had a difficult time getting the Indian Army committed to the war liberating Bangla Desh from Pakistani rule in 1974,[26] and President Bush had similar difficulty getting the U.S. military enthusiastic about Desert Shield and Desert Storm in 1991.[27] And Adolf Hitler had not found his generals and admirals so supportive of his plans for World War II.[28]

It would be a far more supportable accusation that generals and admirals may welcome and enjoy the *preparations* for war, the enlargements of forces and purchases of weapons, for these do indeed lead to faster promotion, and to more of a sense of purpose in society, to a higher status for the military. Generals do not like to see their troops get killed, and admirals do not like to have their ships sunk, but both may like parades and bigger officers' clubs, and faster promotions.[29]

Factoring this picture of the tendencies at work between 1945 and 1949, one would thus not expect large numbers of U.S. Air Force and other officers to be advocating preventive war, even if they would be arguing for larger expenditures on forces to deter such wars (and to win them, if the other side were to launch aggressions). For an officer like General Orvil Anderson to advocate an actual use of force, rather than the mere stockpiling of force, might thus have come as a disquieting shock, just as much to his fellow officers as to his civilian superiors.

The question of preparedness would moreover involve all the forces and officers that might have *less* of a role if nuclear weapons were truly now "the absolute weapon." A debate was to rage before 1949, and just as much thereafter, between relying heavily on strategic bombing and nuclear weapons, vs. continuing major preparations for conventional war, on the ground and on the seas, and in the air by tactical warfare.[30]

A general or admiral making the case for the continuing relevance of warships and infantry or armored divisions would hardly be inclined to attach so much importance to the nuclear monopoly, or to believe that this monopoly was usable to perpetuate itself.

After 1949, for the rest of the Cold War, the case for expanding conventional forces, as exemplified in the thinking of Secretary of Defense

McNamara, derived very importantly from *a respect for* nuclear weapons, a respect for such weapons in Soviet hands and for the damage they could inflict on American cities. But before 1949, it stemmed rather from a skepticism about the impact of such weapons, a skepticism about strategic bombing in general, in either its counter-force or counter-value mode.[31]

The believer in ground forces before 1949 was someone who, perhaps because of his own combat experiences and his career interests, was convinced that no foreign country could be coerced by the mere prospect of being bombed, that is, that any advocate of preventive war, in uniform or not, would be wildly irresponsible.

As noted above, a reasoned advocacy of preventive war might have required, in addition to a more rapid production of atomic bombs, some greater investment in conventional forces from 1945 to 1947 so that West Germany and Western Europe would not be quite so open to a Red Army advance as the immediate Soviet counter-retaliation. Rather than tolerating the de facto total disarmament of American ground forces in Europe, as the American army that had fought Hitler was converted into an occupation constabulary, the officers advocating ground forces in being would have had to be given more of their way.

Yet it still would have been a long psychological leap to move such officers from wanting to have more soldiers ready for combat, to actually endorsing what could be an American initiation of combat.

The Emphasis on "Military" Targets

We noted above the tradition in the Western world's armed forces of seeking to disarm the enemy, in a counter-force emphasis on *military* targets. Such an emphasis has been based on arguments of practicality, and of morality.

There surely have been many wars were the very best use of one's artillery or other firepower was to aim at the enemy's people in uniform; to aim at civilian targets would have been a distraction, a waste of ammunition, it would have allowed the enemy to do better in the contest of military attrition.

Whether or not the best use of one's military is to target the opposing military, we also have a cultural heritage of powerful moral arguments for avoiding civilian targets. God and the church get angry if cathedrals are destroyed, and neutral countries get outraged if marketplaces are shelled. Such destruction violates the laws of war when it is deliberate, and collateral damage to civilians is to be avoided as much as possible.[32]

Since a "policy" of avoiding attacks on civilians is so much required by moral considerations, however, one has to be skeptical about whether generals and admirals will ever openly admit to departing from this cleaner form of warfare. What if practical considerations suggest that one has a better chance of defeating Germany in World War I by starving its civilian population, than by sinking its battle fleet? Will such a shift from counter-force to counter-value targeting be acknowledged? Or will the claim be made instead that food was targeted in the blockade only because it was headed for the stomachs of enemy soldiers?[33]

The same held true for the American economic blockade of Japan in World War II, of course, and then in the conventional (and nuclear) bombings of Japan.[34] Hiroshima was the home base of two Japanese infantry divisions, and thus, so it was claimed, had to be destroyed. The Japanese government more probably surrendered because of the prospect of thousands of civilians dying in such attacks, but someone on the American side could always claim that these were simply collateral damage, unintended but inevitable.

U.S. air war planners had already in 1945 then begun looking for military-industrial targets across the Soviet Union, just in case there were to be a war with the Soviets. It is not so surprising that, in such war plans that were never executed, *every* sizable Soviet city was found to contain military targets.

The same held true, of course, in the conventional bombings of North Korea [35] and North Vietnam,[36] where there was always some "military purpose" being pursued, but where the real purpose might simply have been to tire out Kim Il-Sung or Ho Chi Minh, to make the Marxist regimes unwilling to continue the contest of resolve.

Is there any more of a problem here, then, beyond a simple layer of euphemism and hypocrisy, as every military campaign pretends to be directed at the enemy's fighting capacity rather than its will, or as the "military" nature of the targeting is substantially exaggerated, with the "collateral damage" to civilian targets being welcomed more than anyone will admit? If nothing is involved besides a bridging of the gap between moral standards and actual practice, this is hardly something that will shake the world anymore.

But there was a larger impact here than the simple strain on moral conscience. If the military planners of the United States took their postures of aiming at enemy military power at all seriously, they were then inevitably driven to larger estimates of what would be required to carry this off.

Someone more forthrightly and honestly stressing the brutal counter-value mass destruction aspect of a nuclear attack would be counting, in violation of traditional Western morality, on imposing surrender on an enemy, *without* militarily defeating that enemy. For this purpose, subjecting one or two opposing cities a week to nuclear attack might suffice, rather than destroying 150 in the first night.

But, in the aftermath of World War II, amid the less-than-totally-grounded conclusions that "no one has ever been terrorized into surrendering" (so well matched to the moral injunction that one should not aim to hurt, but to disarm), it always seemed more appropriate to talk about full-scale attempts to *defeat* the Soviet Union.

There is thus a curious logical loop by which those who feared Soviet future intentions the most, who most would see war as inevitable sooner or later, would be more hesitant to threaten a preventive war before larger American nuclear forces were ready.

By this kind of logic, Stalin was *already* threatening to launch a World War III in 1948, even before he had any nuclear weapons of his own, because he was counting on the superiority of his conventional forces, because he was callous enough not to be intimidated by the suffering a strategic bombing would inflict on his cities.

U.S. nuclear weapons, and strategic air power in general, could, in this professional U.S. Air Force view, be brought to bear to defeat Stalin, either after he had launched a war, or perhaps preferably before he felt himself empowered enough to launch it, not because the destruction inflicted would intimidate the callous Soviet dictator, but because the U.S. bombing campaigns would in the end cripple Soviet military potential.

By this kind of calculation, what was being headed off in any preventive war would not have been Soviet acquisition of nuclear weapons, but Stalin's reaching of a power threshold sufficient to support Soviet aggression. And, just as the Soviet acquisition of a few nuclear warheads would not by itself be so decisive, the threat of devastating a few Soviet cities by American nuclear attacks would not be decisive.

By this kind of calculation, larger numbers of American atomic bombs, and larger numbers of air raids with such bombs, would be needed to achieve an effective preventive war, and this would then have to wait beyond 1947 and 1948. The counter-force-oriented view typical of the military is importantly different from that of anyone who saw atomic bombs as unignorable counter-value weapons, and who thought it urgent to keep Moscow from acquiring this kind of weapon *in particular*.

If some civilians thought that Stalin might surrender his own nuclear physicists into American custody, rather than seeing his cities destroyed on a two-a-week basis on the pattern of Hiroshima and Nagasaki, this was in effect to paint him as a less callous dictator, less eager to aggress in general, and certainly unlikely to aggress as long as he had no nuclear weapons of his own.

The 1947 and 1948 musings of a Curtis LeMay and a Bertrand Russell on preventive war are thus importantly different in premises and character, with LeMay's U.S. Air Force reasoning in effect being a case for delay, while Russell's was a case for urgent action.

Someone like Bertrand Russell, who *feared* the pain of nuclear war first and foremost, would be much more ready to entertain thoughts of applying that pain to Stalin, to keep him from acquiring his own force of painful weapons. For those of this world outlook, even a few dozen American atomic bombs, and the bombers to deliver them, were enough, and it would hardly be important to recover each bomber after it had inflicted a repetition of Hiroshima on a Soviet city.

But most Air Force generals and other military planners in the United States were, by morality or by habit, disinclined to talk about war-fighting as the mere imposition of pain.[37] If it was instead the crippling of the enemy's *ability* to fight, a much larger venture was required, with more bombs and more bombers, with repeated missions, and hence great concern about the hazards of Soviet air defenses, and about the recovery of U.S. bombers.

Here we come back closer to the classic calculations of preventive war speculation, whether "now" would be the time to wage war with a better total chance of winning, or whether the optimal time was a decade or two later. Unless one had *all* the military components in line for such a preventive war, the advantage might still rest with waiting.

We have thus two moral factors at work here, not just one: the qualms about the *initiating* of preventive war, and the moral objections to conducting an explicitly counter-value war, intended to force concessions simply by the tormenting of civilian hostages.

This debate about counter-force "war-fighting" applications of nuclear weapons vs. counter-value "deterrent" applications has, of course, continued onwards, ever since the U.S. nuclear monopoly was broken. Those pushing the war-fighting arguments would paint mutual deterrence as morally flawed, as "MAD" was equal to mutual assured destruction, and would paint any Soviet leader as difficult to deter simply by the threat of punishing his civilian population.

A popular argument in the early Reagan administration was that the Soviets might be quite willing to accept the destruction of their cities, as long as the Communist leadership still survived, and as long as Communist political control was spread in the war.[38] Even if victory was now to be meaningless in the destructiveness of the two nuclear arsenals, so Secretary of Defense Weinberger and President Reagan argued, it would be important to arrange that this "victory" would go to the West if there were a nuclear war, because this was the only factor tilting Moscow toward or away from aggression.

Those skeptical of the "war-fighting" arguments saw these as a self-serving military case for expanded forces, for continuing the arms race. One needed more forces to counter enemy forces, if the contest was about "victory" in any sense, than one needed to devastate their cities in a second strike.

It is worth repeating that this debate of the 1980s, indeed in all the decades after 1949, is virtually identical to a debate central to the feasibility of preventive war.

The latter-day case for focusing on war-fighting, and counter-force and victory, matches the earlier argument that it would be very difficult to force Stalin to surrender, that there might thus not be enough nuclear weapons to go around, or enough bombers.

And today's converse argument that nuclear weapons should *only* be used to deter use of the adversary's nuclear weapons, that the United States should settle for finite deterrence and assured destruction, matches the earlier case that relatively few nuclear weapons, and bombers to carry them, might be enough to impose the Baruch Plan on the Soviets.

It is dangerous to become too ad hominem in the analysis of arguments, but such imputations of personal motives inevitably have to play some role in political analysis. The Air Force and Navy have to be bigger if we are preparing for a nuclear contest of total military victory; by comparison there were fewer promotion slots to general and admiral if these services simply settled for being able to destroy cities.

In the debates of the 1970s and 1980 about Soviet intentions and strategy, where the Soviet leadership still did not particularly admit to being frightened of the weapons aimed at its cities, it had to be more than the bureaucratic politics considerations of career advancement that spurred on the "nuclear war-fighting" argument. Yet it is bizarrely possible that making the case for bigger services and more rapid promotion somehow caused military officers in 1946 to overestimate the physical requirements for a preventive war. The arguments are indeed parallel, for whatever this part of the explanation is worth.

Absence of a Casus Belli

When the possibility of a preventive war is introduced, the immediate response today is often that President Truman would have had no cause for war to cite to the American people.[39] Americans were tired of war after the sacrifices of World War II. And they were not in the habit of initiating wars.

In 1946, the Cold War was hardly yet so set in place. Public opinion polls can be misleading here, but they occasionally offer a nice chronological overview of the evolution of an issue, where (even if the absolute numbers are not so decisive, because of possible difficulties with the wording of the question, etc.), the trend of variations over time suggests what is happening. One such polling question posed repeatedly over time was (with minor variations) phrased as "Do you think that Russia can be trusted to cooperate with us after the war is over?" The responses of the Americans polled were as follows[40]:

	Yes	No
Feb 14 1942	38	37
Mar 26 1942	39	39
May 6 1942	45	25
July 1 1942	45	26
Aug 21 1942	51	25
June 18 1943	48	27
April 8 1944	50	22
June 7 1944	47	36
Nov 15 1944	47	35
Feb 20 1945	55	31
May 15 1945	45	38
Aug 8 1945	54	30
Feb 27 1946	35	52
Apr 10 1946	45	38
Sept 25 1946	32	53
Dec 11 1946	43	40
June 26 1949	20	62

As the polls suggest, Americans in 1946 were still uncertain (as compared with 1949) of how much of a challenge to peace would be posed by the USSR.

Yet one could should return to the 1941 policy choices cited earlier. President Roosevelt after 1939 had seen a need to get the United States into the war against Hitler, even when the great majority of Americans were opposed to any such intervention. By pressuring the Japanese on oil supplies, he did not succeed in forcing them to withdraw from China, but instead drove them to attack the United States at Pearl Harbor. By joining in the escort of convoys across the North Atlantic, Roosevelt did for a time constrain how German U-boats attacked such convoys, for Hitler was for the moment eager to avoid provoking the American public. Yet combat did occur between German submarines and American destroyers, cleverly orchestrated so that the American public would see the Germans at fault.[41]

Turning to Truman's situation, Stalin's violations of the letter or spirit of the Yalta agreements were hardly so subtle that Americans would have trouble making an issue of them. While only a tiny portion of the American public could have wanted war immediately with the USSR, American forces and American diplomats could have been similarly interposed to commit the prestige of the United States, so that the USSR either backed down or went to war.

As one example of what might have been a more general policy, but was not, Truman afterwards fondly remembered the warnings he had delivered to Stalin in early 1946 about the Soviet failure to withdraw as promised from northern Iran.[42] Those who argue that the nuclear threat did not amount to very much (or that it at the most could be used for deterrent purposes, rather than for compellence) must confront the interpretation put by Truman and others on this instance. A not-so-veiled threat was delivered of strong American responses if the Soviet forces were not withdrawn; in the event, Stalin withdrew them.[43]

Would Stalin have done the same with regard to Poland? Most probably not. But if the same threats had been made about Poland, and then rejected, would the American public not have seen Soviet behavior as more clearly unacceptable, and war as much more thinkable?

Iran may have been a clearer case than any other at the time, in that Soviet armed forces were definitely trespassing across an international border, having over-stayed the time agreed upon for the occupation of this country during World War II. Iran had been euphemistically defined as an ally rather than an enemy after the joint British-Soviet occupation of 1941, even though the elder Shah had been forced into exile because of his obvious pro-German sympathies.[44] In 1941 it had been important to avoid defining too many states as Axis states, and Iran had thus gotten off easily.

The continued Soviet force presence in Iran in 1946 was not quite as clear and blatant as a violent crossing of a frontier, such as was to occur in Korea in 1950 (after the Soviets had their own atomic bombs), but it was more blatant than what was going on in Poland (where the Soviets had been accorded the right to station troops to maintain logistical support for their garrison in East Germany) or in "defeated Axis states" like Hungary, Romania, and Bulgaria.[45] The 1948 Communist seizure of power in Czechoslovakia was to be executed without any Soviet military forces crossing borders, executed as in the rest of Eastern Europe by more subtle initiatives of secret police operatives, or of civilians armed with weapons as "workers' militias."[46]

One interpretation might thus be that the American nuclear monopoly could be harnessed to deterring as clear a violation of international peace as the violent crossing of a border (or even to an arbitrary prolongation of a presence across the border, as in Iran), but not to affecting anything short of this, for here the United States would be the initiator of the military conflict, rather than the USSR.

Apart from any inherent American reluctance to initiate war, the argument would also be that Americans were particularly sick of war by 1945, regardless of who would have been at fault for launching it. Yet virtually every American, except those very few who were privy to possibility of nuclear weapons, had expected that the war with Japan would go on into 1946 and 1947, and perhaps even longer.

What Japan had initiated with the United States, from the very beginning at Pearl Harbor, was an endurance contest, an aggression based on the hope that the American public would not accept the sacrifices of winning back the positions Japan had seized, but would instead sue for a peace in which East Asia was left to the Japanese.[47]

Despite very stiff Japanese resistance through 1943 and 1944, where each occupation of an island took a substantial toll of American young men, one heard few cries in the United States for settling for less than total victory, for less than "unconditional surrender." And the same held true in 1945, when Hitler's Germany had been defeated, when the treat of an Axis conquest of the world was definitively gone.

If most Americans, without nuclear weapons, were thus ready to keep on matching and overcoming Japanese resolve, until a final bloody amphibious invasion of Japan's main island of Honshu would perhaps occur in 1946 or 1947, would the same Americans, now knowing that they alone had the atomic bomb, but that Stalin might get the bomb as well in a few years (and knowing that the Soviet Union was much more of a threat than Japan to conquer the world) have been so insuperably war weary?

As just noted, President Truman, after leaving office, was to remember 1946 as a year when the Soviets had been compelled to leave northern Iran by the implicit threat that American nuclear weapons might otherwise come into use. Skeptics about the general applicability of nuclear weapons have sometimes scoffed at Truman's version of history, charging it off to the failing memory of a retired statesman, arguing that the American public would never have seen Iran as so important.[48]

If Iran were difficult to relate to American interests as a possible trigger for nuclear war, however, some might in retrospect find it easier to see such relevance in the Berlin crisis of 1948, when Stalin ordered the closing of land routes from West Germany to West Berlin. The immediate Western response was to begin ferrying supplies to West Berlin by air, an effort which Stalin must have thought would fail, because he underrated the logistic capabilities of the American and British Air Forces; the effort then succeeded magnificently, in what is remembered as the "Berlin airlift."[49]

The airlift might thus be one illustration of the power of air forces, but the same months of 1948 saw the deployment forward to Britain of American B-29s, with subtle hints that these might be able to deliver nuclear weapons to the USSR if the crisis went into actual warfare. The Soviets may have tolerated the airlift, rather than interfering with it just as they were frustrating land communications, because they expected it to fail; but Stalin (as Richard Betts has noted)[50] may also have been deterred from such a further escalation by the American nuclear counterthreat.

This is not a book about exactly when and how the Truman administration would have orchestrated a nuclear ultimatum to Stalin. Churchill was not the only advocate of preventive war to regard the Berlin blockade as a particularly salient occasion, but Stalin surely had provoked the West on other issues, ever since 1945. The more important point, for this book, is that such an ultimatum had to come before September of 1949.

More Benign Views of the Soviet Union

Most of the advocates of a preventive war with the Soviet Union after 1945 would have seen the obstacle to this as resting in the moral dictates of American democracy, something to be proud of, but something that would doom the world to a bipolar confrontation of thermonuclear missiles.

But a few would have blamed something else, a gullibility among many Americans about Stalin and his Soviet regime, in the wake of World War II, a gullibility that had arisen during the shared experience of fighting Hitler, a gullibility that had been enhanced by the machinations of a few American Communists who were secretly agents of the Soviet dictator.

Almost from the beginning of the Cold War, there had been discoveries of clandestine Communist agents attempting to steal information about how nuclear weapons were made. Other such people secretly taking orders from Stalin had infiltrated labor unions, Hollywood studios, and universities, pushing an image, before 1945 and after, that Stalin was the people's choice in Russia, that the Soviet Union was a benevolent and peace-loving place, and that anyone seeing a need for a confrontation with the USSR was a provocateur and warmonger.[51]

Movies such as *North Star* or *Mission to Moscow*, still shown on late-night television today, seem very quaint after the experience of the Cold War, and after all the revelations about Stalin that emerged even from within the Soviet Union after Khrushchev took power. Whether or not the plot outlines of these and other movies were dictated by agents from Moscow, such films and novels had something of an impact on American thinking during World War II, a thinking which was not then to be changed immediately thereafter, even when the examples of Soviet violations of Polish self-determination were fairly obvious.

One important purpose of Kennan's "long telegram" from Moscow proposing the policy of containment had indeed been to undo this excessively positive picture of Stalin and his dictatorship, but the years from 1945 to 1949 still had a fair number of Americans seeing Stalin's Russia as far less hostile than Hitler's Germany.

And indeed one can find many Americans today who would, in light of events since 1952, or certainly since 1989, share important parts of this argument, by which preventive war against Communism was a much less appropriate idea than against Nazism, by which any violent attempt to maintain the American nuclear monopoly would have been the tragedy of tragedies, *even if* it had succeeded, perhaps even if it had succeeded with Stalin giving in to American controls before a single Russian city had to be destroyed.

One would have had to be an extreme Cold Warrior to proclaim in 1948, or indeed at any time after the end of World War II, that the Soviet system was just as evil and just as dangerous as Nazi Germany had been (or indeed that it would be more dangerous, once it possessed nuclear weapons). Objective reality, and not just clever Communist propaganda circulated through Hollywood, suggested to Americans that there was at least some difference here in favor of the USSR.

At the very minimum, Americans were uncertain in 1945 and 1946 about how serious a political confrontation they would face after the defeat of Hitler and Japan. Americans were not used to the rough-and-tumble of old fashioned balance-of-power reasoning, by which yesterday's ally almost automatically became tomorrow's adversary, as soon as the previous common enemy had been defeated.[52] Americans were rather inclined to see peaceful relations between nations to be the norm, with wars and armed confrontations the unpleasant exception. As such, one would want to give the benefit of the doubt to Stalin's Soviet Union before planning for wars against it.

Those who lamented the failure of the United States to exploit its nuclear monopoly might thus have blamed the influence of the leftists, and the gullibility of the rest of Americans in the face of World War II propaganda. Yet most Americans were not so leftist or so gullible, but rather people (Dean Acheson is an excellent example) who simply regarded the post-World War II world as a test of uncertain Soviet intentions, a test which Stalin and his countrymen should at least have a fair opportunity to pass. If the United States brandished nuclear weapons too much, if it were too quick to threaten their use, any indictment of Soviet aggressive intentions would become nothing more than a self-confirming hypothesis, with Americans ever afterward worrying about whether the entire action had been unnecessary.

There are a host of unanswerable but interesting questions that emerge in any such comparisons of Hitler and Stalin. Would Hitler's Germany also have become humanized and democratized in only four decades or so? Did anyone before 1989 predict how soon the end of the Cold War would come, with the collapse of the Warsaw Pact and of the Soviet Union? Were all the predictions of risks of thermonuclear holocaust during the mature Cold War wrong, so that nothing would have been headed off by an American preemption of nuclear duopoly? Do we indeed know what kinds of political regimes will control Moscow's nuclear arsenal from here on?

But the moral case *for* preventive war and for the preservation of the American nuclear monopoly has been presented several times already, and it does not depend solely on equations of Stalin's Russia with Hitler's Germany. The tolerance of Stalin's acquiring nuclear weapons made it easier for other countries to acquire them thereafter; imposing the Baruch Plan on Stalin would have meant imposing it as well on any other state, including those which may yet have leaderships more resembling Hitler's.

And, to repeat, the human price paid for delaying the Russian democratization from 1947 to 1991 was also not so trivial.

In summation, some advocates of preventive war between 1945 and 1949 might have seen the problem as American gullibility and naivete, a gullibility affecting the highest levels of office while Franklin Roosevelt was still president, and carrying forward even thereafter. Communist propaganda had lulled the American public into seeing the Communists as very different from the fascist dictators, and the price of this was that Communist dictators like Stalin and Mao were to come into the possession of nuclear weapons.

This is, of course, an image diametrically opposed to the accounts of Cold War origins offered by "revisionist" historians after 1960, accounts by which Kennan and Harriman, and Truman, Byrnes and Acheson, were seething with antipathy to Stalin after 1945.

Kennan may have felt that he had some illusions to dispel in the "long telegram," but American governmental policies showed that the United States was certainly shedding its most naive images of the nature of Soviet society, even if it had for a time been taken in. A gullibility about Stalin's regime does not really suffice as the barrier to preventive war here.

The Russian People as an Ally

Related to American's instincts as a democracy have been the implicit or explicit assumptions Americans have made, throughout the Cold War, about who their adversary was.

In World War II, it had become possible for Americans to see most or all Germans as enemies, since the German enthusiasm for Hitler and the Nazi ideology seemed to have made the war an ethnic conflict.[53] The Japanese people and their culture were similarly to be seen as to blame for the massacres of Chinese at Nanjing, and for the barbaric treatment of American prisoners of war.[54] When German cities were thus destroyed by the combination of British and American air raids, the human suffering imposed could be justified by a logic that the German war effort was sustained by civilian energies and enthusiasm, that the Germans were "all Nazis." The fire-bombing of Tokyo and the nuclear attacks on Hiroshima and Nagasaki were similarly rationalized by arguments that the Japanese were all enthusiastic supporters of Japanese aggression.

The German and Japanese "cause" in World War II was a very explicitly selfish cause, putting the welfare of Germans and Japanese above the welfare of other nationalities, enslaving and victimizing others openly, as part of improving living standards back home.

But the Cold War, from the very beginning, was a much less explicitly selfish exchange. Rather than putting the welfare of Russians on a higher plane than that of other human beings, Moscow was proclaiming that its version of socialism was meant to be an improvement in the lot of workers and poor people everywhere. And the Western side of the Cold War similarly meant to serve the well-being of people everywhere, spreading free speech and free press and political democracy.

The Cold War was thus a contest of competing altruisms, rather than of ethnic selfishness. And this might make a major difference on whether or when one could drop nuclear weapons on a Russian city. Americans explicitly or implicitly assumed that Russians were being governed against their will by Stalin and his Communist successors, just about as much against their will as the Poles or the Czechs.

It was one thing to punish Tojo's accomplices by a nuclear attack on Hiroshima, as a way of getting even for Pearl Harbor and Bataan, and as a way to get Tojo's successors to surrender; but it might be quite another to punish Stalin's victims as a way of getting even with Stalin for his aggressions, or as a way of keeping Stalin from getting nuclear weapons of his own.

The conventional (and nuclear) bombings of World War II had of course been officially rationalized as being directed against "military targets." The moral need to obfuscate the real purpose of aerial bombardment here is an older story, dating even back to the first air raids of World War I. To satisfy consciences and to appease neutral opinion, all the governments involved will claim to be aiming at "legitimate military targets," even where they are in fact instead trying to erode the other side's *willingness*, rather than *ability*, to fight.

Dresden was leveled, again with close to 100,000 people killed in a pre-nuclear air raid, allegedly to cripple German logistics passing through the city, and thus to offer assistance to the advancing Red Army. Yet the more real explanation was the desire to force Germany to surrender by the sheer imposition of suffering, supported by an intuition that all the Germans shared in Nazi guilt, just as all the Japanese shared in the guilt for World War II barbarism.

The distinction here can be illustrated easily enough by comparing the fates of Dresden and Prague, cities not so very far apart geographically. Both of them could have been attacked and burned and leveled if the goal was simply to offer military assistance to the advancing Soviet forces. But Prague was populated by Czechs, allies of the West, while Dresden was populated by Germans, the enemy. And Prague was thus hardly bombed at all, while Dresden was bombed as severely as any city in World War II.[55]

Americans thus had had some difficulty in confronting the real purposes of their bombing campaigns even against the hated Germans and Japanese, having to pretend that the purpose was purely military; but such bombardment would face far more severe problems if directed against Russians, the Russians who would indeed in 1991 confirm that they had been held under Stalin's rule against their will. The Russians might thus already in 1948 have looked more like the 1945 Czechs, and less like the 1945 Germans or Japanese.

Stalin's Soviet Union resembled Nazi Germany in its institutions of secret police and concentration camps, its networks of secret agents abroad, and its expansionist world view. But the evidence, photographic and otherwise, was that ordinary Germans were more enthusiastic about Hitler and his policies than ordinary Russians were about Stalin. And, to repeat, there was nothing about Communist ideology that was remotely as selfish or racist as the ideologies of the three Axis powers in World War II.

When the nuclear duopoly settled into place after 1949, every last Russian and other Soviet population center was indeed to be targeted, always on the grounds that military targets had been found in such cities, with the people that would have been killed, in the response to a Soviet initiation of World War III, simply amounting (as in World War II as well) to "collateral damage."

The basic logic of the nuclear confrontation from 1949 to 1989, and probably beyond, has thus been beset with a number of logical contradictions, of which the most important came in targeting philosophy. The believer in assured destruction and mutual deterrence was relying on the (counter-value) *pain* to be imposed on civilians in nuclear retaliatory attacks, but these would all along have been attacks that pretended to another purpose, the (counter-force) winning of the war by crippling the enemy's potential to fight.[56]

The believer in counter-value deterrence might be skeptical that a war could thus be won by nuclear weapons, that the Soviet armed forces would really be crippled; but he would welcome the "unintended collateral damage," because the mere prospect of this would probably deter the Soviet leadership from ever initiating a nuclear World War III, or even a non-nuclear limited war advance into Western Europe.

Americans were thus capable of planning the nuclear devastation of Russians who were probably not to blame for aggression, and of Poles or Hungarians who were indeed the victims of earlier aggressions, as long as the official intention was not to impose such devastation, but to defeat Soviet armed forces. The array of pretended versus real intention was parallel to the arrays for World War II, but with the important differences that no one hated the Russians as much as they had hated the Germans or Japanese; and the scenario was always that of a war which had not been initiated by the United States.

For the bulk of the Cold War, it is difficult to find examples of American or Western reasoning where the enemy is thus defined as "Russian" rather than "Communist."[57] Stalin, after all, was a Georgian and not an ethnic Russian. The closest one comes is not in the form of hatred for the people, but in theories advanced late in the 1970s by which the Communist Party leadership was relying on Russians to maintain control over all the ethnically disparate portions of the Soviet Union, an "evil empire" in which Brezhnev could not trust non-Russians to be the leaders of, for example, the Kazakh branch of the party.

Hunting for a more reliable way of deterring Soviet adventures, as the Soviet nuclear arsenal and conventional arsenal continued to grow into the 1980s, theories of "counter-power" nuclear targeting were published which put another counter-force spin on how nuclear weapons would be directed against Soviet cities in the event of a war (all this still to be posed only as the *response* to Soviet aggression, and hence something that would never have to be implemented, as long as this improved deterrent actually worked).

Targets would be chosen on an ethnic basis, by this theory, so that fewer non-Russian casualties would be imposed, and relatively more Russian, all with a view to confronting the Kremlin with the prospect that it would lose an important component of its control over the USSR, its Russian enclaves in Kazakhstan or Estonia or Moldova, and so on.[58]

While such theories were discussed, and while the thrust of this thinking was parallel to attitudes expressed by the incoming Reagan administration about the inherent difficulty of deterring Soviet aggression, no such blatantly ethnic target policy was ever proclaimed. Yet, as our earlier comparison of Prague and Dresden already illustrated, some of such differentiation would have been natural and inevitable. Whatever the American theories on how Russian felt about being governed by Stalin, or by Khrushchev, the evidence was even stronger that the inhabitants of Warsaw, Budapest and Prague did not want to be so governed.

In summary, returning to the option of a pre-1949 preventive war, what Americans assumed about the Russian people in 1946 (and what we think we know about them in 1998) might thus have amounted to an insuperable barrier to attacking any Russian city with nuclear weapons, or even threatening such attacks, when the Kremlin had *not yet* set the stage by initiating a war on its own.

What this book is about is not an attempt to apply nuclear weapons to "win" a war Stalin's Soviet Union had launched, but rather an attempt to intimidate Stalin, to deter him from acquiring his own nuclear arsenal and perhaps even to compel him to surrender political power, by the prospect that his cities would be destroyed. This would thus have posed very major moral problems for Americans, because they did not hate Russians as they had hated the Germans and Japanese. [59]

The post-1949 believer in mutual assured destruction was to accept the need to threaten the innocent, the Russian people, as a means of deterring the potentially guilty, the Kremlin leadership, but only because he hoped that this would, decade after decade, keep nuclear weapons from ever being used at all. But most of such advocates of MAD would, on emotional feelings rather than by rational calculations, have been very unlikely recruits for a pre-1949 preventive-war effort to head off nuclear duopoly.

The logic of mutual assured destruction suggests that one can accomplish a very great deal by the mere prospect of destroying cities, such that plans for a counter-force pursuit of "military victory" are unnecessary, as well as being pointless and even dangerous.

But, while this would have been central to the thinking of any venture into preventive war, the moral feelings of the people involved, and the lack of hatred for the Russian population, worked to confuse the logic here.

Overarching World Views

Very few Americans knew about the prospect of nuclear weapons during World War II, until the day that the first atomic bomb was dropped on Hiroshima. For the Americans planning for a postwar world, and for the great bulk of ordinary citizens, the prospects for peace depended on something other than weapons of mass destruction.

The logic of the United Nations can be usefully juxtaposed to that of the League of Nations, and also to that of mutual nuclear deterrence. Americans looking ahead after 1943 could hope that Germany might be defeated by 1945, and Japan perhaps forced to surrender by 1947. To prevent such aggressive nations from emerging again, it would be important that they be totally defeated and occupied, and thus hopefully reformed. And it would be important that the United States this time be enlisted to the structure of collective security, rather than just playing a major role in the design of such a structure, as with the League of Nations, and then failing to join.[60]

The hope after 1943 was thus that the collective security mechanism which had been so challenged in the League of Nations, and which then had failed, could somehow be made to work in a new United Nations Organization. Collective security entailed some fundamental paradoxes and difficulties, from 1919 to 1939, and then in 1945, and now after 1989. The system presumes that international peace, the absence of warfare, is a primary goal, after the bloodshed of the World War I trenches, and so on. The nations of the system commit themselves to pursuing peace rather than pursuing their more narrow interests. If there is an outbreak of war anywhere on the globe, they will intervene against the side which first resorted to armed violence, just as the sheriff in domestic law and order intervenes against the first party in a conflict to use firearms.[61]

But this then offers an opportunity for someone like Mussolini or Hitler, or Saddam Hussein, to probe whether the peace-loving nations are not bluffing in their pledges to intervene. "Since you love peace so much, please get out of my way, as I reclaim territory and property that are rightfully mine," so goes the implicit challenge to the system, a challenge which the world failed to meet in the days of the League.

Clausewitz captured this fundamental paradox of the logic of collective security very well in his comment that "the aggressor is always peace-loving,"[62] noting that our human intuitions remember a war as beginning only when the victimized state *resists* aggression. We remember World War II as beginning in Europe in September of 1939, when Poland resisted Hitler's attack, and not in March of 1939, when German forces entered Prague after encountering no Czech resistance.

The "realist" in international politics thus expresses grave doubts about whether such a system can ever work, whether states that love peace will dare to initiate war to resist aggressors, whether states will not be guided instead by many other interests, alliances, old friendships, and so on. The system of collective security would require that all such friendships and interests be overridden, by the simple objective facts of who had been the first to resort to warfare, with punishment and intervention then being directed against that offender.[63]

Compared to the League of Nations, the United Nations was thus already a notch more "realistic," in that the permanent members of the Security Council were given a veto over the use of international force, thus allowing them to serve their own interests. In the League of Nations Council, the major powers would not have had such a veto wherever they themselves were involved in a dispute. This U.N. veto was inserted in part to assure that the United States would join the United Nations, rather than abstaining as it had with the League, and in part to assure that Stalin's Soviet Union be retained as a key member of the anti-Axis coalition.

The worldview of the enormous majority of Americans, before they were so caught by surprise by Hiroshima, was thus a more cautious hope for collective security once the Axis had been defeated, a hope taking into account an inevitable preeminence in military strength of the major powers, a hope that the wartime coalitions produced by the fear of the Axis could be maintained to prevent a return of anything like the Axis. This was thus already a more "tough-minded," and somewhat less optimistic, approach than had obtained at the end of World War I.

Much of what followed August of 1945 would then come as a surprise on this issue of worldview. The defeat of Japan had come one or two years earlier than anticipated, with much less of a cost in American casualties and economic sacrifice. Nuclear weapons existed in American hands, with an elementary uncertainty about how long it would be until other countries had them also. And the Soviet use of the veto in the United Nations belied the anticipations of a close postwar cooperation among the World War II allies, and undermined prospects of a very effective role for the U.N.

The years since 1989, with the model of the resistance to Saddam Hussein's aggression against Kuwait, might now be seen as a fresh start for collective security, the system that failed between the World Wars, the system which never really got started in the post-1945 U.N.[64] If it were to work successfully into the future, it would amount to another version of the "happy ending" for the Cold War, an ending that would amount to more ammunition against any precipitate American attempt to apply nuclear weapons before 1949.

But, for the years from 1945 to 1949, the over-arching promise of the United Nations amounts to a source of frustration, and distraction or confusion. Americans could become angry at the frequent Soviet resort to the veto, and at the same time remember that this veto was part of the bargain initiating the U.N., a part of the revised vision of collective security which, for those not privy to the Manhattan Project, had looked like the only hope for peace.

If a cold-blooded strategic analyst had concluded that the Hiroshima bomb already made the U.N. obsolete, most Americans would have reacted instead that this successor to the League of Nations needed to be given a chance to see how it would work. The sheer inertia and momentum that attached to thoughts about the new United Nations thus may supply another explanation of the American disinclination to contemplate preventive war.

As noted, clear-headed analysts had foreseen that the Security Council veto would be logically incompatible with the reliable global nuclear disarmament projected in the Baruch Plan.

This veto had stemmed from pre-nuclear calculations of a blending of collective security reasoning with realistic power politics reasoning. But, looking ahead somewhat, this veto was to also become very consistent with the Soviet acquisition of nuclear weapons in 1949, and then the proliferation of such weapons to Britain, France, and China, the other permanent members of the Security Council possessing such a veto.

The overarching logic of United Nations, where it differed from that of the League of Nations, may thus, by its blend of optimism and pessimism, of idealism and realism, have had the unfortunate impact of helping to resign Americans to the termination of their nuclear monopoly. By the time that the U.N. had been "given a chance to work," by the time that the logical arguments were clarified by which a veto was incompatible with preventing nuclear proliferation, the first round of nuclear proliferation had occurred, the round that will always have mattered the most.

American Political Checks and Balances

The analysis of almost any issue of American foreign policy has to include major references to the role of Congress, because the founding fathers of the United States intended for powers to be split in a system of checks and balances, and simply because Congress has often enough been eager to "horn in" on any major issue area, for reasons of ego or voter appeal, or distrust of the incumbent in the presidency.[65]

The necessary secrecy of the original race to get nuclear weapons had seemingly required that the Congress, and the general American public, not be informed at all that such weapons were being sought in the Manhattan Project. Because President Truman did not command as much personal respect as had Franklin Roosevelt, and because the war was over and the basic secret was out, Congress and the American public would then be impatient in 1945 to restore whatever checks and balances had been suspended during the war.

But the role of the U.S. Congress on nuclear matters is interestingly complicated here, with regard to this earliest fear of nuclear proliferation, the fear that a *second* country would get the atomic bomb. As noted earlier, the Congress had been driven also by an opposite fear, that there might be too much military secrecy on nuclear matters, compromising the principle of civilian control over the military, and perhaps missing opportunities for civilian exploitation of nuclear physics.

Both concerns had to be important for Americans. But the second concern was then to come under serious reexamination after the Indian detonation of a "peaceful nuclear explosive" in 1974.

In 1946, the Congress was afraid that an excessive concern for military considerations, that is, for preventing the spread of nuclear weapons and loss of U.S. power advantage, would cause the military to keep nuclear matters too much under wraps, thus missing too many of the beneficial "spinoffs" for civilian purposes.[66] By 1975, the Congress was instead alarmed that nuclear weapons proliferation, to India and to many other countries, had been made too easy as a spinoff *from* civilian nuclear power reactors *to* weapons.[67]

In the aftermath of the USSR having gotten its own bomb, and of three more states doing so explicitly, and a fair number more threatening to slip into possession of such weapons, the Congress had thus become resistant to, rather than supportive of, peaceful nuclear activities. The relevant spinoffs were now working in the opposite direction.

The Congress was never unconcerned about maintaining nuclear secrecy and preventing other states from acquiring the bomb, especially after the first Soviet espionage rings dedicated to nuclear matters were exposed already in 1946. In later years, even after the USSR had acquired nuclear weapons of its own, the Joint Committee on Atomic Energy, until the 1970s probably the most powerful and respected Joint Committee in the history of the Congress, thus continued to oppose any American assistance even to Britain and France in the production of nuclear weapons, in important part for fear that there might be Communists in these national programs who would pass along the technology so that Moscow could improve its weapons.[68]

Any analysis of what actually *did* happen is thus incomplete without factoring in the Congress, and the legislative controls it imposed, after World War II was over and the Manhattan Project had been disclosed. Yet the question then remains on whether Congressional sentiment, and the popular sentiment behind it, would have been an insuperable barrier to the concerted effort required for stopping Soviet nuclear weapons acquisition.

Just as there would have been opponents of any such operation within the Congress, there were also some advocates of such an operation, not in the leadership, not such as to force the hand of the Truman administration into the venture, but illustrative of the fact that the idea was thinkable.

Just as the Truman administration had to enter into the hard work of shaping bi-partisan foreign policy for the Marshall Plan and for the launching of NATO, and just as Franklin Roosevelt had faced a great deal of hard work in selling Lend-Lease and U.S. military prepared-ness, the president would have had to lay a groundwork of greater con-frontation with the Soviets, and then engage in a great deal of coordina-tion and ego-stroking, if a more military nuclear initiative were to be undertaken.

This task would, in retrospect, have to be rated as neither easy nor impossible.

The bombings of Hiroshima and Nagasaki had come as a surprise attack, because wartime conditions had allowed the United States to maintain a very effective curtain of secrecy over the Manhattan Project. By comparison, a nuclear preventive war against the Soviet Union would have come as much less of a surprise, because Stalin already had seen the American bomb used, because the processes of peacetime Congres-sional involvement would have shown what was coming.

Yet, to repeat, a most important part of the schemes being consid-ered here (unlike the Japanese model, where Tokyo was not offered a demonstration of the fate that was in store, before Hiroshima was de-stroyed) would have entailed giving Stalin the option of surrendering before being bombed, of Stalin's at least surrendering the possibility of making atomic bombs of his own. Rather than being an unmitigated obstacle to this kind of an approach, the processes of Congressional involvement in U.S. foreign policy could have been applied to achieve this purpose of compellence.

7

American Morality

The arguments against preventive war listed so far will often seem to overlap. Some readers might thus simply conclude that the *combination* of all such sources for hesitation would be the explanation for the rejection of preventive war, even if no one of them by itself would suffice.

Yet the one *indispensable* element, it would be argued here, is what has already surfaced and intruded in a number of these kinds of logic, the American moral aversion to applying the nuclear monopoly to preserve itself. Deleting that American moral disapproval of war-initiation would have opened up many more lines of speculation, and would have subjected many of the supposed obstacles to preventive war to more critical scrutiny.

When all the various arguments about an alleged American inability to exploit a nuclear monopoly have been considered, we are thus still left with a considerable case for what most Americans have believed about themselves, that the United States is an unusually moral and well-behaving nation, that it was simply too moral to give preventive war the consideration it might have deserved.[1]

This often enough has been painted as a "myth" by the analysts who are unwilling to see Americans going around congratulating themselves, and (especially during the Vietnam War) by critics of U.S. foreign policy in general, critics who were not inclined to characterize the United States as an "unusually good country," or even as an "ordinary country," but rather, because of the alleged defects of capitalism, or because of our Wild West and inner-city traditions of domestic violence, as an "unusually bad country."[2] Yet ordinary Americans may still find very persuasive the interpretation by which America was too moral to exploit its nuclear monopoly.

It was one thing to use a monopoly of nuclear weapons when a war was already underway, a war which Japan had begun with a treacherous sneak attack at Pearl Harbor. A homely, but not atypical, example of American feelings here emerged after Japanese criticisms were voiced when Lyndon Johnson's daughter had inadvertently scheduled her wedding on the anniversary of the bombing of Hiroshima. Caught off guard by a press question on the choice of date, she snapped back "What do they suggest instead, December 7th?"[3]

The 1941 shift from peace to war has been as shocking for Americans as for any other people, or perhaps even more so. Americans remember themselves as not starting wars, and then as plunging reluctantly, but wholeheartedly, into the effort of winning the war after it had been forced upon them.

Hiroshima and Nagasaki were also shocking for Americans, but more happily so, in that World War II ended so quickly, when everyone would have guessed that the war would need to be fought for another year or two. A democratization of Japan and an assurance that Japan would not get nuclear weapons were important results of the use of American atomic bombs, but the most immediate result was that a horrible war was surprisingly and suddenly over.

By contrast, the option we are contemplating here, a preventive war designed to keep the Soviet Union from getting nuclear weapons (and also *perhaps* designed to democratize Russia) would have entailed a move again from peace to war. Even the more power-minded and realistic Royal Navy, so eager to head off any threats to its Britannic rule of the waves, would have had more qualms about a preemptive attack initiating a war against the French, Germans, Russians, or Americans in the nineteenth century, as compared with seeking to wipe out the opposing navy once war was declared.

Americans thus regarded the launching of war as blatantly immoral, and also as psychologically traumatic. The objections voiced, in response to the various preventive war proposals, begin again and again with how contrary this would be to important American values and traditions.

We might turn once again to the fascinating juxtaposition of the 1946 works by Bernard Brodie and William B. Borden, works undertaken immediately after the news of Hiroshima, but reaching such diametrically opposite conclusions about what the real role of nuclear weapons would be.

Brodie and his partners in the edited work largely saw such weapons as this book sees them, as an unignorable way of inflicting mass destruction, while Borden saw them instead as a very rapid way of disarming an enemy and defeating his forces. Yet the two books were agreed on a point central to the discussion here: The American nuclear monopoly would not be maintained, but would be succeeded by a nuclear confrontation, in which one or more *other* nations had such bombs;[4] and both authors opined that an important explanation for this, looking ahead in the fall of 1945 and spring of 1946, was that Americans were too well-intentioned to undertake any kind of preventive or preemptive action.[5]

Neither Brodie nor Borden went into detail in this, and neither even very much addressed the case for preventive war, the case that the nuclear confrontation should be headed off. Each instead took this kind of American attitude as a given, as a premise that was so self-evident that it did not need much elaboration.

Interesting, and to be discussed further below, each also avoided citing the Soviet Union as the obvious next possessor of such nuclear weapons, dealing instead with a generic nuclear adversary of the future, that might as easily have been a Germany or a Japan, or a Britain.

Unrelated to nuclear issues (most 1944 military planners were of course not privy to the Manhattan Project), the U.S. Army Air Force's wartime plans for the postwar world were also not targeted on the Soviet Union as the likely enemy, as plans were made for the development of large arrays of bombers, with the likely enemy being a resurgently militaristic Japan or Germany.[6]

Similarly, the bulk of the novels and analyses speculating about a nuclear war in the years immediately after 1945 did not cast the USSR as the likely enemy.

Double-Edged Morality

The United States, it will be argued here, was guided very much by morality, and generosity, and respect for law, as it decided what it could do, and what it could not do, with nuclear weapons after 1945.

We introduced earlier above the argument that the Truman administration may have been deterred from exploiting the nuclear monopoly by its concern for the welfare of the West Europeans. But if this is indeed any part of the explanation for restraint, it already illustrates these liberal democratic instincts. Such feelings may have blocked any American initiation of war, just as they would explain an American willingness to escalate to the nuclear level if the Soviet Union had initiated such a war.

The NATO countries, including West Germany, were indeed to be seen as "the fifty-first state" after the launching and expansion of NATO, for purposes of gauging whether the U.S. would take risks, including the risks of nuclear escalation, on their behalf.

France and the Low Countries would have benefited from such a status already in 1945, and West Germany, after the joint experience of the Berlin blockade and airlift, began to benefit from the same kind of American feelings after 1948.[7]

If Brezhnev and his advisers were ever to take seriously the argument advanced by Pierre Gallois [8] and others, that the United States would never have cared enough about Western Europe to be ready to escalate to the use of nuclear weapons against the Warsaw Pact, he might thus have sobered himself to give up hopes of any easy "limited war" Communist reunification of Germany, by remembering this part of the explanation for American restraint between 1945 to 1949.

If one credits the Soviet potential grip on Western Europe as being the crucial counterweight and deterrent to any American exploitation of the nuclear monopoly, this would already be proof that Americans care a great deal about the countries from which most of their ancestors came, and about countries that are governed democratically.

One can not very easily have it both ways on this logical point, that Americans were inhibited by the vulnerability of Europeans before 1948, but would not have identified enough with them to make extended nuclear deterrence credible after 1949.

In the event, for whatever reason, such extended nuclear deterrence apparently remained credible enough after 1949, until 1989, when the collapse of the Warsaw Pact presumably eliminated the need for it. Despite Gallois, despite all the American analyses of "limited war" by which an American president would "of course" not be willing to initiate the use of nuclear weapons, if Moscow had them and had not yet used them, the explanation for the military security of West Germany and the NATO central front remained as much nuclear as conventional, right until the Berlin Wall was torn down.

And the American willingness to use nuclear weapons for the contingency of a Soviet tank attack may have been very parallel to the unwillingness to use such weapons to head off Soviet nuclear proliferation, an instinctive identification with other peoples, and a concern for international legality, an aversion to launching wars.

Preventive War and the "Democratic Peace"

The end of the Cold War saw political democracy emergent in many more separate countries than ever before in history, and this has led into an extensive discussion on the assumptions of a "democratic peace," the assumptions that democracies will not go to war with each other, and will generally be less likely to go to war with anyone else.[9]

Such optimism has been challenged by the self-styled "realists" of international relations analysis, who would respond that the world may have never seen a war between two democracies, only because, until so recently, there were so very few democracies in the world. Now that we have so many countries around the world governed by systems of free elections, this viewpoint would argue, we will soon enough see military tensions and wars erupting where they face each other.

It is not only the "realists," generally deprecating the importance of domestic politics for international confrontations, that have voiced skepticism here.[10] Some very careful analyses have thus now been undertaken by analysts less committed to one worldview or another, in a continuing debate on the nature of democracy as an international actor.

But many political scientists, and most ordinary people, would indeed continue to be optimistic now about the international style of democracies, and would thus be optimistic about the post-Cold War world, about the avoidance of nuclear arms races and nuclear war in the future.

Such an optimism would be consistent with the rejection of the very idea of preventive war. If the Cold War was destined to end with the replacement of a Communist dictatorship in the Soviet Union with a political democracy, what would ever have been the point of using nuclear threats to prevent Moscow from acquiring the atomic bomb?

Yet such an optimism, well-taken or not, also very much illustrates and reinforces the interpretation of the American 1945-1949 decisions being offered here. The United States may have rejected preventive war not because it was so inherently unnecessary and such an inherently bad idea, but because the United States was a democracy, and because democracies do not initiate wars.

8

Preventive War After 1949?

This book focuses on the years of the American total nuclear monopoly, the years from 1945 to 1949. In 1949, the United States concluded that it had reliable evidence that the Soviets had tested a nuclear device, and President Truman made a public announcement of this on September 23. To introduce a personal note, as one very rough and ready indicator of the importance of events, this author can remember where he was standing when he heard that President Truman made this announcement.

Perhaps this book should then simply end in 1949, as the monopoly was gone, never to return. The nuclear monopoly would remain as what was to be feared, if the other side could ever achieve it for itself, but it was not there any more for us to exploit, or to maintain.

But why not still consider a preventive war attack on the Soviets immediately after this news, when the Soviet retaliation would still be small, and when the threat had now been confirmed? There was indeed a wave of discussion of such options, inside the government and outside, continuing into the first years of the Eisenhower administration, that is, as late as 1954.[1]

For someone locked mainly on to the question of victory, of who had any forces remaining after all the attacks had been made, these were still to be years of American "nuclear superiority," with the world not shifting into a parity, or Soviet "nuclear superiority" until the missile gap of the end of the 1950s, or until the massive Soviet investments in throw-weight at the end of the 1970s. A traditional preventive-war calculation would have attached great significance to these post-1949 trends, now that the first detected Soviet detonation had verified the thrust of Soviet intentions.

And even someone more fixated on the counter-value aspects of the confrontation might still not have ruled out a preventive war attack here, since so few Soviet atomic bombs, and means for delivering them, would have had to be available in 1949 or 1950.

Yet, to repeat, this author was, and is, impressed enough by the examples of Hiroshima and Nagasaki to sense that even a few atomic bombs are a serious deterrent. After September of 1949, there was the very real risk that any attempt to dictate nuclear disarmament to the Soviets, as it had been dictated to the Japanese, would mean the destruction of New York or some other American city. The delivery systems for Soviet nuclear weapons were nothing like what were to be developed later. The victim of Soviet nuclear retaliation was likelier to be London or Paris, which the Soviet Tu-4 bombers could strike more easily. Yet, utilizing a submarine or a freighter, could not some last-gasp desperation mission still also get a bomb into New York Harbor?

The new sensitivity of the United States and its allies is illustrated in a large number of magazine articles published in 1949 and 1950 on the impact of a nuclear attack on an American city.[2]

Some of the subsequent post-1949 U.S. government "analysis" of preventive war could indeed be questioned as to its seriousness, and might, in an ad hominem way, even be introduced as evidence of the American moral aversions to such preemptive action.

To draw a somewhat folksy analogy, this might all be like the happily married man on a train who notices an attractive female smiling at him. He does not respond, and she gets off several stops later. After she has left the train, *when the moral danger is safely behind him, and nothing bad can happen*, he amuses himself for the remainder of the trip speculating about what it might have been like, following up on her signs of interest.

The American antipathy to the idea of starting a war was great. Once the Soviets had the atomic bomb, when it was almost assuredly too late for such an American war-initiation to have occurred, it may then have seemed interesting, and *morally safer*, to muse on whether such a campaign could have had gains outweighing the costs.

"War plans," and other studies of contingencies within a government, are thus notoriously hard to evaluate as to their importance, when staff officers are allowed to acquire experience in contemplating options that will never be taken seriously, when someone's favorite course of action is often presented in tandem with dummy alternatives to be rejected. "We can disarm unilaterally, we can launch a preventive war, or we can adopt the commonsensical middle-of-the-road military budget we are recommending."

Yet, one still has to consider *some* serious possibilities here of the preventive war option, even after September 23, 1949. If such an act should have been thinkable on September 22, when (as noted earlier) there had to be some inherent possibility that the Soviets might already have assembled a nuclear weapon or two, was such action to be totally unthinkable on September 24th?

And, if one was morally ready to destroy several, perhaps even several dozen, Russian cities, in a preventive-war contest of wills with Stalin, would one really have had to back off at the prospect that one or two American cities would also suffer?

It would have helped if one had some good intelligence on where Soviet bombs were being produced and stored, and where the putative delivery systems for such weapons would be based, so that the first use of American nuclear weapons could now be meaningfully counter-force, rather than counter-value, that is, intended to eliminate the existing Soviet nuclear capability, rather than only to intimidate Moscow into surrendering that capability.[3] But the mere fact that the Soviets were so close to nuclear weapons in 1949 had caught the United States by surprise, suggesting that the details would be hard to come by, on where U.S. bombs should be aimed to eliminate the threat of Soviet bombs.

The outbreak of the Korean War brought to the surface more of such speculation about preventive war, already discussed above, most noticeably by Secretary of the Navy Francis Matthews and Air Force General Orvil Anderson.[4]

But, for most people, the Korean War conveyed exactly the opposite message, namely that Stalin had felt safe in sending Kim Il-Sung's forces southward, that Russian nuclear weapons were understood, in Moscow and in Washington, as cancelling out the impact and applicability of U.S. nuclear weapons. Where U.S. nuclear attacks would previously, before 1949, have been the response to tanks made in Russia, the Russian-made tanks advancing through South Korea had to be repulsed by tanks made in the United States, as nuclear weapons had to be held in reserve.

The Korean War opened a grand and painful discussion of "limited war" in the United States.[5] But limited war is logically nothing more than the opposite side of the coin of mutual deterrence, what later came to be labeled mutual assured destruction. Rather than being the occasion for a serious enthusiasm for preventive war, the Korean War, launched as it was by forces under the influence of Moscow, had instead to be seen as a symptom of the end of any U.S. nuclear monopoly. For some, the Korean War might have made 1950 look appropriate for preventive war, but for most it made it look too late.

An antidote to skepticism about the significance of the nuclear monopoly would thus be to look at the more tangible American reactions *after* the monopoly was lost. By hindsight, the Soviet acquisition of such weapons made a tremendous difference. Our question in this book is whether it should not have captured more attention, and action, by foresight.

One immediate reaction did not lead to very much concrete action. President Truman commissioned a National Security Council study under the direction of Paul Nitze, which would be numbered NSC-68.[6] NSC-68 saw the Soviet nuclear acquisition indeed to be a major blow to the security of the free world, and called for a substantial enhancement of Western military preparations, both in the nuclear and conventional field. NSC-68, before its text was actually declassified, was widely touted as having been the original formulation of the limited war argument, by which nuclear forces would now deter each other in a simple pattern of mutual assured destruction, while conventional armored forces would then be free to lunge at each other.

The actual text [7] did indeed advocate larger conventional forces, but it also showed considerable sympathy for counter-force war-fighting arguments at the nuclear level, rather than merely assuming that destructive nuclear forces would deter each other, and it thus called for substantial expansions of American forces here as well.

In the event, President Truman congratulated Nitze and his colleagues on the quality of the NSC-68 product, but elected for the time not to implement its recommendations for increased defense expenditures, indeed planning further cuts for the spring of 1950.

It was the North Korean invasion of South Korea in June of 1950 that then brought home to the Truman administration, and to the American public at large, the apparent fuller significance of the end of the nuclear monopoly. As the Korean War was fought as a "limited war," many ordinary Americans seconded the complaints of General MacArthur that it was somehow unreasonable to fight with only a portion of the American arsenal, attacking targets in North Korea, but not in China or

Siberia, and so on. But the answer for such complaints would again and again be the reminder that the Communist world now had nuclear weapons too.

A very different kind of indicator of the significance of the Soviet breaking of the monopoly was the sentence imposed on Julius and Ethel Rosenberg, after they were convicted of having delivered nuclear secrets to the Soviet Union, as the death penalty was imposed on both of them (such a penalty in 1953 still being unusual for a female), and as all pleas for clemency were to be denied. In the words of Judge Kaufman, what the two of them had been convicted of was to be regarded as considerably worse than murder.[8]

The Soviets had not announced their 1949 nuclear test, leaving it to the United States to publicize the test after it had been detected, with Moscow even then not confirming that this test had occurred, or that it had been the first such Soviet test. The Soviet posture was thus to be one of blurring the 1949 accomplishment, and more generally to leave an impression that such a Soviet nuclear arsenal might have already been in place earlier.

The opening of records since 1989 confirms that August 29, 1949 was indeed the first Soviet nuclear weapons test;[9] but, given the lateness and uneven quality of American monitoring systems, and the closed nature of the USSR under Stalin, and Molotov's vague claim, Americans could not so surely have ruled out the possibility that the Soviets could have already had a bomb earlier.

David Holloway differentiates between two possible American responses to a more open Soviet accomplishment here, either that the United States would have considered preventive war, or that it would have accelerated its own nuclear weapons program, and he suggests that both of these concerns would explain Stalin's decision not to announce the 1949 test publicly.[10] Yet, the rest of the Soviet behavior pattern may indeed fit fears of preventive war, more than fears of American nuclear weapons production.

Stalin indeed had delayed the first test until he had enough fissile material to produce a second bomb,[11] precisely on the argument (one relevant to any proliferator today) that a nuclear test detonation must not amount to a verified unilateral total abolition of one's own arsenal.

If one wished to slow down the accumulation of nuclear weapons in the American stockpile (we indeed know that it had been slowed down a great deal in 1946 and 1947), it would not make sense to claim weapons of one's own, as Molotov in effect had done. The very best hope of those who wanted to eliminate the American nuclear arsenal, and/or to keep it from being enlarged, was that the good example set thereby might be emulated by the USSR.

If one wished to reassure the USSR against a preventive war, however, Moscow then needed to maintain an impression that 1949 was not some special initiation of a Soviet retaliatory threat to targets in the West, but merely another sample of it.

The worst apprehension of some outsiders was that Stalin would never have announced his nuclear program, hoping to lull the West, just as the West had lulled Hitler. When it was too late, when the Soviet Union had in some significant way surpassed the American nuclear arsenal, the Soviet nuclear accomplishment could then have been announced as had been the Manhattan Project, by its actual application in an unanticipated nuclear attack.

But the Molotov speech does not fit this model. Perhaps Stalin's worst fear indeed was thus what this book is all about, an American-launched preventive war.

9

Lessons, For the Future, and From the Future

One of the important "lessons" of this first round of nuclear proliferation, as noted, emerges in what it may have proved about the character of the United States, as Americans were tested by the opportunities
and challenges of 1945 to 1949.

But another such lesson might come in what Americans would deduce as the policy implication of this experience, that is, whether they
would let another such monopoly slip out of their hands in the future, if
it ever again became attainable.

"Would the U.S. Have Let the Opportunity Pass Again?"

Americans would see the Korean War, and the matching exposure of
the NATO countries to a similar attack by Soviet-built tanks, as the
confirmation of their own worst predictions about the behavior of Stalin
and his successors.

The NSC-68 study might be seen as having predicted limited-war
attacks like the Korean War. Other analysts, noted above, would even
before 1949 have foreseen major trouble once Stalin had bombs of his
own. But many Americans, perhaps a majority, might have had a more
open mind about whether Moscow would roll its tanks forward when
the opportunity arose.

The pessimists were thus more reinforced in June of 1950 than the
optimists. There had not been blatant aggression when Stalin had no
nuclear weapons of his own. But now that he had bombs with which to
deter the use of American nuclear weapons, he was free to exploit the
inherent military advantages of the Soviet geopolitical position at the

135

center of the Eurasian continent, and to exploit the enormous manpower the Communists governed in Russia and China, translating into hundreds of divisions, equipped over time by many thousands of tanks.[1]

The memory or "myth" of 1945-1949, accentuated by the Korean War of 1950, and by all the rest of the Cold War, thus inevitably posed the same question that has explicitly been posed since then by all the theories of mutual deterrence: *If* Americans were ever again to have an opportunity to prevent the USSR from threatening their cities, would they let it slip a second time? That is, could Americans really walk away from the pre-1949 years as having "proved" themselves, or had they instead merely "educated" themselves, made themselves less "idealistic" and more "realistic"?

This author must confess himself to be a believer in mutual deterrence, mutual assured destruction, for any time after 1949. This is a position that would attach more importance to preventing a thermonuclear World War III than to winning it, or to exploiting any deterrent benefits from the risks of escalation to World War III. This is a view that the U.S. should avoid putting Moscow into worried concerns about whether it could retaliate after an American first-strike, because such fears could make the Moscow leadership unnecessarily tense and nervous during any political dispute, setting the stage for a "war nobody wanted."[2]

The typical formulation of any analysis of mutual nuclear deterrence, right to the very end of the Cold War, and even today, has thus stressed that *both* sides must have a second-strike ability to impose massive counter-value retaliation, if "strategic stability" or "crisis stability" is to be maintained. By a logic endorsed publicly by Secretary of Defense McNamara in the 1960s,[3] and presented very clearly already in the 1959 book by Oskar Morgenstern, *The Question of National Defense*,[4] it was to the United States' interest to be able to retaliate for any Soviet attack, no matter how cleverly the Soviet attack was executed, but it was also important, *for the United States*, that the Soviets be able to retaliate for any American attack, no matter how cleverly the American attack was executed. It would be crucial that the Soviets not feel threatened by our counter-force capabilities, not be put into a position of "use them or lose them," not be made nervous about the possibility of an American nuclear attack.

But such a formulation, however "fair-minded," also suggests that the United States would *this time* attack if it did not face such retaliation, that 1945-1949 was what Americans somehow now would see as a great missed opportunity. Advocates of "assured destruction," of whom Secretary McNamara was one of the most prominent and important, regarded it as understandable that Moscow would fear an American nuclear attack if the Soviet ability to retaliate were ever to be too low. To avoid any Soviet "nervousness" about such an American sneak attack, it was important for Moscow to have some assured second-strike forces of its own, and McNamara publicly welcomed the deployment of reliable Soviet submarine-based missiles, having then to face some criticism in Congressional hearings for allegedly welcoming the Kremlin's ability to kill millions of American civilians.

Pre-1949 and Post-1949 Strategic Stability

This book is, in part, an attempt to explore the links between pre-1949 and post-1949 strategic logic, the logic of nuclear monopoly vs. that of nuclear duopoly. Continuing with this exploration, we might look for any traces of such a sympathetic reasoning about crisis stability before 1949, when the Soviets *might* already have some nuclear weapons, and most probably were seeking to acquire them.

And then the reverse logical relationship also has to be explored. Would Americans feel a greater need to reassure the Soviets against an American counter-force capability after the experience of 1945 to 1949, or would they feel less of a need?

In the first linkage, one can find yet another layer of inhibition to American consideration of preventive war. Merely promoting a discussion of preventive war before 1949 would have produced leaks, given the decision processes of American democracy, leaks which might have panicked Stalin into some drastic preemptive action of his own, leaks which at the minimum would have accelerated whatever efforts the Soviet Union had assigned to acquiring a nuclear arsenal.

The proposal that has been dissected here has hardly been that of a sudden nuclear surprise attack on Soviet cities, but rather of a series of ultimata tied to something like the Baruch Plan (which of course would also have given the Kremlin a chance to do something else, besides surrendering or waiting for the threatened American nuclear attack).

Yet the fear of panicking Moscow into a preemption devastating to American interests was surely to be greater once the USSR had nuclear weapons, than at any time before. The entire concept of "strategic stability" or "crisis stability" really gets clarified only when *Soviet* bombers with A-bombs and H-bombs are facing American bombers with such weapons.

Shifting to this latter period, American advocates of a war-fighting capability (of a stress on counter-force rather than counter-value targeting doctrines) were not only citing moral grounds after 1949, or the premise that this alone would deter the Soviet leadership. They also were importantly arguing that there was no need to be so concerned to reassure the Kremlin against the prospect of a U.S. surprise attack, or of an otherwise unprovoked American nuclear attack, precisely because the United States had *proved itself* in the years of the nuclear monopoly.[5]

This kind of argument often did not have to be explicated, as most Americans automatically assumed that their own country never began wars, that being a political democracy made one a helpful and peaceful member of the international system. If the United States "of course" had not launched a preventive war before 1949, this was intuitively seen by most Americans as the simple product of the nature of their society.

The result, in the 1950s and afterward, was that U.S. Air Force planners and many other strategic analysts were to challenge the abstract symmetry of the arguments for strategic stability, the arguments by which it would be destabilizing for the United States to be able to destroy Soviet missile silos or SLBM-carrying submarines, or to shield civilians as proposed in President Reagan's SDI Strategic Defense Initiative.[6]

There was good reason, in this view, to ward off *Soviet* counter-force capabilities, as these would very naturally make Washington nervous. But there was far less reason to ward off American counter-force capabilities, or to welcome Soviet counter-value retaliatory capabilities, since Washington had already, by its past behavior, passed the tests necessary to relieve any nervousness in Moscow.

We come thus to yet another illustration of how the logic of mutual nuclear deterrence, or mutual assured destruction, matches the logic for preventive war before 1949.

The arguments of Donald Brennan (perhaps the first to refer critically to *mutual* assured destruction, thus to coin the acronym "MAD," to suggest that it was fundamentally crazy), and of other advocates of technological defenses against bomber and missile attack, were that it was unacceptably immoral to base peace on the mutual vulnerability of civilian populations, and that this was also possibly not enough to deter Moscow.[7] And the same American analysts would argue that there was no need to leave American cities vulnerable, that Moscow had no need to be nervous, or to be able to inflict nuclear retaliation, because the United States had proven itself as a peace-loving democracy over the years, especially when it had possessed a nuclear monopoly in the years before 1949.[8]

But, if the argument of this book were to get any hearing at all, Moscow might have had reason to be nervous, because Americans would have been lamenting the opportunity they missed between 1945 and 1949. If the strategic and moral calculations presented above have any standing, an American President seeing *another* chance to push the "adversary" nuclear genie back into the bottle might have been tempted to do so, because the Korean War, and everything else that happened after 1949, had demonstrated the trouble hostile nuclear proliferation could cause.

The lesson of the 1945 to 1949 period, and then 1950, may thus have been twofold, that Americans proved themselves as peace-loving, but that Stalin's system had also proved itself itching to aggress. If so, Americans might have been more ready to take the preemption initiative, *if* an opportunity were ever again to appear, than they had been earlier. No such opportunity ever showed up, because of the massive Soviet expenditures on nuclear warheads and the systems to deliver them.

Implications of Non-Use Post-1949

The breaking of the U.S. nuclear monopoly was followed by the production of more than 40,000 nuclear warheads by each of the superpowers, and by the explicit entry into the nuclear-weapons "club" of Britain (1952), France (1960) and China (1964). India detonated a "peaceful nuclear device" in 1974, and in 1998 escalated the South Asian confrontation with five detonations of explicit nuclear weapons, to which Pakistan responded in kind. Israel is widely assumed to have acquired nuclear warheads without test-detonating or openly announcing them.[9]

Yet, despite what almost any professional military officer would have extrapolated from the patterns of the past, all these weapons were built, and none were ever used in anger. Hiroshima was the first city to be hit with a nuclear weapon, and Nagasaki three days later was the last. Most of us would regard this as a very happy end of the story, compared to the normal patterns of earlier history, where the weapons that got built got used.

Yet is it the end of the story, since the world has all along regarded itself as skating on thin ice here? One writes about the non-use of nuclear weapons with one's fingers crossed, hoping that the pattern will not erode.

What does this then tell us about the mini-debate of 1946 and 1947, on whether nuclear weapons were powerful enough to be applied to maintaining their own monopoly? The lesson of "no first use" is that the world is (quite rightly) enormously averse to the damage that *any* nuclear weapon can inflict, not just the enormously more destructive fusion weapons, but even the most basic fission weapon. The non-use of such weapons is a sign of how much everyone is afraid of them.

An analyst who predicted that Stalin could shrug off nuclear attacks, and who deduced that nuclear attacks were somehow not so crucial to the Japanese surrender, would logically then have had to predict that these weapons would be used soon enough in warfare, once they were available on both sides of the conflict.

But the contradictory impression is what later history would seem to support, that these weapons were too horrible to introduce because their matching use by the other side was too painful to bear; this strongly supports the view that, in 1947, even a few of the Hiroshima-size A-bombs might have been too much of a threat for Stalin to rebuff.

The Baruch Plan in Retrospect

If asked to describe what this book is all about, the author sometimes would lean toward the short answer of: "imposing rather than proposing the Baruch Plan." As we now hear the growing concerns about whether nuclear proliferation can be contained, there emerge wistful comments that the Baruch Plan should have been pushed harder in 1946.

The Baruch Plan, derived from the Acheson-Lilienthal study of the possibilities of an international control of nuclear energy, means different things to different people.[10] Some revisionists and other skeptics about U.S. postwar foreign policy see it as never intended to be taken seriously, because the United States wished to maintain its own nuclear weapons monopoly, and proposed an unacceptable international monopoly of all nuclear facilities as an alternative that Stalin's Russia, if no one else, was sure to reject.[11] Yet this begs the fact that most Americans were sure that Stalin's country was seeking nuclear weapons, and would probably acquire them within ten years or so, if international arrangements were simply rejected.

Some of the "missed opportunity" kinds of analysis instead focus on the changes made by Bernard Baruch in the original proposal as drafted by Acheson and Lilienthal.[12] Four changes in tone or substance are normally noted here, each of which allegedly made it difficult or impossible for Stalin to accept the proposal: The Baruch Plan envisaged private operation of peaceful uses of nuclear power (under political regulation, of course), rather than an international governmental operation, and it called for eventual total disarmament of *all* weapons, not just nuclear weapons. It also spelled out punishments for violation of the ban on production of nuclear weapons; and the most significant change of all was probably the clarification by which the veto of the United Nations Security Council could not be applied to issues involving the renunciation of nuclear weapons.[13]

The more normal American analysis of Stalin's rejection of the Baruch Plan focuses not on any Western failings, of course, but on the duplicity and closed nature of the Soviet regime. The Soviet counterproposal was for total nuclear disarmament first, and then for international management progressively installed later. One did not have to be rabidly anti-Communist to see such a proposal as a preposterous test of Western gullibility.[14] If the United States agreed to disarm its nuclear stockpile, while the Soviets agreed not to build one, the *New York Times* and the *Washington Post* and all the other agencies of the American free press could have been counted upon to police American compliance; would *Pravda* and *Izvestia* have been as free to blow the whistle on any secret Soviet nuclear weapons program?

For decades into the future, the Soviet-American "disarmament debate" was to persist in such a form, as Moscow would call for disarmament without inspection, knowing that the United States might have an uphill battle in rejecting such proposals—-in avoiding the implication among neutral observers that it was "blocking disarmament," but knowing also that if the United States ever accepted such a proposal, it would be much easier for the Soviet Union than for the U.S. to cheat in the implementation of the disarmament terms.

Because the Soviets wanted their own bomb, and wanted to use everyone's aversion to a nuclear confrontation to trick the world into letting this become a *Soviet* nuclear monopoly, a great opportunity for international nuclear arms control was thus presumably lost. This is still the view that most Americans would find plausible.

One can find some other reasons, also demeaning to Stalin, for why he might have had to reject the Baruch Plan, because he would have had to fear what any international nuclear administrators ensconced on his territory might do to destabilize his rule over the USSR. Because Stalin ran such a closed society, a Soviet Union where the number of Western visitors in the 1940s each year might number only in the hundreds, the intrusion of an international management structure, guaranteeing one and all that no Soviet nuclear weapons were being built, might simply have been politically unacceptable.[15]

Yet there is another argument about the difficulties of the Baruch Plan that would lay less particular blame on the American side, or on Bernard Baruch's changes in the plan, and also less particular blame on Stalin, but would simply note some of the inherent aspects of the American nuclear monopoly that had already come into being.

Skeptics about an American magnanimity in proposing the Baruch Plan could note that the United States, even if it had divested itself of its own nuclear weapons (in exchange for achieving international control over everyone else's nuclear resources), would have retained the knowledge and practical experience of being the only state ever to complete production of such weapons. A shadow of *potential* monopoly would thus have hung over the Baruch Plan, if adopted, a shadow running as follows: What if such deep political disputes ever erupted that the United Nations and the entire structure of international nuclear management had broken down? There would have been an immediate race by all the powers to acquire nuclear weapons, a race that the United States would most probably have won, on the basis of its prior experience of mistakes to be avoided. Would the anticipation of this kind of a potential race for the bomb not then have hung over all the world in the Baruch scheme?

By such an interpretation, whether or not the management of nuclear operations was subject to a Security Council veto (the veto that the USSR had used so often on other matters in 1945 and 1946) made only a marginal difference. In a major crisis, involving conventional war, or even the threat of such a war, any of the major powers could have declared that it was no longer bound by the Baruch Plan, with or without a veto, and could thus have begun the race to reintroduce nuclear weapons into the world.

The last such race to invent nuclear weapons had led to their being used, against Japan rather than against Germany. The precedent of such use, and the prior accomplishment by which the United States alone had acquired the experience of producing such weapons, might then have inhibited all concerned, regardless of the legal formulae involved.

Dean Acheson, in opposing the modifications Baruch and his advisers had made in the original Acheson-Lilienthal Plan, indeed argued that such politico-military realities made the issue of the veto irrelevant.[16]

Were Baruch and other Americans thus silly in insisting upon a legal fine-tuning of the United Nations Charter? Why not offer a Baruch Plan with a continuation of the veto, since any major crisis producing such Soviet defiance of world opinion would have led to a breakup of the plan, with each nation reverting to attempts to produce atomic bombs, and with the veterans of the Manhattan Project then able to win such a race?

If Stalin had accepted the original Acheson-Lilienthal arrangement, would he not still have been trapped by a de facto American nuclear monopoly? And, if he had rejected it, there would have been one less bit of business in the haggling, one less detail on which Stalin might win any world sympathy for his rejection.

But this kind of interpretation may indeed be excessively "realistic," for it misses what may be still the most plausible explanation for all of what we are examining here, the American commitment, extracted from successful domestic experience, to legality, to adherence to commitments and treaties.

Whatever the Soviet provocation, it would thus have been easier for the U.S. to initiate such a new nuclear race if the veto was not part of the legal structure. In one case Washington would have the law on its side, and in the other it would not.

It would take a very hard-headed and realistic "power-politics" analysis to see the United States as applying its simple nuclear *potential* here, regardless of whether United Nations Security Council unanimity was required for a change of course. (The same hard-headed analysis would presumably have advocated a preventive war if this ban on a Soviet nuclear weapons program were rejected by Stalin.)

Baruch, and the others who called for an elimination of the Security

Council veto, could have argued that the relative unthinkability in Washington of an "illegal" preventive war showed how important it was to get the law clarified.

Imagine a world where the United States had rid itself of any and all components of nuclear weapons, in compliance with the structure of the original Acheson-Lilienthal proposal, and the Soviets were merely *suspect* of having a clandestine bomb program, in effect of reaching for a new nuclear monopoly of their own. If the appropriate steps to investigate such a clandestine program were then delayed and ensnared by a Soviet veto, would the United States have been so daring as to terminate the nuclear ban unilaterally? Or would it have fallen into the worst trap of all, where the Soviets had won the race to be the first to bring nuclear weapons back on to the scene?

The Issue of "International Sharing"

Some parallel revisionist arguments, sympathetic to the alleged problem of Stalin's regime in accepting the Baruch Plan on good faith, would go back still further, to the process by which the U.S. and Britain conspired in the knowledge and pursuit of the possibility of nuclear weapons, but did not share these secrets with the USSR during World War II.

The discussion of the later feasibility or nonfeasibility of various versions of the Baruch Plan is thus sometimes broadened to the general issues of nuclear sharing, including options dating back to the very outset of the Manhattan Project. This option of "sharing" indeed draws much more wistful discussion in retrospect than one ever sees for the option of "preventive war," our theme in this book.[17]

Advocates of greater sharing suggest that American and British failures to make the right moves in 1943 or 1944 made it impossible for Stalin and the Soviets to accept the Baruch Plan in 1946, where otherwise there might have been a chance of thus heading off what became a nuclear arms race. But it is not always clear what such "sharing" would have meant, as it changes from period to period. And this issue then becomes the mirror-image of analysis of the monopoly.

When Niels Bohr suggested that the Soviets simply be told of the Manhattan Project in 1944, this would have been sharing the facts *that* a bomb was being built, and not for the moment the facts on *how* such bombs were to be built.[18] Winston Churchill was vehemently opposed to giving even this much information to Stalin, most probably on the logic that merely knowing the possibility of the bomb would stimulate an earlier Stalin effort to build such weapons, and thus hasten the day when the Soviets had them.

As it happens, the Soviets already understood the possibilities here, and had through espionage learned that the United States had a bomb project underway. Stalin had thus committed the USSR to a serious bomb program in 1943, after the battle of Stalingrad. The Bohr proposal would have entailed giving Stalin information he already had, but it would have eliminated the hostile signal of an (unsuccessful) attempt to keep all this a secret.

Yet if Stalin were to see the Manhattan Project as a hostile anti-Soviet act when there was this fruitless attempt to keep it secret from him (the Americans and their partners had more success in keeping the Manhattan Project unknown to the Germans and Japanese), would he have been so reassured if Roosevelt and Churchill had instead told him of the bomb project? Would Moscow, in the absence of a sharing of *how* the bomb was built, not have seen this version of "sharing" as nothing more than the brandishing of a threat?

Once the bomb had been used on Hiroshima, of course, the "international sharing" question was moved along to a different level, since the possibilities of nuclear fission and the accomplishments of the Manhattan Project were now known to all. One could then instead "share information" on the (relatively low) size of the U.S. nuclear weapons stockpile, and on U.S. intentions with regard to the acquisition and use of nuclear weapons in the future. Yet would Stalin not have been inclined to treat such reassurances as unreliable, or as contingent on his behavior, and thus again as a deterrent threat of sorts?

Or the possibilities of sharing could have moved still much further along, perhaps to helping the USSR get bombs of its own, or to the establishment and maintenance of a more binding international decision process on the uses of what had been the American nuclear arsenal, or to eliminating the U.S. arsenal, in something like the Baruch Plan, in exchange for the avoidance of a Soviet bomb program.

The agreements between Roosevelt and Churchill had envisaged an Anglo-American sharing that would have amounted to either a "safety catch" for each power, by which neither could use these weapons without the other's approval, or a "trigger" for each of them (what was actually to emerge by 1952), where each was independently capable of launching a nuclear attack with weapons of its own.

By the logic of mutual deterrence, to become so familiar after 1949, the nuclear trigger of the second, opposing force could become an assurance against the use of the first nuclear force, that is, could become an *indirect* "safety catch."

Yet if this were to have been what "sharing" with Stalin would have meant in 1945, would it have been anything more than accelerating the nuclear confrontation forward from 1949 to 1945, speeding the day when nuclear devastation could be inflicted on *both* sides, and where all the safety of the world depended on the effectiveness of mutual deterrence?

One normally presumes that the later critics of the Truman administration's outlook have something other than this in mind as the "lost opportunity" of heading off what was to follow. But their preferred alternative then would presumably have been a world where *no* power was able to inflict nuclear destruction on another. The question then, just as the question now at the end of the Cold War, is whether such a world is physically possible, or how it could be attained in a manner that would not immediately inspire rounds of self-confirming distrust.

Sharing a More Finite Deterrence

Many critics of the Baruch Plan would thus suggest that an opportunity was missed to head off the nuclear confrontation altogether, if only the plan had been handled differently, if only America had been less hostile and confrontational with Moscow. But others would contend that a Soviet nuclear force was inevitable, yet something that could have been moderated in size, in what would have been an earlier success at "arms control," if only the political approach had been tuned differently.[19]

One could thus outline a quite different argument against any preventive war in 1946 or 1946, a kind of analysis which would have looked ahead very presciently to the four decades following 1949, by which there was nothing so terrible to be headed off in the loss of the American nuclear monopoly. Either the nuclear weapon was not that important a weapon, or it would deter itself in confrontations of mutual assured destruction. For either reason, it would not be used, Hiroshima and Nagasaki would not be repeated.

By such a logic, it might be perfectly understandable and predictable that the USSR would assign major effort to matching the American nuclear stockpile, but the world would not come to an end once this had happened. And the thought of waging war to head this off, or even threatening to wage a war, would remain unthinkable.

Extrapolating from this kind of analysis, an argument might then be made for skipping even the half-hearted attempts to retain the monopoly, on the ground that secrecy produced suspicion; a policy instead of sharing information about nuclear weapons might have reduced the fears in Moscow, and anywhere else, during the period of the U.S. monopoly, and might have lowered the totals of nuclear weapons that would be accumulated on all sides.

An "international control" designed to keep Moscow or London from *ever* having nuclear weapons would be bound to fail, by this view; and any attempts to achieve it would only drive the second and other nuclear weapons states to push for much larger arsenals, with the U.S. then having to match these in turn, producing the enormous ranges of "overkill" that were eventually to appear.

Such a counter-factual case is interesting (even if it must remain just as unprovable as all the other counter-factuals), that a different American approach, more resigned to Soviet nuclear weapons possession (perhaps even actively engaged in sharing weapons), would have guided the world into a steady state of finite deterrence, rather than of mutual overkill. By this view, thermonuclear weapons could have been headed off,[20] perhaps policed through a test ban, and the accumulation of large numbers of ordinary atomic bombs could also have been headed off.

At the level of political atmosphere, one might also argue that a Soviet Union which had been *given* the information about how to make weapons, rather than having to develop and *steal* this information for itself, would have come into the post-1945 world with very different attitudes, would have been less hostile to, and suspicious about, the West. The argument is sometimes thus that a similar impact would have been achieved if the Soviets were at least *told* of the Manhattan Project in 1942 or 1943, rather than in 1945 after Hitler had been defeated, so that Moscow would not have needed to learn about the Anglo-American effort through espionage.

Yet the risk remains, as noted above, that Stalin would have regarded information about the bomb, short of an actual sharing of weapons, as a brandishing of the bomb. And even a sharing of weapons technology might have been viewed as a trick, as Stalin and Beria had even feared that some of the gleanings of their espionage nets were disinformation.[21]

One must be a very intense critic of American policy in 1945 to claim that Stalin could have been easily weaned into becoming a cooperative partner after the defeat of the Axis, and to claim that Stalin would have slowed or halted his efforts to acquire nuclear weapons, when there was no Western ability to monitor the pace of such efforts.

A world without nuclear weapons might thus well have had to be a world where Einstein's theories had turned out to be wrong. A world without nuclear weapons, as an alternative to a nuclear confrontation, would have to overcome the obstacles noted, obstacles that were noted even in 1945.

In retrospect, all of this kind of reasoning must still deal with the intensely paranoid and power-oriented nature of Stalin, and indeed of later Soviet leaders. Skeptics will respond that Stalin would simply have exploited any such policies to achieve a large nuclear arsenal earlier, and that he would have reached for thermonuclear weapons in any event.

And, what is even less certain is whether such a mutual posture of finite deterrence or minimum deterrence would have been reliable, whether it would have smothered the visions and fears of splendid first strikes and preemptive strikes as reliably as what actually appeared in mutual assured destruction.

The retrospective argument against preventive war will often incorporate the fact that no nuclear war occurred after 1949, so that there was less of a disaster to be headed off. But one must then be careful about where the credit for mutual deterrence is to be directed; for some of it may indeed have to be assigned to the maintenance of nuclear forces well above what anyone would call "finite."

Most of those who today lament the lack of a greater "sharing" between 1943 and 1949 would not be so content with a world where each side can impose assured destruction on the others. This book shares the premise that there are serious dangers to the world *whenever* nuclear forces confront each other, dangers of false alarms and preemptive attacks, dangers of failures of command and control, compounded by the further dangers of nuclear proliferation to additional separate states.

What this book has been about is a different alternative, a world with one nuclear-weapons state.

If one is anxious about the contemporary relevance of these choices as they were made, one has only to turn to current questions on the future of nuclear weapons, and how they are to be eliminated.

Pessimists about the possibility of total nuclear disarmament see insuperable issues of verification ahead, as Russia and the United States, and the three other declared nuclear weapons states (Britain, France, and China), and now India and Pakistan, and the various undeclared and potential nuclear proliferators, *all* have to be trusting and trustworthy, and as the International Atomic Energy Agency (IAEA) will have the thankless task of checking, and refuting, all the rumors that would emerge that one state or another was cheating, or that one state was so fearful that another was cheating that it had decided to cheat in preemption of this.[22] Much of the task here will pertain to how one "shares" information and shares responsibility, in ways that amount more to a safety catch for each state than to a trigger.

In a sense, the Americans who were so unready to consider a preventive war before 1949 were indeed expressing an opinion on sharing, that is, that such sharing was inevitable. Despite some of the offhand statements of President Truman, the criticism that Americans somehow expected that no one else could master nuclear physics is basically knocking over a straw man. Almost every strategic analysis that has been noted here, inside the government and outside, presumed that other countries would develop nuclear weapons sooner or later.

The American policy of proposing the Baruch Plan, but of not *imposing* it, amounted to a liberal and generous attempt to head off such widespread nuclear proliferation. And the American resignation then to the Baruch Plan's rejection suggested a reconciliation to the inevitable here. A sharing of "the secret" of the atomic bomb was inevitable, either because nuclear science was bound to be taught around the world, or because Soviet espionage rings were bound to be effective, or both.

It is not the case that the United States lost its nuclear monopoly because it never dreamed that anyone else could make atomic bombs. Rather most Americans never dreamed that a preemption of this by a use of nuclear weapons could be morally appropriate.

Stalin's Attitudes in Retrospect

The opening of Russia since 1989 has produced a tremendous flow of disclosures on what the intentions of Stalin had been, and on what the Soviet leader knew about the United States and its arsenal, but there are numerous contradictions in such disclosures, suggesting that not every memory or report is to be regarded as reliable.

One kind of conclusion certainly looms out fairly clearly, however, that Stalin was very much impressed by nuclear weapons, rather than somehow indifferent to them, that he assigned major effort to acquiring such weapons for the USSR, and that he felt substantially inhibited by the American monopoly of such weapons, even when the American stockpile was small.[23]

The calculations of U.S. Air Force planners before 1949, and afterwards, were that the U.S. would have to be able to apply nuclear weapons to defeating and crippling the Soviet armed forces, if it wanted to win a World War III, or if it wanted to reliably deter the Soviet launching of such a war. The believer in minimum deterrence or mutual assured destruction was regarded as not understanding the callousness of the Soviet leadership, under Stalin or his successors. Advocates of a reliance on counter-value mutual deterrence were accused of projecting American feelings, the feelings of a democratically elected government concerned about the people it represented, on to a Soviet government which felt no such concerns or constraints.[24]

We have lots of reason to assume that Stalin was callous, ranging back to his treatment of Ukrainian Kulaks. Yet the evidence unearthed since the fall of Communist rule is that Stalin would also have been very much in dread of even a single nuclear weapon detonated over Moscow or Leningrad, just as many Americans were to be in dread of a single Soviet atomic bomb detonated over New York.[25]

Perhaps such a bomb over the Kremlin would have killed the dictator himself, or the most trusted members of his entourage, or otherwise threatened his hold on power. Or perhaps it would simply have stripped away too much of what had been accomplished under Communism.

As a sign of how much importance Stalin thus attached to nuclear weapons in particular, and to fears that the United States might launch exactly the kind of preventive war campaign being outlined here, some of the earliest Soviet reactors and uranium enrichment facilities were relocated to make them less easy targets for an American B-29 attack.[26]

The version of preventive war which more traditional air planners in the West were contemplating, to be postponed because the resources were not yet available, would have required that *all* of Soviet industry and military potential be vulnerable to an American attack. But the more narrow view of preventive war would have concentrated on only two kinds of targets, the larger Soviet cities, and the Soviet nuclear facilities that could produce bombs to destroy American cities.

Central to the theme of this book would thus be the question of whether Stalin was afraid the United States might go ahead with a preventive war. Stalin would have had before him the evidence of the reduction of American conventional forces which had occurred so precipitously after the German and Japanese surrenders in 1945; and he might also have some clues that, despite the general tone of U.S. governmental pronouncements, no large nuclear weapons force had been assembled.

To reassure him, Stalin would certainly have had the evidence that very little public discussion of preventive war, or threats of such war, had emerged in the United States, as the Baruch Plan had been proposed by the Americans, but as no real effort had emerged to impose it.

Yet Stalin, to close the logical loop, would also have had the insights of what he himself would have done with a nuclear monopoly. The Soviet Union in 1945 was wrapped in secrecy. Stalin's style, and the style of his associates, was hardly to credit adversaries in the capitalist West with a great openness, but rather to suspect secret plans and plots there as well. At early stages, this had even caused Stalin and Beria to suspect the reliability of the nuclear information being conveyed back by their agents in the West, on the theory that this might well be disinformation designed to lure the USSR into wasting precious resources on a foolish pursuit of nuclear weapons.

Once the atomic bomb had been proven, at Alamogordo, and then at Hiroshima and Nagasaki, Stalin leaned much more in the direction of trying to copy the American bomb as much as possible, rather than pursuing a bomb based on Soviet scientific self-reliance.[27] Similarly, when the three B-29s had come into Soviet possession by being interned after abortive air attacks on Japan, Stalin did not conclude that these were an American trick intended to divert the Soviet aircraft industry into a wasteful production path. He instead ordered that this American bomber be disassembled to be reverse-engineered into as close a copy as possible, avoiding all Soviet innovation for the moment.[28]

When the Soviet Union was finally ready to test a nuclear device in the summer of 1949, Stalin voiced the concern, as noted above, that such a test, once detected, would bring American threats and perhaps preventive war, as the U.S. would try to erase the Soviet nuclear stockpile. His elementary caution was thus to require that the first bomb not be tested until at least one more such bomb was ready, so that Moscow would not again be facing an American monopoly. Stalin also, of course, elected not to announce the test publicly, but perhaps to hope that the test would escape American notice for the moment.

Stalin's demand that *one* more bomb be ready raises some of the most fundamental questions of nuclear confrontation and strategy that are with us all along here. Why not wait for ten or twenty more bombs? Would one bomb be meaningful against the American force that already numbered in the one hundreds?

This one additional bomb would not have been directed at any "military target" if it had to play a retaliatory role against an American attack. It would have been directed somehow against New York or some other large American city. Was Stalin somehow seeing this as meaningful "assured destruction" in 1949? This is at least how the author of this book, in retrospect, would see it, as the threat of a single nuclear strike against a city like New York (or perhaps instead London) was already qualitatively different from the situation where *no* such nuclear attacks were possible.

Stalin thus feared American preventive war in 1949, but he feared it less if he could confront the world with a nuclear force in being, even if that force were small. His policy decisions reinforce the logic of this review, by which the years *before* 1949 are crucial. And there is evidence that he feared an exploitation of the American nuclear monopoly as early as 1945. We now have accounts of the actual wording of his instructions to his nuclear physicists, after the news of Hiroshima came in:

A single demand of you, comrades. Provide us with atomic weapons in the shortest possible time. You know that Hiroshima has shaken the whole world. The balance has been destroyed. Provide the bomb—it will remove a great danger from us.[29]

Stalin's reference to the Soviet Union being in great danger thus belies all the accounts of the time by which he was unimpressed by nuclear weapons, or unaware of their power. Perhaps it was only worst-case analysis on his part, but it also suggests that he did not share the view of the American mainstream, that a preventive use of a monopoly of nuclear weapons (a preventive war and/or a series of ultimata backed by the threat of such a war) was such a totally unacceptable idea.

One could thus summarize some of what we have learned about Stalin's perceptions as follows: Regardless of whether Americans might today regard the preventive war option as crazy, Stalin did not see such a venture as so crazy. In statements reported more recently, as well as in the efforts discovered much earlier that he assigned to breaking the monopoly, Stalin indeed showed signs of being very afraid of just such an American initiative.

Skeptics about the applicability of nuclear weapons might envisage all kinds of ways in which the Soviet system could respond to such an American attack, or shrug it off, but Stalin in truth could not shrug it off, whatever his pretense at Potsdam.

10

Some Counter-Factual Speculations

In retrospect, we now often take it for granted that the United States nuclear monopoly was not to endure, that the Soviet Union would acquire its own weapons after four years, to be followed by Britain, France, and China, but the central theme of this book is that alternatives were possible. If one thus rearranges any of the sequence of proliferation here, a larger portion of what we assume about the nuclear balance might also be reexamined.

How much of the hostility between Moscow and Washington can be explained by the nuclear confrontation that had emerged after 1945, and especially after 1949? Some would have argued, during the Cold War, and now even after, that the horrendous threats of mutual assured destruction amounted to a continuing insult between the superpowers, and this is one more argument for trying to eliminate such weapons entirely.[1]

An alternative proposition would be that the existence of such thermonuclear weapons, and their continual threat of assured destruction, made little difference for the hostility between the opposing ideological camps.[2]

And yet another alternative would be that such threats of nuclear escalation actually muted and reduced the hostility; if nuclear weapons had not existed, would not the West have had to expend many more resources and encumber the lives of many more young men with preparations for a conventional defense (and would this not in turn have sparked the Soviets and their allies to increase their spending as well on conventional weapons)? [3]

155

By looking at counter-factual alternatives, we might thus be more able to sort out whether mutual assured destruction has played an important part in *causing* hostility between the superpowers, rather than attributing this hostility primarily to preexisting issues of politics.

And a parallel counter-factual possibility could be explored on whether political hostility (rather than being the product of mutual assured destruction) was somehow a prerequisite to the very theory of mutual deterrence. If Stalin had not been so politically threatening, would all of our thinking on the need for assured second-strike retaliatory forces perhaps never have emerged?

Britain Instead of Russia?

Several interesting scenarios might be introduced as part of testing conclusions and propositions here. For example, what if Britain, rather than the Soviet Union, had been the second power to acquire nuclear weapons? Would there have been as much political hostility directed toward London in the sorting out of mutual nuclear deterrence, as there was toward Moscow? Would anyone in the United States, if it had become obvious that London would be the second to cross the line into possession of atomic bombs, have floated the same preventive-war trial balloons that emerged vis-à-vis Moscow? [4]

It is thus interesting to speculate, as a counter-factual *gedankenexperiment*, whether mutual deterrence reasoning would thus fall into place between *any* two nuclear weapons states, even if they were in as much political agreement as the United States and Britain.

In the abstract, the deterrence problem may in fact have a life of its own, whether or not the crucial questions ever get posed explicitly. What would Britain do if the United States Air Force attacked British cities? Almost everyone would respond that this is the most silly of questions, since nothing like this could ever happen. But if an answer were required, it is obvious enough: Britain would have to launch nuclear retaliation against the cities of the United States. And the same if British nuclear forces had ever initiated an attack on American cities, another such "silly question": the strategic forces of the United States would have to retaliate against British cities.

The most relevant issue, for the purposes of this book, would then be what it was that made such questions seem so "silly," such that they would almost never get raised. Believers in democracy might argue that no two such self-governing countries will ever get into wars with each other, or even be in the business of threatening and "deterring" each other. Believers in the political importance of culture and tradition might point to the shared English language, or the Magna Carta and the English Common Law.

But a "realist" analyst of international power politics might be skeptical of all such explanations, arguing instead that it was the shared fear of Soviet nuclear attack that kept Americans from ever worrying about the potential of the British V-bomber force, and kept Britain from ever worrying about attack by the U.S. Strategic Air Command. This is all very parallel to traditional balance-of-power reasoning, by which shared enemies can defuse power rivalries for the moment, and by which the defeat or disappearance of such an enemy can reactivate them.

One can find examples of such logic that have surfaced. The national stereotype about France is that it has a culture inclined to abstract Cartesian reasoning, thus ready to explore all possibilities with a cold logic, and not to dismiss any questions as "silly." As evidenced by the French all-azimuth strategy, pronounced under President de Gaulle and still capturing some endorsement in Paris even after the end of the Cold War, *any* nuclear weapons state thus has to consider what *all* the other nuclear weapons states might do, and what its own response would be. Rather than being a silly question, Paris has dignified the question of appropriate responses to an American or British nuclear attack, with answers.[5]

As elementary logic would dictate, as the French example demonstrates, the question of mutual deterrence would be unavoidable, once the world has more than one nuclear force. And, contrary to the older balance-of-power logic of the realists, this is a reasoning which has to be directed to all azimuths at all times. One can not forget what the third nuclear force might do, merely because one is the most concerned about the second.

Logical abstractions aside, we still have the task here of comparing the treatment accorded Stalin's proliferation venture, with the treatment others might have drawn. Compounding our puzzle, several of the earliest and most important analytical treatments of the nuclear strategy question are interesting, as noted, in that they look forward to early proliferation, that is, to an early point where the U.S. will face a nuclear rival, but that they do *not* paint the USSR very definitely into this role.

Neither Bernard Brodie nor William Borden had pointed specifically to the USSR as the likely future nuclear adversary, simply suggesting rather that one country or another would fill this role. The problems thus seemingly had raised themselves in the aftermath of Hiroshima and Nagasaki, without any specification of the political disputes driving them.

In this chapter we are now speculating on whether the abstract logic of mutual nuclear deterrence has been a cause of political hostility, or whether deterrence instead requires political hostility as a prerequisite.

American hostility to the Soviet Union rose in the same years that it became clear that the USSR would be the first adversary to match American nuclear capabilities. Because we can not separate these two trends in time, we might be tempted to see them causally interlinked. If we had seen Britain or Canada instead become the second nuclear weapons state, we would have a test of alternative possibilities.

The United States needed access to uranium in the Belgian Congo after 1945, which entailed Britain's releasing its claim to some of this raw material. The Truman administration had quietly also wanted the Atlee government to waive whatever restraints the wartime Churchill-Roosevelt agreements (unbeknownst to Congress) might have imposed on future American *use* of nuclear weapons. In exchange for the British concessions, the U.S. government thus in 1946 and 1947 quietly waived whatever reciprocal restraints the wartime agreements had imposed on Britain even *producing* nuclear weapons.[6]

In the abstract, however, the United States after 1945 was unenthusiastic about *any* other country acquiring nuclear weapons, including Canada or Britain. It had no particular qualms about these English-speaking democracies, of course, so that the opposition was hardly pushed very much. Yet some portion of the secrecy with which the Labour government launched the postwar British nuclear weapons program stemmed precisely from its not wanting to draw great American attention.[7]

When Klaus Fuchs turned out to have been a Soviet spy, this in some ways complicated the relationship, and in other ways simplified it, as the withholding of American assistance to Britain could be seen as a distrust not of *British* nuclear weapons, but of the leakages that might yet enhance the Soviet nuclear arsenal.[8]

Would an emergence of mutual nuclear deterrence between Britain and the United States thus have led to political conflict? Some versions of a "realist" power-politics analysis would have predicted so, on the grounds that the two strongest powers in the world are bound to be rivals, simply by the structure of the international system. If London rather than Moscow had become the first possessor of a nuclear check on the U.S. nuclear force, would the United States not have had to direct all its scenarios to war with Britain, rather than war with the Soviet Union?

The typical American, who hardly studies very much history, would regard this as inconceivable, given the "special relationship" that had existed between the two English-speaking democracies. But someone with a longer view would cite the War of 1812, and all the naval war plans and plans for the invasion or defense of Canada which continued to be drawn up, in Washington and in London, at least until the beginning of the twentieth century, and perhaps even longer.[9]

The defeat of World War I had produced a naval arms race of sorts between Britain and the United States, as President Wilson had declared that the United States must have a navy "second to none," while Britain had always demanded for itself a two-power standard, by which its fleet was equal to the next two fleets in the world combined. One did not have to be a mathematical genius to see that these two post-1918 national demands could not be simultaneously satisfied, and thus that a wide-open naval arms race would emerge. Having eliminated the menace of the German fleet, the English-speaking partners against the Kaiser might now turn against each other.[10] In the event, by means of the Washington Naval Disarmament Conference convened by President Harding, this naval race was headed off.

Just as the defeat of the Kaiser, or the earlier defeat of Napoleon, could turn allies against each other, so could the defeat of Hitler. Those assigning the highest priority to such power constellations would thus blame much of the Cold War on the disappearance of Germany as a factor, and would also assign great significance to what concerns us here, to the very new power factor of nuclear weapons. Yet, which was the new enemy to be for the Americans, to replace Hitler? Is there something about the confrontation of *nuclear* weapons that determined the new alignment of conflict?

Rather than getting into a conflict with Stalin about the delays in the removal of Soviet troops from Iran, might the American focus then have become the delays in British withdrawal from India? Rather than becoming exercised about the denial of self-determination in Poland,

might Americans instead have become worked up about Northern Ireland? It is interesting to remember that there were British troops in
Saigon in 1945 helping the French reestablish their authority, while
there was a tiny American mission in Hanoi and in Saigon supporting
the claims of Ho Chi Minh.[11]

Two kinds of analysis of American foreign policy would thus tend to
attach great importance to nuclear weapons. The starkest form of "realist" power-politics theory would, as noted, dismiss the domestic at-
tributes of how Washington, London or Moscow were governed, as unimportant for international relations, focussing instead on the threats and
temptations of hegemonic power.[12] By this kind of a theory, the United
States might well have been drawn into hostility against *any* state challenging its nuclear monopoly. Yet, by this kind of a theory, it is all the more of
a mystery that Stalin's Russia was allowed to acquire nuclear weapons.

A very different kind of analysis, also noted at the outset, is the "revisionist" interpretation of the Cold War that styles itself as Marxist or
at least as "radical" in its ideology. This is a view, of course, that traces
the Cold War ultimately to the problems of capitalism. But, as a symptom of the trouble-making propensity of capitalism, it would also attach tremendous significance to nuclear weapons, and to the threats
allegedly posed against Stalin's Russia by the unchallenged American
possession of such weapons.

Nuclear weapons should have been done away with, such was the
message from Moscow, and from those sympathetic to Moscow, as in
the so-called Stockholm Peace Petition.[13] And if they were not done
away with, great credit should be given to anyone, inside Russia or
outside, who helped the Soviet Union get such weapons for itself.

Nuclear weapons, like weapons in general, tended to poison the atmosphere between the United States and the Soviet Union in this view
(in a view indeed shared by many non-Marxists). Such weapons were
an aspect of militarism, which was part of the problem of the capitalist
lack of sympathy for socialism.

It is obvious that this book is not very sympathetic to such a Marxist
or revisionist interpretation of nuclear weapons and the Cold War. And
the peculiar ways in which the American nuclear monopoly did not get
utilized also poses major problems for the power-politics interpretation
of these years.

At the end of this speculative venture, therefore, one is tempted to
conclude that there would have been an elementary development of

mutual deterrence reasoning between Britain and the United States, if Britain had indeed been the second power to acquire atomic bombs; but the political impact of this, in terms of poisoning relations, and exacerbating conflict, would most probably have been no greater than the impact of the French 1960s proclamation of an "all-azimuth" strategy.

Is Deterrence More Appropriate between Democracies?

There is one last, quite bizarre, possibility to be considered about a British-American confrontation, a possibility perhaps not so irrelevant to the future of Russian-American relations.

By a certain kind of moral logic, noted earlier, it was always wrong to prevent World War III by aiming American nuclear weapons at Russian cities, because this would have been threatening the innocent to deter the potentially guilty. Since the Russian people had not elected Stalin or his successors, and since one could assume that they would not do so if they had a choice, they were innocent. Since they would not have approved of the Soviet aggression that triggered nuclear retaliation, they would be the wrong victims of retaliation.

By such a logic, mutual deterrence is morally acceptable only when the people threatened have responsibility for the acts being punished, when they elect the regime being deterred. That is, mutual assured destruction, or mutual deterrence, becomes appropriate only between democracies.

That this is not simply an abstract and silly moral calculation is illustrated by the way Americans and Britishers, in justifying the bombings of German cities in World War II, had convinced themselves that most Germans were Nazis, that Hitler in effect was a popularly elected leader. And the same with the calculations by which Americans had concluded that most ordinary Japanese supported the imperialism and cruelty that their government had set under way.

When there are no ideologies pitting the parties to a confrontation against each other, the issue is more likely to be seen as one of culture, or simple nationalism, with the masses on the opposing side sharing in the guilt for having generated the conflict in the first place.

Imagine a future world where Boris Yeltsin or his successors, quite freely elected, get into military conflicts with the United States. There are theories by which such conflicts are either unlikely or impossible, but such theories are not what we are testing here.[14]

If such confrontations and conflicts were to break out, with each of the powers continuing to maintain nuclear arsenals, the question is rather whether mutual assured destruction would then be less likely and acceptable *between democracies*, or whether it might actually be more morally acceptable, and hence more likely. If the Russians, for example, back the Serbs in the former Yugoslavia because of simple nationalism, because of the cultural identifications described by Samuel Huntington in his "Clash of Civilizations" article,[15] while the United States backs the more "Western" Croats, would it not be easier for Americans to see all the Russians as culpable here, no longer the "secret ally" to be rescued, but rather the "guilty party."

Returning to our British-American model, it is thus thinkable that a nuclear duopoly between these two English-speaking powers would have made mutual assured destruction counter-value targeting even more readily acceptable, since the British were not being governed against their will, but rather were the source of the national feelings affecting any disputes with Americans about Ireland, Palestine or India, and so on.

In the actual Cold War, Americans fastened less often on Russian culture and mannerisms as they girded themselves for conflict, fixing instead on the arrogance of the Communist leaders in governing others against their wills (allegedly for the benefit of those governed, but by a very particular view of benefit, never to be tested at the polls). In the hypothetical Cold War being broached here, of Britain and the U.S. confronting each other in a nuclear duopoly, one might have seen Americans taking offense more often at British mannerisms and cultural arrogance, at something shared by all the people on the other side.

All things considered, this author would bet on democracy for its international implications, just as he would most assuredly bet on it for its domestic benefits. Yet democracy has proven itself more on the domestic front than on the international, if only because the international arena, until the end of the Cold War, has comprised too few democracies for a fair test to be administered.[16]

It is a good bet (but only a bet, and not a sure thing), that democracies will generally get along well, so that crises and arms races and wars will not occur between democracies. But it is indeed a logically sure thing that mutual assured destruction is more morally appropriate between democracies, than between a democracy and a dictatorship.

Can Nuclear Confrontations be Forgotten?

The alternative possibilities we are reviewing here, for the years after 1949, as well as the years before, may shed light on one more possibly important question for the future, whether the existence of nuclear forces and inherent destructive threats has to burden the consciousness of the states involved, or whether this psychological and political burden can be eliminated.

As noted, Americans have never thought very seriously about the mutual nuclear deterrence that might be in place between themselves and the British, or between themselves and the French. Americans do not always even think so very much about the nuclear deterrence in effect with Communist China. And perhaps the day will soon be at hand when no one thinks much about the assured destruction that Russia can inflict on the United States.

The announcements by Boris Yeltsin that Russian nuclear warheads are no longer targeted on the United States, neither on American weapons nor on American cities, might not be very reassuring for someone who knows how speedily such weapons can be retargeted back to their old aim-points again. But these announcements have surely had some political impact among people at large, pushing thoughts about nuclear war and nuclear deterrence away from public consciousness.[17]

The United States was once directing great attention to the development of nuclear weapons in China, with Secretary of Defense McNamara using the Chinese threat as the rationale for a rudimentary American ABM system. Within a decade or two, it was remarkable how little American attention was assigned to the Chinese arsenal. By the logic of power-minded "realists," this occurred only because Beijing and Washington came to be allies of sorts, in face of the growing nuclear strength imputed to the Soviet Union at the beginning of the 1980s.

But the question for the future, extrapolating from some of the non-bipolar nuclear interactions of the past, will be whether such confrontations always have to be present, whether the United States will always have to focus on one nuclear adversary or another. The hope of a believer in democracy would be that such power rivalries indeed do not have to be inevitable, and that the looming menace of nuclear devastation also does not have to be a barrier to friendship and normal relations. If a nuclear confrontation of sorts has to persist very far into the future, because of the inherent difficulties of verifying a total elimination of such weapons, the example of the American-British "confrontation" might be the model for Russian-American interactions.

Americans have, in a way, "forgotten" the French all-azimuth strategy, and have "forgotten" that their lives could be ended without warning by French, British, and Chinese nuclear forces. If there were to be some sort of a political poison in the nuclear threats posed by such forces, it is hard to find. And perhaps, without any other threat being required as a distraction, Americans and Russians can thus also forget about the threats they pose to each other's survival.

The Race Being Run

In the event, all of the above speculation about Britain's role is of course very counter-factual. Stalin had already launched a major effort to develop nuclear weapons in 1943, and Britain was thus indeed doomed to be the third nuclear weapons state, rather than the second. There was not really any meaningful race between the British and the Russians to be second, perhaps because Stalin had more reason than Britain to fear an American monopoly, perhaps because Stalin would even have liked to be first to have the bomb, ahead of the Americans.

The United States, thinking that it had to avoid coming in second to Hitler, came in first, but a mere four years ahead of Stalin, the four years we have been retrospectively dissecting here. Had the United States not been afraid of Hitler's (basically nonexistent) efforts, it might in fact have come in second to Stalin, with perhaps stupendous consequences for the world. One has to be an extremely revisionist scholar of the origins of the Cold War to interpret the motivation of those working in the Manhattan Project, or even the motivation of the American leadership funding and authorizing it, as directed against any particular enemy other than Nazi Germany. It was because the United States had feared what Hitler would do with a monopoly of such weapons, that it did not have to face what Stalin would do with such a monopoly.

As noted earlier, there has been an interesting debate, ever since 1945, on whether the German failure to get going on a Nazi nuclear weapons project was due simply to Aryan incompetence, as the non-Jewish and non-liberal nuclear physicists who had remained in Germany after 1933 were too unimaginative to make any serious progress toward a fission bomb, or due to a moral reluctance among such physicists to design something so destructive for a regime like Hitler's.[18] Any post-1945 German claim of moral reluctance has tended to be denounced as self-serving, by the alumni of the Manhattan Project, many of these being physicists who had themselves been refugees from Nazi-occupied Europe, people who lost relatives in the Holocaust. Yet the denunciations are somewhat in conflict with the presumption of the same Manhattan Project, and of the people working in it, that there was a race to be run against the physicists of Nazi Germany, a race which the United States would have to work very hard to win.

Such retrospective assessments of Nazi Germany are of course very relevant to the assessment of the USSR. If one goes about afterward scoffing at any "secret" to nuclear weapons, noting that the Soviet Union was bound to be able to master the techniques of producing fissionable materials and atomic bombs, it is difficult to paint the Germans as simply incompetent here, rather than as also somewhat reluctant.

The takings of position about the German World War II "nuclear effort" are thus somewhat self-serving on both sides, the staking out of positions with a view to what history will remember. Germans like Heisenberg have wanted to be remembered as competent, and as moral. The victims of Nazism who produced the bombs used on Hiroshima and Nagasaki, bombs which *would have* been used on German cities (and which *were not* used on Russian cities) want to be remembered as having had good reason to push the Manhattan Project at full speed; but at the same time they want to remember having had a Nazi enemy that was in no sense, and at no level of decision-making, too moral to produce nuclear weapons, but was rather, because of its bizarre emphasis on "Aryan physics," too inept to do so.[287]

In the aftermath of the Cold War, we are now being treated to a parallel debate among Russians about who should capture more of the credit for the Soviet acquisition of atomic bombs, and then of thermonuclear hydrogen bombs.[288] Russian scientists will make the claim that it was their ingenuity and prowess that produced such weapons, that there was no "secret" of such weapons production that could not be mastered by patriotic physicists trained in the scientifically first-rate universities of the Soviet Union. Alumni of the USSR's intelligence networks will counter that it was their espionage efforts that brought back indispensable shortcuts from the American effort, speeding the Soviet acquisition of a nuclear arsenal.

Either version of history testifies to the importance Stalin attached to nuclear weapons, despite his protestations of indifference to the power of these weapons, when he did not yet have them.

Russian physicists will label it as the height of Western arrogance for Americans to believe that Soviet nuclear espionage was crucial to making atomic bombs possible in 1949. Yet this would only confirm the peril that the world faced in Stalin's Russia. If they are right, given the priority that Moscow attached, after Stalingrad, to developing atomic bombs, Soviet nuclear weapons might have emerged by 1949 *even if* there had been no Manhattan Project in the United States.

There are Americans who explicitly, or implicitly, accept a view of Cold War history by which Stalin was only responding to American initiatives in seeking weapons of mass destruction, that he would probably not have pursued atomic bombs if the United States had not acquired them first.[21] Yet, just as it is a mistake to believe that only Americans had thought of how one *produced* nuclear weapons, it would be a mistake to assume that only Americans had thought of how such weapons could be *exploited*.

If Hitler had moderated his foreign policy in the 1930s, and Japan had done the same (so that World War II would not have broken out as it did, with the United States being pulled in by the end of 1941), which country in the world would have been the first to develop nuclear weapons?

A Weimar Germany, a Germany that had not driven away so many competent scientists by anti-Semitism and limitations of intellectual freedom, might well have been the most *able* state in this realm. But, without the fear of a Hitler reaching for nuclear weapons, would the United States have been the most *willing*? Or would the most willing state instead have been the USSR?

Counter-Factual: If Hiroshima and Nagasaki had been Spared

This is not the right place to get drawn very extensively into the debate about whether the U.S. bombing of Hiroshima and Nagasaki was necessary for getting Japan to surrender.[22] The author is convinced that these nuclear attacks did make an important difference. Japan had, ever since 1941, been banking not on defeating the U.S. militarily, but on exhausting the willingness of American citizens to bear the costs of pushing Japanese forces back; and the Japanese might still in 1945 and

1946 have hoped that the heavy casualties imposed on American amphibious landings would achieve something much better than unconditional surrender.[23]

Those who argue otherwise have sometimes presented a case that the use of American nuclear weapons against these two Japanese cities, unnecessary for winning World War II, was meant instead to intimidate Stalin's Soviet Union, that is, that this was the first blow of the Cold War.[24]

This entire book argues against this interpretation. If the two atomic bombings were the first shots of American nuclear intimidation, why were there no follow-on shots, why was the nuclear arsenal allowed to shrivel, and so on?

Yet it is interesting, as a counter-factual, to speculate about a world where Japan had, like Germany, somehow surrendered before the Manhattan Project had produced its weapons, or instead where the proposal had been adopted that the Japanese government simply be allowed to witness a nuclear test, and then chose to surrender, rather than letting any city suffer such a fate.

One can project out such a world in some very contradictory directions. Perhaps no one would have taken as seriously the *hypothetical* destructive potential of an "atomic bomb," if this had not been accompanied by the real photos of the burned human victims in the two Japanese cities. If the atomic bomb was an inadequate deterrent, to be shrugged off like other aerially inflicted destruction (one of the arguments noted above), it might have been all the more so as an enormous test-bed flash of light. It must be remembered that, even after the 1945 real-life bombings, the American public's reaction to the Bikini test was to describe it as a "dud," as a disappointment, less frightening than people had anticipated.[25]

Working in exactly the opposite direction, we might instead project that the experience of Hiroshima and Nagasaki somehow increased the barriers to any unilateral American use of such weapons against a Russian city, or even the threats of such use. Having used the bombs twice in the heat of the anger of World War II, many Americans were then repulsed by what this had actually done to fellow human beings, amid a substantial feeling of guilt thereafter. It is not unfair to say that Japanese spokesmen have been adept at nurturing this American guilt since 1945; at least some of the Japanese claims in later years, that Japan was "about to surrender anyway" in August of 1945, have been intended to reinforce such guilt, with the implication that the use of such weapons was unnecessary, as well as brutal and immoral.

Would Americans then have been *more* willing to threaten Stalin with horrendous nuclear destruction after 1945, if no such destruction had ever occurred in real life, because they felt no guilt and less revulsion? Or would they have been less willing to do so, because the entire subject of "nuclear warfare" was too hypothetical and abstract? And would Stalin, or anyone else who had to be threatened with such weapons, have been less prone to intimidation? Those who argue that Japan did not need to have two cities bombed to achieve a surrender, but only needed to be warned of the potential of such a bombing, are in effect endorsing a view that even *the abstract prospect* of such destruction would have been effective. But the critics of the bombings can be quite self-contradictory here, arguing that the bomb should have been *demonstrated* to the Japanese, but arguing that its actual use made little or no difference in the timing of the Japanese surrender, *and* that the threat of such use could have had no impact on Stalin.

It is hard to deny that the actual use of such weapons made the bombs much more awfully real. Would analysts like Bernard Brodie and William Borden, or like Bertrand Russell, have been projecting out the implications of nuclear weapons, if these weapons had not been used twice "in anger"? The proposition of this entire book is that there was some urgency to heading off the acquisition of nuclear weapons by other countries. If all the United States had done was to test such a bomb in New Mexico, would there have been nearly as many Americans who in any way worried about "the end of the monopoly"?

Yet how limited can imagination be, in a world of hostile ideological confrontations, and international power politics? German nuclear physicists apparently had difficulty in impressing Hitler with the possibilities of an atomic bomb, but probably only because he was too preoccupied with his plans for winning wars, and killing people, with the means already at hand. It did not require the Hiroshima experience to induce Stalin to get his nuclear weapons program underway, with high priority already in 1943. And Franklin Roosevelt had been persuadable, in the abstract, that the Manhattan Project was a worthwhile investment.

We might try to trim off this round of speculation basically as follows: The nuclear confrontation after 1945 would have been different in some important ways if the bomb had never been used "in anger," with the net impact most probably being to make an American attempt to retain a monopoly even less likely, but with hardly any reduction in the Soviet desire to break the monopoly.

Counter-Factual: Soviet-Launched Preventive War

As a very different counter-historical proposition, we have already noted the speculative test of what Americans thought Stalin and the Soviets would have done with nuclear weapons, if *he* had possessed them first.

George Kennan's formulation of containment is widely remembered for depicting Stalin as less of an adventurer and gambler than Hitler. Stalin and his associates, in this view, were eager to project Moscow's power, and quite unscrupulous about it, reinforced by an ideology predicting the spread of revolution and of Communism around the world. But they were realistic enough to be averse to warfare where it could be avoided, and were more patient than the Nazis, precisely because of the Communists' long-run confidence based on this ideology.

Yet Kennan's analysis was of a Stalin who did not have nuclear weapons, facing a United States that did, the "real world" after 1945, and his advice was premised on this entire background. Would Stalin have seemed as patient and containable, if nuclear weapons were impossible, if the United States did not possess the means for destroying all the cities of the USSR? Would Stalin have been as patient and cautious, trusting in his dictums of ideology for the long-run victory of Communism, if instead *he* held a nuclear monopoly, facing the possibility that the United States was working to break this monopoly?

Anyone counting on ideology to override the power temptations of nuclear weapons has to remember how Stalin's ideological pronouncements of the 1940s were scoffing at the importance of nuclear weapons, at the same time that he was assigning high priority to the production of atomic bombs, and to the production of the Tu-4 to carry them.[26]

Rather than speculating further about the counter-factual world where Stalin's USSR has invented nuclear weapons before the U.S., we might turn then to scenarios which were to capture much more attention some years *after* 1949, whether Moscow might seize the opportunity to *create* such a monopoly, by a preventive war first-strike intended to catch all the American nuclear forces before they could be used.

This certainly became a preoccupation of United States planners in the middle 1950s, as the RAND Corporation won a reputation for its analyses of possible American vulnerabilities to a Soviet counter-force attack, that is, an attack intended to achieve a Soviet nuclear monopoly.[27] The central image of the nuclear confrontations of the Cold War is that one had to be endlessly vigilant and alert here, lest the very worst fate of all be suffered, a sneak attack on the pattern of Pearl Harbor, a sneak attack catching virtually all of the U.S. nuclear arsenal at its bases, thus sparing almost all Soviet cities from retaliatory attack (leaving Moscow then free to threaten American cities with nuclear destruction, unless they submitted to what had been imposed on Poland and Czechoslovakia, etc.).

In standard nuclear strategic discussions, for the bulk of the Cold War, the dream of the enemy (the worst fear for our side) is a "splendid first strike," a first strike which totally eliminates the possibility of nuclear retaliation, or which so much reduces this retaliation that the costs can be accepted as the price of achieving a world domination. All of the U.S. effort here had to be directed to guaranteeing that the U.S. second strike would always be so destructive as to make a Soviet first strike unattractive.

The historical picture is sometimes that American planners were insufficiently alert to these risks even in the middle 1950s, until analysts such as those at RAND prodded them to disperse the bombers of the Strategic Air Command more widely. Rather than reviewing the later history of the bomber gap and then the missile gap, the intention here would be to factor such considerations into the time of the American nuclear monopoly, the years before 1949.[28]

Americans had gone through the traumatic experience of Pearl Harbor, and were aware that the Soviet Union had invested espionage assets into trying to learn about nuclear weapons. One might thus ask how much of the concerns for maintaining a second-strike retaliatory force, the concerns that became so central in the 1950s, should have been at play already in the 1940s. And how would such concerns interact with the possibilities of preventive war?

How salient therefore would have been any apprehensions of a Soviet sneak attack in the years before 1949, an attack where the Soviets would have accumulated nuclear weapons in stealth, and then introduced them in a sudden attack on the U.S. bomb stockpile and bomber force?

We introduced above, as one strand of logic that could always be arrayed against an American-launched preventive war, the unignorable possibility that Moscow might have already crossed the line. If *any* of the U.S. reluctance to launch a war was thus based on an assumption that Stalin might already have the atomic bomb, it would have been prudential for the United States to accelerate the production of its own nuclear weapons, rather than merely pretending that such bombs already existed in quantity. With the additional prod of the Berlin blockade and other Communist pressings of the situation in Europe, this was indeed undertaken in 1948.[29]

And, it would similarly have only been prudential to consider the worst case situation where Stalin's Soviet Union might attempt to launch the mirror image of what we are contemplating here, a preventive nuclear attack designed to achieve and maintain a *Soviet* nuclear monopoly.

We certainly see this articulated in all the later anxieties of the 1950s and 1960s about bomber and missile "gaps," and in the scenarios circulated late in the 1950s by Albert Wohlstetter and his RAND colleagues about a "delicate balance of terror."[30] But is there sufficient reassurance against this in 1947 and 1948?

As late as 1948, the United States Air Force, separated since 1947 from the U.S. Army, had only a very limited number of B-29 bombers that had been structurally reinforced and otherwise prepared to carry nuclear weapons, with all of such aircraft stationed at a single air base in New Mexico.[31] The best information on the "stockpile" of U.S. nuclear weapons is that these were all kept, disassembled into components, at a single other location in New Mexico.[32] If Stalin and his colleagues had already possessed nuclear weapons as early as 1948, and has been as inclined to roll-of-dice gambles as, for example, the Japanese leadership at Pearl Harbor, would it have been beyond their intelligence capability to determine that Soviet forces needed only to destroy these two targets to eliminate the U.S. nuclear force, thereby giving Moscow rather than Washington the nuclear monopoly thereafter?

The Soviet Tu-4 bomber, a reverse-engineered copy of the B-29, might have been expected to be comparable to the original, losing something because of the inherent problems of copying, gaining because the extra years might permit some Soviet-discovered improvements.

As it happened, Stalin was so eager to obtain this four-engine bomber that he ordered that it be copied *exactly*, without any attempt to improve it by independent Soviet technological innovations, just as he was to order that the first Soviet atomic bomb be copied exactly from what had been gleaned through Soviet intelligence.[33]

The B-29 original being copied was hardly such a perfect airplane, having been rushed into mass production during World War II when the United States was in a hurry to carry the air war to Japanese cities. Particular difficulties emerged with the engines of the B-29, which did not really produce enough power for the weight of the airframe, and had a tendency to overheat. It was not until the B-50 appeared in the U.S. Air Force in the latter 1940s, a considerably improved version of the B-29 with more powerful engines, that the United States had a heavy bomber with the reliability that it wanted. Given the strictures that Stalin had imposed against deviations from the American design, the Tu-4 would almost certainly not have exceeded the B-29 in reliability.

That so many Tu-4s, between 700 and 1,000, were produced might suggest that Stalin was not endorsing a finite deterrence interpretation of nuclear weapons, since getting atomic bombs to London or Tokyo, or even to Seattle or New York, would not have required hundreds of such bombers, but only dozens at the most.

But the quantity production of such airplanes might also, of course, be seen as a hedge against delay in achieving nuclear weapons for the USSR, so that London could be threatened with massive conventional air attack (i.e., with the fate of Tokyo in March of 1945, devastated by an incendiary attack of 300 B-29s, rather than with the fate of Hiroshima and Nagasaki in August).

Alternatively, the larger number of Tu-4 bombers could be seen as Stalin endorsing, or more persuasively *pretending* to endorse, the grand counter-force theory of strategic bombardment and nuclear war so many American Air Force officers were inclined to accept, the view most of such officers also imputed to the Soviets. If Stalin could convince American planners that only a counter-force use of strategic nuclear air power made sense, by suggesting that he himself saw things this way, the chances of an American preventive war attack would be reduced.

For the grand counter-force, counter-military capability, kind of air war, one needed to be able to recover one's bombers for multiple missions, such that calculations about the Tu-4, as about the B-29 and all the bombers in the Western air forces, would project their range based on a need to return, such that larger numbers of bombers would be needed.

For anything emphasizing the simple and horrendous destruction of a nuclear destruction of London or New York, however, one could dispense with the round-trip calculations, projecting out the maximum range of only a few such airplanes on a one-way mission. And the same held true for any emphasis on striking just the nuclear stockpile of the opposing side.

Besides a conventional fire-bombing of London, or attacks on industry, or the atomic bombing of any Western city, there was thus one more significant scenario that needed to be factored in here, whether the Tu-4, on a non-return, one-way mission, perhaps refueled once or twice in flight, could have delivered a Soviet atomic bomb to the airbase in New Mexico where all the nuclear-capable B-29s of the United States Air Force were based, and to the weapons lockers not so far from this base, where all the American nuclear weapons, disassembled into components, were stored.[34]

The United States, despite rumors that had emerged of the reverse engineering of the interned B-29s, was not really aware of the serial production of the Tu-4 until late in 1947, when several of such airplanes appeared at an air show. Even then, the conclusion was that these might have been the same American aircraft, being flown by now in Soviet markings, or at the worst the flight of a few prototypes.

Once the existence of more sizable numbers of Tu-4s had been established, however, the obvious question would then have had to be whether such aircraft could threaten perhaps the most important target of all, the United States nuclear force.

Projections of the simple round-trip range of a Soviet copy of the B-29 would have put New Mexico out of range. Yet it can not be stressed too often that round trips would really be of no importance, if the mission were so ultimate as the elimination of all the American B-29s adapted to carry atomic bombs, and/or all the stored components of American A-bombs. Just as one did not introduce the question of "round trips" for missiles when the missile gap was to pose the same ultimate question at the end of the 1950s, so the round trip mission dimension would become irrelevant here, as the crew of the successful or unsuccessful Soviet sneak attack could parachute into Mexico to await the results of their venture.

Such a Tu-4 attack might seem tied to a Soviet air-refueling capability. With the end of the Cold War, it is now known that the Soviets indeed experimented with such refueling techniques, with uneven results. Yet a projection of one-way range, even *without* refueling, suggests that the Tu-4 might have been able to make a strike from Siberia to New Mexico.

One might be accused of simply designing a fanciful Hollywood scenario here, rather than developing a counter-factual analysis of the impact of nuclear weapons on the international political system:

Imagine Stalin taking some of the Tu-4 bombers that had been produced, and coupling them with two nuclear weapons in a go-for-broke attempt at world domination. Perhaps the aircraft could just barely execute the attack without any refueling at all. Or one could make the attempt using in-flight refueling techniques over and over again, in the manner of the 1982 RAF V-bomber air attacks on the Argentine forces in the Falklands,[35] with eight bombers keeping four going, and four refueling two, and so on. The end of all this would be the attack on the two key locations in New Mexico, with the final one or two bombers then having their crews parachute into Mexico; again, there would have been no need to bring their aircraft back intact to Russia, since what had been brought back would have been much more, a nuclear monopoly for Stalin, and with it the ability to dictate a Baruch Plan in reverse, the ability to dictate the Communization rather than the democratization of the globe.

Most would scoff at such a scenario because of the horrendous gamble it would have entailed, especially if Stalin had been misled into believing that the U.S. possessed a much larger stockpile of nuclear weapons, a stockpile not all collected at one location. But we know that Soviet espionage was fastened on to the U.S. nuclear program in these years, and that the Kremlin, despite its professed indifference to nuclear matters, actually attached great significance to the atomic bomb. We know less about whether Stalin was informed on exactly how small the existing U.S. arsenal was in 1947, or the shape it was in.

The model of the Japanese decision to attack at Pearl Harbor was to become a centerpiece of American concerns in the 1950s about a delicacy of the balance of terror.[36] The Japanese had attacked, in a daring gamble with limited chances of success, because they saw growing American pressures for a Japanese withdrawal from China. Stalin is remembered as more cautious than Hitler or the Japanese military leaders.

But, if the Soviet dictator could have looked ahead to what was to happen in 1989 and 1991, to the end of the Cold War, might he not have been similarly willing to gamble everything on heading this off?

In the event, Americans did not worry very much about a Soviet counter-force attack with a few nuclear weapons in 1948, even though they worried much more about later bomber gaps and missile gaps.

Why might we then have concluded earlier above that the same Americans could have been discouraged from launching a preventive war by the small possibility that Stalin already had some bombs, such that a U.S. initiative would have exposed a few American cities to counter-value retaliation? Is there an inconsistency in these two impressions of the American alertness to Soviet nuclear progress?

Yet these impressions are not really so inconsistent. Delivering one or two Soviet atomic bombs to destroy New York or San Francisco would always have seemed easy, compared with using such a rudimentary Soviet force carefully enough to destroy *all* the U.S. nuclear arsenal.

11

The Belated Non-Proliferation Barrier

The world became very sensitized to the nuclear proliferation problem after 1960, when a fourth country had acquired nuclear weapons, and a fifth was about to. The argument of this book is that such a concern was much more relevant before 1949, and should have been more articulated more completely in this earlier period. Some further discussion of the parallels and the linkages would seem to be in order here.

Does the Second Lead to the "Nth"s?

Responding to the shock with which the suggestion of preventive war is normally received, one sometimes tries to cite a list of horrendous things that might have been headed off by such an immediately immoral move. For openers, the thermonuclear World War III so much feared in the years from 1954 to 1989, and still to be feared, would have been impossible if a repetition of Hiroshima and Nagasaki had headed off nuclear duopoly.

Those rejecting the very thought of preventive war might now claim enough retrospective confidence in the responsibility and deterrability of the Soviet Union, and of the United States, to dismiss the thermonuclear holocaust threat between the two superpowers, even while the same international relations analysts would have assigned this threat great importance before 1989. Since we made it through all the Cold War without violating the post-Nagasaki nuclear taboo, why even begin to lament the failure to head off the nuclear confrontation?

Yet allowing Moscow to become the second nuclear weapons state may have gone hand-in-hand with allowing Britain and France, and then China, to become the third and fourth, and the fifth, possessors of nuclear weapons; and this has opened the possibility in turn of still further horizontal nuclear proliferation to India and Pakistan, and so on, amid the concern that one of these separate nuclear arsenals will sooner or later come into the control of a madman, of someone indifferent to the nuclear retaliation of others.

No reasonable analyst of international arms control can, at the end of the twentieth century, guarantee that nuclear weapons will not continue to proliferate, or that they will not come into use, any more than one can assume that such weapons can with any reliability be eliminated from the current arsenals.

If the United States had taken measures to prevent the Soviet Union from acquiring nuclear weapons, it would surely have had to do the same for Communist China, and probably even for a China that had not become "Communist China," and it might similarly have had to take such steps for France and for Britain. Turning the logical pattern around, when no such measures had been taken vis-à-vis Moscow, it is hardly a surprise that no strong pressures were applied to the third, fourth, and fifth, and that the American support for a non-proliferation effort did not really emerge until the 1960s.

The thrust of this entire book is that the most important distinction was between monopoly and duopoly. To repeat a personal note, this author can remember very well where he was standing when he heard the news that President Truman had announced the discovery of a Soviet nuclear program. By comparison, he can not at all remember where he was when he heard of the British and French first detonations. (And, to turn to a newer line of concerns, he *can* remember where he heard of the Chinese detonation in 1964, and the Indian detonation in 1974).

Once the Baruch Plan had been definitively rejected, as by the 1949 news that Moscow had nuclear weapons of its own, many Americans thus became resigned to a world where such weapons would become like any other weapon, spreading to other countries as well. The British might justify their own program this way, producing nuclear weapons so that they could help out their American allies in a common effort, much as the RAF and USAAF had helped each other by pooling efforts in bombing Germany during World War II.[1] The French would instead justify their program later by the reasoning of Pierre Gallois, by which the United States, once Moscow had its own nuclear weapons, could not be counted upon to escalate to the nuclear level if Soviet tanks where rolling toward Paris.[2]

The emergence of a second nuclear weapons force (the first instance of "proliferation," although the term was not yet used) thus paved the way for further and more extensive (someday possibly horrendous) nuclear weapons proliferation, in at least two ways. As noted earlier, it diverted the American logic of mutual deterrence and hostility away from London or Paris, because one focussed, as in an earlier day of the calculations of conventional balances of power, on a "principal enemy." But the first two nuclear forces also *protected* the emergence of "nth" nuclear forces, at least in that no preventive war actions could be taken against them. Because American nuclear forces checked those of the USSR, there was no question of Moscow ever preempting British or French nuclear weapons acquisition. And because of Moscow's bomb, the Chinese Communists may have been safe against U.S. preemption.

The first two nuclear forces in the world have thus largely been seen as checking each other. This might indeed be seen as an argument that additional nuclear forces were *unnecessary*.

But this duopoly has also, until some greater risks of much more widespread nuclear proliferation have emerged, made additional nuclear forces *possible*, to be assembled largely free of threats of preventive war, that is, free of the threat that we have been speculating about here for the 1945-1949 period.

The Later Non-Proliferation Barrier

One encounters some important exceptions to this rule, however, as the issue of preventive war was then to be partially reopened in two very interesting cases, the approach of Communist China to nuclear weapons in the early 1960s, and the fears that West Germany might seek such weapons in the same decade. The U.S. would never have tolerated any Soviet military effort, or even Soviet military threats, to keep Britain or France from acquiring atomic bombs. The logic by which the second deters the first, and the first deters the second, thus opening up the doors for the third through nths, thus would seem to be supported.

But the negotiation of the Partial Test-Ban Treaty in the early 1960s apparently saw the Kennedy Administration trying to persuade Moscow to apply pressure on Beijing to forego nuclear proliferation. The wording of the PTB withdrawal clause, to be repeated exactly in the later Non-Proliferation Treaty (NPT), allowed for parties to withdraw if "extraordinary events, related to the subject matter of this Treaty, have jeopardized the supreme interests of its country."[3]

This was intended as a signal that if China detonated a nuclear device, the U.S. and Britain would be released from the test-ban. Perhaps Soviet assistance was still required to facilitate a Chinese nuclear test. Or perhaps Moscow still had important influence with the Chinese Communists, through the fraternity of Marxist-Leninist parties. Both of these, of course, were to be very inaccurate assumptions.

Or perhaps the Soviets could be prodded to intervene militarily, at least to threaten to intervene, to preclude the completion of a Chinese weapons program. Or, and here of course the real facts will always be hard to pin down, the USSR could be persuaded to tolerate American military intervention, and/or threats of intervention, to keep China from acquiring weapons of mass destruction, the same China that was about to horrify the world by plunging into the excesses of its Cultural Revolution.

There are thus rumors of American trial balloons in the 1960s about such intervention[4] (and then in the 1970s rumors of *Soviet* trial balloons, as to whether the U.S. would oppose a Soviet counter-force attack on the rudimentary Chinese nuclear force).[5] In later years, Americans and Russians would each hint to the Chinese that the other had been tempted to take such action;[6] and Chinese analysts, from the perspective of an elementary analysis of power politics, might be inclined to accept both sets of rumors.

If such ideas were even remotely explored in Washington prior to the 1965 Chinese detonation, this would of course reinforce the argument for preventive war before 1949. A Chinese nuclear force would not be important for its counter-force impact on the international confrontation of strategic and military forces. It was rather to be opposed because of its counter-value threat to Soviet or American cities.

To underscore this counter-value impact, the Chinese Communists' declarations, from the moment that their bomb had been tested, were to stake out a position of "no first use" for nuclear weapons, making the Chinese declaration of NFU the clearest and most repeated of any of the open nuclear weapons states.[7]

To pronounce that nuclear weapons would only be used if another state had used them, and never otherwise, was quite consistent with what some Americans were recommending for a U.S. posture. But it was also to underscore that these weapons were uniquely horrible in the pain they inflicted on ordinary life, so horrible that they would be held in reserve, so horrible that even a few bombs in an "nth" arsenal might be enough to deter and cancel out the supposed "military significance" of any much larger opposing nuclear arsenal.

To repeat a central paradox, the endorsements of mutual assured destruction and of no-first-use of nuclear weapons are consistent with attaching primary importance to heading off even the most rudimentary nuclear force in someone else's hands (as in today's opposition to nuclear proliferation, *and* as in heading off the nuclear proliferation that Stalin achieved in 1949).

The Soviet opposition to West Germany acquiring nuclear weapons never produced concrete threats of a military strike at German nuclear facilities. Nonetheless one saw more veiled threats that warfare could indeed emerge if a country so tarnished by the Nazi record, the losers in World War II, were to reach for weapons of mass destruction.[8]

An opposition to Germans, or Japanese, having control over such weapons was to be found as well in the West, of course; it is not so accidental that the abstract question of non-proliferation began to jell after nuclear technology became more plausible for Germany and Japan.

Again, as in the case of all nuclear programs since the Soviet, the outsider apprehension was hardly that a few bombs in German or Japanese hands would tip some military balance. The last time that nuclear weapons were really interpreted in terms of such comparative war-fighting capabilities came in some of the American assessments, after 1949 and before, of Soviet nuclear weapons. Instead the fear, in Moscow, or in London or Sydney, was that it was too early to rule out a repetition of the worst of German or Japanese World War II behavior, too early to conclude that democratization and demilitarization had eliminated all the risks of a truly mad round of unprovoked mass destruction.

The current open possessors of nuclear weapons then came, in time, to rally behind the more general non-proliferation effort, and the Nuclear Non-Proliferation Treaty (NPT).[9] When this aversion to proliferation was augmented by the naked Iraqi aggression against Kuwait launched by Saddam Hussein in 1991, the world then finally saw the second bombing campaign in history intended to head off a nuclear weapons program[10] (one should remember, as the first, General Groves' inputs to

Allied target choice, in the World War II bombings of German-occupied Europe).

Again, the model of what might have been tried against Stalin was
what had been done against Saddam Hussein, and/or against Hitler's
Germany, and such an effort in 1948 might have kept the issue of Iraqi
or West German or Indian nuclear weapons from ever emerging.

One might be quite optimistic now about the evolution of democratic politics in Russia, and about the development of international
relations between Russia and America, or Russia and everyone else,
without this very much relieving the current concerns about nuclear
proliferation. And the strongest case against such proliferation remains
that some country, sooner or later, perhaps because of domestic unrest
or a civil war or military coup, will use weapons of mass destruction
without any reason, oblivious to the retaliation that will come.

If decade after decade passes without this happening, the retrospective case for having headed off all nuclear proliferation will seem weaker
and weaker. The day that it does happen, however, will make this argument look very strong.

The nuclear proliferation risk is often described with the metaphor
of putting a "nuclear genie back into the bottle." The contention of this
book is that only a nuclear cap could have pushed back the nuclear
genie, that only the threat of nuclear weapons in the hands of a power
like the United States could have sufficed to prevent the development
of other nuclear arsenals.

More on the Special Case of Britain

Returning to our speculation about a world where it is Britain that is
preparing to detonate its first device in 1949, with Moscow having no
chance to do so until 1952, it is thus possible that the United States
would have applied strong pressure against this, on the simple logic
outlined just above, that a second nuclear weapons state (however
friendly and democratic) would open the door for a less friendly and
democratic third. Yet could we imagine Washington even threatening
war to head this off, if the government of an Atlee or a Churchill had
been determined to acquire nuclear weapons of its own? [11]

Here the answer is probably the closest to obvious for all the "silly
questions" we have been posing. Since the United States did not launch
or even threaten preventive war to keep Moscow from getting nuclear

weapons, "of course" there would have been no prospect of doing so against Britain.

Yet someone might protest that the Soviet detonation had, after all, caught the U.S. by surprise in 1949, and that Stalin had not really dared announce it in advance, or even immediately after it had occurred. British preparations to detonate in Australia would instead have been known in Washington, allowing more galvanizing of opposition (including perhaps even the threat of moves to prevent it by warfare?). Or, if Britain had taken steps to try to keep all this secret from the United States, would this not have activated much more of the logic of hostility that was discussed above as possibly derived from the logic of nuclear duopoly? Would all the recriminations about British vs. American views of decolonization, and so on, then have taken on more life again?

Yet another counter-factual possibility then has to be raised. *If* Britain had beaten Stalin to the bomb, joining the U.S. in the priority position, would the British government have been more inclined to deny such weapons to Moscow, and been more able then to enlist the U.S. into a joint effort to force non-proliferation on Stalin and everyone else? While there is hardly any reason to assume that Atlee and the Labour Party would have shared in this, we have noted Churchill's suggestions of preventive war.

Rather than opening the door to the third through the nth possessors of nuclear weapons, the particular "second" in London might, by this scenario, have galvanized the first into imposing a ban on any further spread of such weapons, and nuclear weapons would thereafter have remained a monopoly of the democratic English-speaking "special relationship" (i.e., what Churchill might have envisaged in 1942 when he initiated his informal agreement with Franklin Roosevelt to pool Britain's talents into the Manhattan Project).

A British nuclear weapon by 1949 would at least have shaken Americans out of any excessive confidence in "the secret" of producing such weapons. But such a more benign form of nuclear proliferation would have left it still "not too late" to prevent the potentially aggressive dictators of this world from acquiring weapons of mass destruction. The inputs of a more traditional realpolitik-oriented British statesman like Winston Churchill might have thus made the difference in getting Americans to look at preventive war more seriously. And Britain would have had the means to launch such a war on its own, if it had acquired as many nuclear warheads by 1951 as the United States could have accumulated by 1947, and if Stalin's Russia still had not quite acquired any.

12

Some Conclusions

George Kennan predicted that containment might work in a decade or two. In the event, it "worked" after more than four decades. A reasonable prediction in 1945 was that the USSR would possess nuclear weapons within a decade. Blending even the more optimistic of these two predictions, the world would still have had to experience a hostile nuclear confrontation between Washington and an unreformed Moscow for at least a decade, a decade in which a horrible nuclear exchange would all along have been a possibility.

In the event, the world went through *four* such decades of nuclear confrontation, from 1949 to 1989. With Moscow now reformed with a non-Communist government, the confrontation has changed, so that far fewer Americans worry about it. But the thermonuclear holocaust still remains physically possible.

There are analysts who today argue that the nuclear confrontation urgently needs to be terminated.[1] This book may in fact be agreeing with the desirability of this, but amid grave doubts as to whether a nuclear-free world can still be achieved.

The thrust of this book is that the situation of 1945 to 1949 offered one way to avoid such a confrontation. Are there really now other ways?

The "Delicate Balance"

Atomic bombs and hydrogen bombs have not been used since Nagasaki. This is a simple matter of fact, to be set against any and all counter-factual conjecture. Most Americans might conclude that this would, per se, settle the issue of a pre-1949 preventive war, to dismiss the possibility as totally unnecessary, as well as crazy and immoral.

Most readers, when first confronting the theme of this book, might simply begin by asking how serious anyone could be about the possibility of preventive war. For all of the reasons cited, this is often just dismissed as an option. And what can possibly be the practical policy implications of reopening these questions some fifty years later?

This entire book has thus been an exercise in considering counterfactuals, what the world might have been like if preventive war had been given a more serious hearing,...and what America or the rest of the world would have had to be like for such a hearing even to occur.

This author indeed sees a military counter-force attack to reestablish the American monopoly, to eliminate all other nuclear weapons forces, as impossible after September of 1949, and thus as very definitely impossible today; so the policy implications might then be written off as nil.

And yet..., the logics of the planning for the nuclear forces, in all five of the declared nuclear weapons states, still presume that an adversary might be tempted to try such a counter-force "splendid" first strike, if the opportunity should ever present itself.

One of the most powerful arguments against MIRVed missiles is also one of the more important arguments against a very rapid and major nuclear disarmament, that we have to be concerned for what is known as crisis stability or strategic stability, that we have to avoid offering any power the temptation (and avoid subjecting any power to the fear) of such a counter-force attack. The possibility of eliminating the entire adversary nuclear threat, and not suffering unacceptable damage in the process, may be more totally dismissed when the adversary possesses the "overkill" of thousands of nuclear warheads; but that possibility might seem to come to life again, once the warhead totals settle down into the hundreds.[2]

As discussed above, some of the Americans who ruled out preventive war before 1949 might have considered it after the experiences of the 1950s, (when preventive war might be much less feasible, but when the Soviet Union seemed more definitely threatening and aggressive.) If certain American analysts express a sympathy for a Khrushchev or Brezhnev having to fear an American nuclear attack, this author can not totally disagree.

One of the reasons that preventive war deserved more of a hearing before 1949, therefore, would be that thermonuclear exchanges were not so totally impossible between 1949 and 1989, and may not be so totally impossible even after 1989. If the fears of preventive war, and fears of preemption, have been at all real in the decades of "bomber gaps" and "missile gaps," and of crisis diplomacy, some of these fears will persist.

Bernard Brodie once disparaged the case that Albert Wohlstetter and his RAND Corporation team had made about the dangers of counter-force first strikes, with the comment that whatever else the balance of terror had been, it had not been "delicate."[3] By historical hindsight, one could thus dismiss any preventive war by contending that nuclear war would never have broken out, that the superpowers would definitely have been mutually deterred by the retaliatory capacities they faced. This is a viewpoint that sometimes contends that the only real nuclear risks today emerge from sloppy command-and-control arrangements, from the inherent risks of accidents or insubordination when *so many* nuclear warheads have been generated.[4] Or perhaps the only risk came from the febrile imaginations of people like Albert Wohlstetter or Curtis LeMay, excessively tuned to the possibilities of Pearl Harbor-type sneak attacks from the other side, and excessively inclined to speculate about the feasibility of similar sneak attacks by our side.

Today's advocates of substantial and rapid nuclear disarmament would argue that nuclear force totals in the hundreds are more than sufficient to deter any rationally motivated nuclear aggression. To preclude irrational initiations of nuclear warfare, their urgent recommendation would be for a rapid reduction in the totals of nuclear weapons, and perhaps then for the total elimination of such forces.

Leaving aside the kinds of argument that become articles of faith, however, most analysts would admit that there are at least *some* issues of trade off here. Reductions in the likelihood of nuclear war, from the 1950s to the present, have at least *to some extent* stemmed from the high destructiveness of such war. If one markedly reduces the destruction in a strategic bombing exchange, there will be decision-makers, somewhere, who will again begin to contemplate the possibilities, rather than rejecting them out-of-hand.

Imagine a world where the total of uranium would have been much less than actually uncovered, so that the total of bombs produced by the various powers might have come only to five hundred A-bombs, and imagine a world where thermonuclear weapons would have proved impossible. This would have been a world where "nuclear winter" would

never have loomed as a possibility, and where the survival of civilization and the entire human race would not have come into question.
But would this have been a world where the deterrence of nuclear conflict was so assured?

Atomic bombs and hydrogen bombs have not been used since
Nagasaki. Today's advocates of rapid reductions in the numbers of such
weapons sometimes argue that it was *only* the large size of the nuclear
arsenals that ever threatened their use; but just the opposite might be
the reality.

Democracy and Deterrence

But we need to look at one more major causal variable here, for the
end of the Cold War in 1989 did not only entail a reduction in the perceived risks of conventional or nuclear conflict, but also the spread of
political democracy to all of Eastern Europe, and then to what had been
the Soviet Union itself.

As democracy has spread, is the risk of nuclear war all the more
unlikely, so that any options for preventive war became all the more
unnecessary in retrospect? To put the question another way, if the typical American reader regards the preventive war idea as outlandish, might
this say as much about the democratic environment in which that American was nurtured, as it does about the idea? [5]

By some kinds of analysis, everything that happened was bound and
determined to happen. Atomic bombs and hydrogen bombs have not
been used since Nagasaki. And political democracy is now the system
of government in four out of five of the declared nuclear weapons states,
in particular in Russia, the successor to the Soviet Union as the second
nuclear "superpower."

If the American example has spread in domestic political practice,
the example of free speech and free press, and freely contested elections, does this same example then include an aversion to even thinking
about initiating war, that is, ruling out preventive war and "splendid
first strikes"?

We thus have the makings of an interesting paradox here. Perhaps it
was short-sighted, in terms of selfish national interest, and perhaps even
in terms of the whole world's interests, for the United States not to
consider more seriously the option of artificially maintaining its nuclear
monopoly. But, if this short-sightedness stems from the very nature of

democracy, all the other countries joining in the democratic process may also be steered by it, whereupon the earlier decision becomes wise rather than myopic.

Someone who "knew" that democracy would spread around the world at the end of the twentieth century also "knew" that the technical possibilities of weapons of mass destruction would not pose any insuperable problem, because the democratic states would not think of using them.

This book has argued that the failure even to threaten preventive war before 1949 has to be explained more by moral absolutes than by rational calculations in the American government. Yet the spread of such moral absolutes would then belatedly add something to the rational calculus. There might be no need to prevent the spread of nuclear weapons to another democracy, or to another state that will in the end become a democracy.

Advocates of more total nuclear disarmament often make a great deal of the power of example. If the United States and Russia agree to reduce their nuclear arsenals, this would, it is argued, reduce the perceived importance of nuclear weapons; and it might also reduce the chances that other states, especially the other democracies, but perhaps all countries, will produce their own atomic bombs in another round of nuclear proliferation.[6] Argentina and Brazil offer some encouraging examples here, both states having edged toward a nuclear weapons capability while they were governed by military juntas, and while the superpowers were expanding their nuclear arsenals, but both now offering reassurances to each other, and to the outside world, that no such weapons are being produced.[7]

The arguments are helpfully circular here. The greater the power of example, the greater the hope for a future without nuclear war, and without even thoughts or threats of such a war. The greater the power of example, the greater the argument against preventive war before 1949, because nothing so bad needed to be headed off. And what a nice example the American attitudes of 1945 to 1949 then indeed provided!

Continuing Concerns

Yet the first glimmers of concern then pertain to the strength of this power of example. If democracies in Argentina and Brazil are imitating the United States and Russia (or are more simply intent on avoiding an arms race, where each nation knows that the other would match any atomic bombs that were produced, but where each also knows that "they" may abstain as long as "we" abstain), the democracies in Pakistan and India hardly seem to be leaning in the same direction.[8]

And the skeptic about a democratic world safe from military threats would be all the more likely to point to Iraq[9] or North Korea;[10] regimes free of having to run for reelection may see great advantages to acquiring nuclear weapons, if the outside world does not intervene to prevent this.

As noted above, much will be shaped here by the risks of exceptions to the rule. Democracy is spreading, and with it an expectation of peace. But also spreading, ever since 1945, has been the physical capability for making the kinds of weapons that can so easily destroy a city.

John Mueller offered an interesting analysis of international relations in 1989,[11] arguing that war, not just nuclear war, but conventional war as well, had become obsolete by the twentieth century. This was not tied, in his analysis, to the spread of democracy, since he, along with the rest of us, did not foresee the collapse of the Warsaw Pact and the Soviet Union. Rather Mueller, and others who share this analysis, have drawn analogies with two other institutions that once were also regarded as inevitable: slavery and dueling. A general common sense would soon enough see war as just as silly as dueling and slavery, and this would even appear in non-democracies.

Mueller indeed deprecated the particular role of nuclear weapons in deterring war, arguing that war would have been relatively rare after 1945, as compared with before, even if atomic bombs had been impossible. Several of his reviewers[12] agreed with the general thrust of the case about the fading likelihood of war, but disagreed about the unimportance of nuclear weapons in this "common sense" spreading around the world. Because nuclear weapons exist, and are so destructive, the common sense is that they should not be used, and perhaps that wars in general should not be considered, since wars could always now *lead to* nuclear use.

Mueller had to deal with the phenomenon of Nazi Germany, of course, in his projection of the declining relevance of war, but argued that Hitler was a fluke and an aberration, being the only person, even among the Nazi leaders, who really wanted a war to occur, while other Germans merely hoped to cash in on the political gains, the returns of using the threat of war to frighten the democracies.[13]

Yet it opens a dangerous door to say that sensible people will hate war, but might welcome the benefits and concessions that come when they can bluff about liking it. This is what the other Nazis perhaps thought Hitler was doing, imitating the pattern that Mussolini had already demonstrated in the 1920s. Will there not always be another Hitler or Mussolini, or Stalin or Saddam Hussein, posing the Clausewitzian challenge to collective security noted earlier, perhaps posing it with nuclear weapons? And, if the American and Russian and other declared nuclear weapons arsenals were reduced to very low levels, would this really reduce the temptation for such leaders to reach for nuclear weapons? Or might such reductions actually increase their temptation?

One can tie Mueller's case about war in general, and the exception of Hitler, quite closely to the nuclear factor. Would there have been a Manhattan Project if there had been no Hitler? Would there have been no atomic bomb project anywhere in the world? If Hitler had never come to power, Churchill also would never have done so. Would Britain have taken the initiative of reaching for atomic bombs under any other prime minister?

But if Hitler was a fluke and an exception (bad luck for the Germans and the world), was Stalin also such a fluke and an exception (bad luck for the Russians and for the world)? To repeat some of the speculations noted earlier, might Stalin's Soviet system not have launched its equivalent of a Manhattan Project, even if Germany was governed by Weimar, and even if the United States was not driven by fears of German nuclear capability. The "power of example" here might not have been powerful enough to hold everyone back.

Would there have been a different American attitude toward nuclear sharing after 1945 if Stalin had in no way resembled Hitler, if he had been merely as rough around the edges as today's Yeltsin? Perhaps yes, if the post-1945 USSR would have tolerated free elections in Poland and around Eastern Europe, and so on; but this is not the actual Soviet Union of the years before 1949.

The pessimistic version of the future would thus be that there will always be Hitlers or Stalins somewhere, such that the power of example will not sweep all before it. If the example of democracy and the example of American pre-1945 nuclear restraint do not prove persuasive *everywhere*, the risks remain of someone else confronting the world's cities with destruction.

What Kim Il-Sung or King Jong-il, or Saddam Hussein, can do with even a very few atomic bombs is today a major concern for the world, something to be headed off, rather than something simply to be adjusted to, or soothed by a policy of nuclear sharing. What a Hitler could have done with even a few atomic bombs was similarly a major concern for Churchill and Roosevelt during World War II. And what Stalin could do, with only a few atomic bombs, turned out to be the launching of an invasion of South Korea, an invasion which was to be the model for all the fears that drove NATO for the next four decades.

Optimism and Pessimism

To repeat, that so little consideration was given to preventive war before 1949 may be a testimony to the peaceful world-outlook of a democracy like the United States. With the spread of democracy since 1989, one could hope that this world-outlook will prevent wars, and threats of war, in the future, and thus retroactively make all the more appropriate America's abstention from a drastic use of the years of the nuclear monopoly.

But the case that *more* consideration should have been given to preventive war still looms in at least two forms.

First, anything less than a perfect and total spread of such democracy will leave in place one regime or another that will resemble Hitler and Stalin in its attitude toward power politics, in what it would do with nuclear weapons if it had them. Second, the post-1989 spread of democracy was not predicted, and perhaps was not so inevitable.

One should never forget how unexpected were the demise of the Warsaw Pact, and the breakup of the Soviet Union. Partisans of opposing approaches to American foreign policy are arguing now about who should be given the credit for the "free world victory" here,[14] but it is very difficult to find any analysts, even as late as the 1980s, who really predicted that the Cold War would end, that political democracy would soon encompass some seventy countries or more, rather than the basic and beleaguered eighteen of the years of the Cold War.

If the collapse of Communism was *not* so inevitable, the spread of freedom after 1989 might have been a very happy accident for the world, but an accident no one could have banked on. A reasonable planner in the 1940s would have had to foresee that the Soviet bloc could persist well into the next century; and can any reasonable planner even today see the termination of Communist rule in China as a sure thing?

Going to Zero?

Many Americans and others may now still call for a total elimination of nuclear weapons, as the United States and Russia remain officially committed to total nuclear disarmament (indeed to general and complete disarmament—GCD—in *all* categories of weapons), by various U.N. resolutions, and by the wording of Article VI of the Nuclear Non-Proliferation Treaty (NPT).

Reducing the current arsenals from tens of thousands of warheads to thousands, and then to hundreds, is thus widely viewed as merely a step in the transition to zero. After decades of American arguments about the role of verification if such disarmament is to succeed, there is a general acknowledgement of the need for safeguards to ensure treaty compliance. But advocates of such total disarmament, seeking to eliminate the risk of nuclear war, will argue that verification is indeed manageable, that cheating and rumors of cheating will not be an inescapable obstacle, especially with the spread of the democracy which makes societies generally more open.[15]

The spread of democracy is the prompt for nuclear disarmament in several ways, as many analysts and ordinary people who regarded such a venture as doubtful before 1989 would favor it now.

First, the conversion of Eastern Europe and the former Soviet Union to democratic rule reduces the likelihood of war, and reduces the need for any "extended nuclear deterrence" to shield the NATO countries against the risks of a Communist tank attack. Second, the spread of democracy makes countries much more open, making it more difficult for nuclear weapons programs to be launched or renewed in secret. Third, the overall tone of democratic government increases compassion for other peoples, and diminishes the appeals of militarism. This is a tone which reinforces the idea that it is "silly" even to speculate in the abstract about a nuclear confrontation between Britain and the United States. It is a tone which makes *politically* much more meaningful the Russian and American declarations that the two superpowers' nuclear missiles are no longer targeted on each other.

Countering these arguments for general disarmament, and even for very deep cuts in the totals of nuclear weapons, are the skeptics about the impact and relevance of democracy where international rivalries are concerned, skeptics about the attainable reliability of safeguards.[16] Such a worldview argues that the dual-use nature of nuclear science will inevitably leave countries close to the possession of nuclear weapons, since the knowledge of how to make bombs out of plutonium or enriched uranium can no longer be corralled and withheld.[17]

"Total nuclear disarmament," in this more pessimistic view of the future, would simply be a world where a number of countries were months or weeks away from possessing nuclear weapons. Such a world, in terms of what we label "crisis stability" or "strategic stability," might then even be worse than the current world of large nuclear arsenals, because the temptations might be greater to initiate and win a new nuclear race, or the rumors and fears would be more potent that another state was about to cheat and reach for a new nuclear monopoly.

The nations of the world might thus be watching each other with concerns just like those of the 1940s about latent potential, and about the gap to achievement of nuclear weapons, with results perhaps being grimmer this time, as whoever was "the first" in acquiring atomic bombs might not be as restrained as the United States was in 1946 and 1947.

Perhaps preventive war before 1949 was unnecessary because mutual assured destruction was to be a truly reliable guarantee against nuclear war for the next four decades, as Bernard Brodie was right that the balance of terror was never so "delicate"; but this becomes an argument then for keeping nuclear forces so robust that retaliatory destruction can never really be questioned. Skeptics about reliable nuclear disarmament thus sometimes call for retaining nuclear arsenals at least at the levels negotiated by President Bush.

The world might very much welcome a time when there were no nuclear weapons at all the world, or even near at hand, that is, where the number of states possessing nuclear weapons was not eight or seven or six, not the basic two, but zero. But however attractive zero might be, the same world will still be gripped by a great aversion to the next lowest number of nuclear weapons states—one. Fear of someone else becoming the *one and only* nuclear weapons state might then ignite races that could even lead to the *use* of such weapons, rather than merely their possession.

Crisis stability would be in great danger, by this argument, when the world was at "zero" nuclear weapons, because of all the inherent risks that cheating might be underway somewhere or other. And it would be in danger already as the existing nuclear powers were scheduled to go through the last rounds of nuclear disarmament, as the remaining totals were getting down below one hundred.

In one country or another, there might be a "clever briefer," an ambitious officer who caught the ear of the political leader with a scenario by which his own country could successfully cheat, and thus establish a new monopoly of nuclear weapons, thereby to dominate the world. Or, the briefing would be of a scare scenario building on rumors that another state was cheating.

Or, perhaps the scariest of all, even in a world of democracies, would be a briefing by which another state was painted as being influenced by false rumors that *we* were cheating, and as thus preparing to cheat on its side (to which the appropriate response, of course, would be that our own country has to cheat in preemption, has to retain some nuclear weapons illegally, or quickly build some new ones).

In an "anarchic world," another state erroneously assuming that we are evil may be just as much of a threat as a state which itself is evil.

Internationalizing Nuclear Forces

As a third option, an alternative to total nuclear disarmament, or to the maintenance of large forces facing each other, one sometimes sees proposals that nuclear forces could now be transferred to international management, perhaps indeed to the United Nations, in the same years that national nuclear forces were being progressively reduced.[18] Any state cheating on the nuclear disarmament agreement, either a new entrant into the field, or an old player that had resurrected its arsenal, would thus not be achieving any new monopoly, but would have to confront a larger nuclear weapons force, governed and directed by the world as a whole.

This is very much in step with the reasoning of Hobbes on the sources of peace and law and order in domestic society, as the "realist" theorists of international relations contrast such law and order with the "anarchic" world of force and diplomacy. Effective government, in the view of Hobbes and many other political analysts, has never meant abolishing the capacity for violence, but instead establishing a *monopoly* of such violence, a "sovereign" to whom all can safely submit, without then having continually to fear violence from others.

In the best of worlds, this monopoly of violence is directed by the people, in a democratic government by the consent of the governed. But what is crucial, even if the government be a monarchy or a dictatorship, is that there be a *single* government, for without this life is "nasty, brutish and short."

This government does not continually have to display its capacity for violence. British police typically patrol their beats without carrying guns. But it is crucial that the police at least possess some guns in reserve, which they can bring out to defeat any criminal group that introduces guns.

World peace, and world government and law and order, will thus only come, in this view, when there is one world army that could defeat any other, or one nuclear force that could overwhelm, and perhaps thus deter, the emergence of any other.

In the best of worlds, to close our analogy with British police practice, the nuclear weapons that were retained in the possession of the United Nations would also not be brandished, but held in a sort of escrow reserve. But what would be crucial, just as in the case of the British police, is that any "race" to deploy weapons could be won handily by the forces of law and order, rather than by their criminal rivals, that is, that the nuclear arsenal under U.N. auspices be timely enough, and awesome enough, to deter any future Hitlers and Saddam Husseins from acquiring nuclear weapons of their own.

Under such circumstances, the temptations of nuclear cheating, and the rumors that another state was cheating, might possibly abate. Under such circumstances, a desirable prospect noted earlier above might be reinforced, that the world might largely "forget" about inherent nuclear threats.

Some of the analysts advocating such an international monopoly of nuclear weapons, as an alternative to a (lamentably unattainable) total nuclear disarmament, refer back to how the Baruch Plan might realistically have worked. If the latent possibility that nuclear weapons might be produced and used always has to hang over the world, then the solution might have to be a single nuclear force more or less in being, one that would be used to punish any renegade trying to acquire such a force for himself.

What Might have Been

Yet it would then be very easy, from this perspective on what is possible in the world, to cycle back to a more positive interpretation of preventive war as Bertrand Russell or Winston Churchill or any of its other advocates envisioned it.

What would the United States, employing nuclear weapons, have done with a world it had conquered, except to democratize it as Japan and Germany had been democratized, and then to allow this world to prosper? Once the Baruch Plan had been imposed, rather than merely proposed, would the world not have reached, some four decades earlier, the happier situation envisaged by this third view of what may be possible?

The argument of this book is that American morality and altruism, the altruism that explains the Marshall Plan and the assistance Germany and Japan received after being defeated in World War II, also explains the rejection of preventive war against the USSR, explains more of this puzzle than any of the other arguments. It is not such a great stretch then to ask what such a United States would have done if it had been able to overcome these moral feelings, what it would have done in the peace terms it would have imposed on Stalin's Russia. The best guess is that the Russians would have benefited, and the world would have benefited.

Indeed, if anyone dreams of the United Nations one day taking charge of nuclear weapons, this is what would probably have become of the American nuclear monopoly, if only it could have been maintained.

The loops of logic and paradox are thus complicated here. The spread of democracy *may* make nuclear weapons unimportant, and thus in retrospect may make preventive war unnecessary. The existence of democracy in the United States may explain the absence of preventive war, thus reinforcing our expectations for what democracy will do to the foreign and military policies of other countries.

But that same tone of democracy might have eased much of any concern about the purposes of a preventive war in 1947. The inmates of the Soviet gulags would indeed have welcomed a more aggressive American foreign policy in the years before 1949, and many an ordinary Russian might also have done so, certainly *if* American *threats* of nuclear action had sufficed to head off the full-blown Cold War, and had sufficed to topple the Soviet regime this much earlier.

And certainly another source of lament for the "missed opportunity" of the American nuclear monopoly would come from any victims of nuclear attack after this book is published. If the world goes another fifty years without nuclear weapons being used, and then another fifty, the case for having headed off nuclear proliferation before 1949 will seem very weak indeed. But if the nuclear genie, for all the reasons cited, can *not* be pushed back into the bottle, and if mutual deterrence and the taboo against using nuclear weapons do not survive, the retrospective case will look much stronger.

The options of the next century will never be what they were in 1946 and 1947; this earlier period is thus relevant not for identifying any future military options, but for the clues it offers about how political decisions were made. This in the end is a book about moral intuitions as much as about cool-headed strategy. The moral intuitions that so typically stopped all American consideration of preventive war may now be the world's best hope, but only if these intuitions are indeed part-and-parcel of democratic government, and if they indeed spread, and spread.

Notes

Chapter 1: Introduction

1. For the variety of United States explanations for the Strategic Defense Initiative, see Donald R. Baucom, *The Origins of SDI* (Lawrence: University Press of Kansas, 1992).
2. Such Soviet responses are expressed in Dmitri Mikheev, *The Soviet Perspective on the Strategic Defense Initiative* (Washington, DC: Pergamon-Brassey's, 1987).
3. An illustration can be found in Pierre Gallois, *The Balance of Terror* (Boston: Houghton Mifflin, 1961).
4. For good examples, see Michael Mazarr and Alexander T. Lennon (eds.) *Toward a Nuclear Peace* (New York: St. Martin's Press, 1994), and Joseph Rotblat, Jack Steinberger, and Bhalchandra Udgaonkar (eds.), *A Nuclear Weapons-Free World: Desirable?, Feasible?* (Boulder, CO: Westview, 1993).
5. On Bertrand Russell's advocacy of preventive war, see Barry Feinberg, *Bertrand Russell's America* (New York: Viking Press, 1974).
6. Hans Morgenthau, *Politics Among Nations* (New York: Alfred A. Knopf, 1967).
7. Kenneth Waltz, *Theory of International Politics* (Reading, MA: Addison-Wesley, 1979).
8. The definitive example here is, of course, V. I. Lenin, *Imperialism* (New York: Vanguard Press, 1926).
9. For good examples of such a "liberal" analysis, see Philip Quigg, *America the Dutiful* (New York: Simon and Schuster, 1971) and David Louis Cingranelli, *Ethics, American Foreign Policy and the Third World* (New York: St. Martin's, 1993).
10. On the Akhramayov suicide, and related issues of Soviet/Russian command and control, see Stephen M. Meyer, "How the Threat (and the Coup) Collapsed," *International Security* Vol. 16 No. 3 (Winter 1991-1992), pp. 5-38.
11. The difficult negotiations with Ukraine and the other successor states about the return of nuclear warheads are outlined in Roy Allison, *Military Forces in the Soviet Successor States* (London: IISS Adelphi Papers No. 280, 1993).

12. On the general problems of accounting for formerly Soviet nuclear materials and nuclear expertise, see Bruce Blair, *The Logic of Accidental Nuclear War* (Washington, DC: Brookings, 1993).

13. The difficulties of determining North Korean nuclear intentions are discussed in Michael M. Mazarr, *North Korea and the Bomb* (New York: St. Martin's Press, 1995).

14. Gar Alperovitz, *Atomic Diplomacy* (New York: Vintage, 1965) and Gregg Herken, *The Winning Weapon* (New York: Alfred A. Knopf, 1980).

15. Adam Ulam, *Dangerous Relations* (New York: Oxford University Press, 1983), p. 12. For a very nuanced and informed retrospective overview, see John Lewis Gaddis, *We Now Know* (Oxford: Clarendon Press, 1997).

Chapter 2: The Option Specified

1. The text of the Truman announcement can be found in the *New York Times* (August 7, 1945), p. 1.

2. On the concern about keeping the atomic bomb secret from the Soviets, see Richard Rhodes, *Dark Sun* (New York: Simon and Schuster, 1995), pp. 128-131.

3. On Soviet nuclear espionage, see H. M. Hyde, *The Atom Bomb Spies* (New York: Ballantine, 1981).

4. On the Hyde Park Aide-Memoire, see Margaret Gowing, *Britain and Atomic Energy* (London: Macmillan, 1964), pp. 341-347.

5. Henry Dewolf Smyth, *Atomic Energy for Military Purposes* (Princeton, NJ: Princeton University Press, 1946).

6. On the deliberations about the McMahon Act, see Robert Gilpin, *American Scientists and Nuclear Weapons Policy* (Princeton, NJ: Princeton University Press, 1962), and Thomas Morgan, *Atomic Energy and Congress* (Ann Arbor: University of Michigan Press, 1956).

7. The responses to the Indian 1974 detonation are analyzed in Michael J. Brenner, *Nuclear Power and Non-Proliferation* (New York: Cambridge University Press, 1981).

8. On the hopes of purchasing the bulk of the world's uranium, see Jonathan Helmreich, *Gathering Rare Ores* (Princeton, NJ: Princeton University Press, 1986).

9. Thomas C. Schelling, *Arms and Influence* (New Haven, CT: Yale University Press, 1966), pp. 69-92.

10. On the choices faced by President Bush on Iraq, see William J. Perry, "Desert Storm and Deterrence," *Foreign Affairs* Vol. 70, No. 4 (Fall, 1991), pp. 66-82.

11. The evolution of the Baruch Plan is outlined in Larry G. Gerber, "The Baruch Plan and the Emergence of the Cold War," *Diplomatic History* Vol. 6, No. 1 (Spring, 1982), pp. 69-95.

12. The broader concept of preventive war is discussed in Richard Betts, *Surprise Attack* (Washington, DC: Brookings, 1982), pp. 145-146.

13. For a prominent example of such an argument, see Robert S. McNamara, "The Military Role of Nuclear Weapons," *Foreign Affairs* Vol. 62, No. 1 (Fall, 1983), pp. 57-80.
14. On the alleged naivete of any attempt to hold back the "secret" of making nuclear weapons, see Gregg Herken, *The Winning Weapon* (New York: Alfred A. Knopf, 1980), chapter 5.
15. On the dismantling of these Japanese nuclear laboratories, see *The New York Times* (December 1, 1945), p. 5.

Chapter 3: The Option in Perspective

1. Thomas Hobbes, *Leviathan* (New York: E.P. Dutton Edition, 1950) especially chapters XIII-XV.
2. Karl Von Clausewitz, *On War* (Princeton, NJ: Princeton University Press translation, 1984).
3. Alfred Thayer Mahan, *The Influence of Seapower Upon History* (Boston: Little Brown, 1890).
4. Giulio Douhet, *The Command of the Air* (New York: Coward-McCann, 1942).
5. On the political accomplishments of the Roman Empire, see Peter Arnott, *The Romans and Their World* (New York: Macmillan, 1970).
6. F. J. Hinsley, *Power and the Pursuit of Peace* (New York: Cambridge University Press, 1963).
7. Bernard Semmel, *Liberalism and Naval Strategy* (Boston: Allen and Unwin, 1986).
8. See Paul Kennedy, *The Rise and Fall of British Naval Power* (New York: Charles Scribner's Sons, 1976).
9. See Jonathan Steinberg, *Yesterday's Deterrent: Tirpitz and the Birth of the German Battle Fleet* (New York: Macmillan, 1965).
10. For arguments that Germany wanted war in 1914, see Luigi Albertini, *The Origins of the War of 1914* (London: Oxford University Press, 1952).
11. For parallel arguments more blaming the Entente powers for wanting a war in 1914, see Berndadotte Schmitt, *The Coming of the War: 1914* (New York: Charles Scribner's Sons, 1930).
12. Such a "no-fault" explanation for the outbreak of World War I might be found in Ludwig Reiners, *The Lamps Went Out in Europe* (New York: Pantheon, 1955).
13. Bernard Brodie (ed.), *The Absolute Weapon* (New York: Harcourt Brace, 1946).
14. On Pilsudski's calculations here, see Richard M. Watt, *Bitter Glory* (New York: Simon and Schuster, 1979), pp. 321-323.
15. The assassination issue is discussed in Harris Lentz, *Assassinations and Executions: An Encyclopedia of Political Violence* (Jefferson, NC: McFarland, 1988).
16. On the American self-image here, see James M. McCormick, *American Foreign Policy and American Values* (Itasca, IL: F. E. Peacock Publishers, 1985).

17. The motivations of the people working on the Manhattan Project are outlined in McGeorge Bundy, *Danger and Survival* (New York: Random House, 1988), chapter 1.

18. The German nuclear effort is described in David Irving, *The German Atomic Bomb* (New York: Simon and Schuster, 1968), Mark Walker, *Nazi Science* (New York: Plenum Press, 1991), Samuel Goudsmit, *Alsos* (New York: A. Schuman, 1947) and Alan Beyerschin *Scientists Under Hitler* (New Haven, CT: Yale University Press, 1977).

19. George F. Kennan ("X"), "The Sources of Soviet Conduct," *Foreign Affairs* Vol. 25, No. 4 (July, 1947), pp. 566-582.

20. On the overall dimensions of Stalin and his regime, see Adam B. Ulam, *Stalin: the Man and His Era* (New York: Viking, 1973).

21. Kennan's views on nuclear sharing are outlined in *Foreign Relations of the United States* Vol. 5 (Washington, DC: U.S. Government Printing Office, 1946), pp. 885-886.

22. On Churchill's views on preventive war, see Lord Moran, *Winston Churchill: The Struggle for Survival* (London: Constable, 1960), p. 315.

23. See David Holloway, *Stalin and the Bomb* (New Haven, CT: Yale University Press, 1994), pp. 61, 88.

Chapter 4: Outright Advocates

1. On the musings of Bertrand Russell on a preventive war against Stalin's Soviet Union, see Ronald William Clark, *The Life of Bertrand Russell* (London: Jonathan Cape, 1975), Barry Feinberg, *Bertrand Russell's America* (New York: Viking, 1974), and Irving Louis Horowitz, *The Idea of War and Peace in Contemporary Philosophy* (New York: Paine-Whitman, 1957), chapter VI.

2. The latter-day image of Russell is exemplified in Peter Limqueco, *Prevent the Crime of Silence* (Stockholm: International War Crimes Tribunal, 1969). See also Norman Moss, *Men Who Play God* (New York: Harper and Row, 1968), pp. 165-168.

3. Quoted in Clark, *op. cit.* p. 518.

4. Ibid. pp. 527-530.

5. On his more general role, see Leo Szilard, *Leo Szilard: His Version of the Facts* (Cambridge, MA: MIT Press, 1962).

6. Brodie's comments on Szilard are noted in Marc Trachtenberg, "A Wasting Asset: American Strategy and the Shifting Nuclear Balance 1949-1954," *International Security* Vol. 13, No. 3 (Winter 1988-1989), p. 8.

7. On the pre-Hiroshima Groves fears about Soviet espionage, see Michael Amrine, *The Great Decision* (New York: G.P. Putnam, 1959), p. 234.

8. Grove's musings about positive action to head off Soviet nuclear weapons acquisition are noted in Gregg Herken, *The Winning Weapon* (New York: Alfred A. Knopf, 1980), pp. 112-117.

9. See Thomas Powers, *Heisenberg's War* (New York: Alfred A. Knopf, 1993), pp. 209-211.

10. On the bombing of Oranienberg, see Richard Rhodes, *Dark Sun* (New York: Simon and Schuster, 1995), pp. 155-156.

11. The Groves quote is cited in Marc Trachtenberg, *op. cit.* p. 5.

12. On the typical estimates of how long it would take for Stalin's USSR to produce an atomic bomb, see William Poundstone, *Prisoner's Dilemma* (New York: Doubleday, 1993), p. 134.

13. General Anderson's public and private endorsements of preventive war can be found in O.A. Anderson clipping file, Air University Library, Maxwell Air Force Base, Montgomery, Alabama. For a favorable commentary, see Nathan F. Twining, *Neither Liberty Nor Safety* (New York: Holt, Rinehart and Winston, 1960), pp. 18-19. See also Russell D. Bushire and William Christopher Hamel, "War for Peace: The Question of American Preventive War Against the Soviet Union," *Diplomatic History* Vol. 14 No. 3 (Summer, 1990), pp. 367-389.

14. On this point, see Air War College lecture by General Anderson on September 26, 1950, Air University Library, Maxwell Air Force Base, Montgomery, Alabama.

15. *The New York Times* (September 2, 1950), p. 8.

16. Golden cited in Poundstone, *op.cit.*, pp. 135-136.

17. A very readable account of Von Neuman's career is presented in Poundstone, *op. cit.*,

18. On this more traditional "war-fighting" emphasis, see Robert Jervis, *The Illogic of American Nuclear Strategy* (Ithaca, NY: Cornell University Press, 1984).

19. On the broader RAND involvement, see Marc Trachtenberg, *op. cit.*, pp. 8-9.

20. Norstad's role here is discussed in Richard Rhodes, *Dark Sun* (New York: Simon and Schuster, 1995), pp. 224-226.

21. Ibid., p.226.

22. Ibid. pp. 269-271.

23. The Churchill Fulton, Missouri speech, and the reaction it drew, are described in Fraser Harbutt, *The Iron Curtain: Churchill, America, and the Origins of the Cold War* (New York: Oxford University Press, 1986).

24. Speech of Winston Churchill, New York City, March, 25, 1949, reprinted in *Winston Churchill: His Complete Speeches* Vol. VII (New York: Bowker, 1974), pp. 7795-7801.

25. Speech of March 1, 1955, *Winston Churchill: His Complete Speeches* Vol. VIII (New York: Bowker,1979), pp. 8625-8633.

26. Speech of January 23, 1948 cited in *House of Commons Debates* 1948 p. 561.

27. Churchill's Llandudno speech of October 9, 1948 is cited in *The New York Times* (October 10, 1948), p. 4.

28. For a commentary on LeMay, see Thomas Coffey, *Iron Eagle: The Turbulent Life of General Curtis LeMay* (New York: Crown, 1986).

29. For discussion of LeMay's accomplishments, see Samuel Huntington, *The Common Defense* (New York: Columbia University Press, 1961), pp. 308-312.

30. On the pre-U-2 overflights, see Rhodes, *op.cit.* pp. 564-567.

81. Such comments are noted in Richard Betts, *Nuclear Blackmail and Nuclear Balance* (Washington, DC: Brookings, 1987), pp. 161-163.

82. Bernard Brodie (ed.), *The Absolute Weapon* (New York: Harcourt Brace, 1946).

83. William B. Borden, *There Will Be No Time* (New York: Macmillan 1946).

84. Ibid., pp. 224-225.

85. On the Oppenheimer case, and Borden's role in it, see Joseph Alsop and Stewart Alsop, *We accuse! The Story of the Miscarriage of American Justice in the Case of J. Robert Oppenheimer* (New York: Simon and Schuster, 1954).

86. The NSC-68 recommendations are discussed in Samuel F. Wells, "Sounding the Tocsin: NSC-68 and the Soviet Threat," *International Security* Vol. 4, No. 2 (Fall, 1979), pp. 116-138.

37. The Matthews speech, and the uproar it caused, are discussed in Poundstone, *op. cit.* pp. 145-155.

38. See, again, Bernard Semmel, *Liberalism and Naval Strategy* (Boston: Allen and Unwin, 1986).

39. Some of the important distinctions here are elaborated in Robert Jervis, *The Meaning of the Nuclear Revolution* (Ithaca, NY: Cornell University Press, 1989).

Chapter 5: Arguments Against: Practical Considerations

1. The small numbers of nuclear weapons produced, and the secrecy about such numbers, are analyzed in David Rosenberg, "U.S. Nuclear Stockpile, 1945 to 1950," *Bulletin of the Atomic Scientists* Vol. 38, No. 5 (May, 1982), pp. 25-30.

2. See Gregg Herken, *The Winning Weapon* (New York: Alfred A. Knopf, 1980), p. 21.

3. A total absence of bombs ready for use is suggested in Richard C. Hewlett and Oscar E. Anderson, *The New World 1939-1946* (University Park: Pennsylvania State University Press, 1962), pp. 624-632.

4. On how closely-held the bomb numbers were, see David E. Lilienthal, *The Atomic Energy Years* (New York: Harper and Row, 1965), pp. 119-120, and Harry S. Truman, *Years of Trial and Hope* (Garden City: Doubleday, 1965), p. 302.

5. The pessimistic, and optimistic, assumptions about a global shortage of uranium are discussed in Jonathan Helmreich, *Gathering Rare Ores* (Princeton, NJ: Princeton University Press, 1980).

6. This summary point is made in Hewlett and Anderson, *op. cit.,* p. 173.

7. See Rosenberg, *op. cit.*

8. For an overall account of this Soviet espionage, see Ronald Radosh and Joyce Milton, *The Rosenberg File* (New York: Vintage Books, 1984).

9. See Richard Rhodes, *Dark Sun* (New York: Simon and Schuster, 1995), especially chapter 3.

10. David Holloway, *Stalin and the Bomb* (New Haven, CT: Yale University Press, 1994), p. 115.

11. The United States Strategic Bombing Survey is analyzed in David MacIsaac, *Strategic Bombing in World War II: The Story of the United States Strategic Bombing Survey* (New York: Garland, 1976).

12. For conflicting interpretations of the Japanese surrender, see Lester Brooks, *Behind Japan's Surrender* (New York: McGraw-Hill, 1967), Robert Butow, *Japan's Decision to Surrender* (Stanford, CA: Stanford University Press, 1954) and Herbert Feis, *Japan Subdued* (Princeton, NJ: Princeton University Press).

13. Truman's arguments on casualties avoided including Japanese casualties are discussed in John Ray Skates, *The Invasion of Japan: Alternative to the Bomb* (Columbia: University of South Carolina Press, 1994), pp. 76-77.

14. A very nuanced and multi-faceted analysis of Vietnam is to be found in Mark Clodfelter, *The Limits of Air Power* (New York: Free Press, 1989).

15. Examples of this kind of Japanese statement can be found in Laura Hein and Mark Selden (eds.), *Living With the Bomb* (Armonk, New York: M.E.Sharpe, 1997).

16. On the variations in USAAF approaches to targeting Germany, see Wesley Craven and H. L. Cate, *The Army Air Force in World War II*, Vols. II and III (Chicago: University of Chicago Press, 1949, 1951).

17. On the RAF logic here, see Charles Webster and Noble Frankland, *The Strategic Air Offensive Against Germany* (London: H.M.S.O., 1961) Vol. III.

18. Such American disquiet about the RAF approach is noted in Craven and Cate, *op. cit.* Vol. III, pp. 638, 725-727.

19. The USAAF shift to area counter-value attacks on Japan is described in Wesley Craven and J. L. Cate, *The Army Air Force in World War II*, Vol. V (Chicago: University of Chicago Press, 1953), pp. 669-674.

20. For projections of callousness on to Stalin, see Richard Pipes, *Russia Under the Bolshevik Regime* (New York: Charles Scribner's Sons, 1974).

21. On Hitler's unwillingness, as compared with Goebbels, to tour bombed German cities, see Helmut Heiber, *Goebbels* (New York: Hawthorn Books, 1972), pp. 298-300.

22. For an example, Richard Pipes, "Why the Soviet Union Thinks It Could Fight and Win a Nuclear War," *Commentary* Vol. 64, No. 1 (July, 1977), pp. 21-34.

23. See Richard B. Foster, "On Prolonged Nuclear war," *International Security Review* Vol. 6, No 4 (Winter 1981-82), pp. 497-518.

24. This author's longer argument on the inherent ability of a totalitarian dictator to hide his real beliefs about something like the power of nuclear

weapons can be found in George Quester, "On the Identification of Real and Pretended Communist Military Doctrine," *Journal of Conflict Resolution* Vol. X, No. 2 (June, 1966), pp. 172-179.

25   On the official pronouncements of the Soviet Union about nuclear strategy, see Herbert Dinerstein, *War and the Soviet Union* (New York: Praeger, 1962) and Raymond Garthoff, *Soviet Military Doctrine* (Glenco, IL: Free Press, 1953).

26.   See David Holloway, *Stalin and the Bomb* (New Haven, CT: Yale University Press, 1994), pp. 116-118, and Richard Rhodes, *The Making of the Atomic Bomb* (New York: Simon and Schuster, 1988), pp. 682-693.

27.   Holloway, *op. cit.* pp. 127-129.

28.   On the capabilities, and difficulties, of U.S targeting intelligence, see David A. Rosenberg, "The Origins of Overkill," *International Security* Vol. 7, No. 4 (Spring, 1983), pp. 15-23.

29.   This overall cast of U.S. Air Force thinking is outlined in Robert Jervis, *The Illogic of American Nuclear Strategy* (Ithaca, NY: Cornell University Press, 1984).

30.   On the limits of U.S. intelligence on Soviet fissionable material sources, see John Prados, *The Soviet Estimate* (New York: Dial Press, 1982), pp. 19-23.

31.   Thomas Powers, *Heisenberg's War* (New York: Alfred A. Knopf, 1993), pp. 209-213, 338-339.

32.   On the public reactions to the Bikini tests, see Lloyd J. Graybar, "Bikini Revisited," *Military Affairs* Vol. 4, No. 3 (October, 1980), pp. 118-123

33.   The impact of the first H-bomb test is described in James R. Shepley and Clay B. Blair, *The Hydrogen Bomb* (New York: David McKay, 1954).

34.   On the actual sequence of who "won" the race to possess H-bombs, see Norman Moss, *Men Who Play God* (New York: Harper and Row, 1968), pp. 62-63.

35.   The debate on whether it was wise, or necessary, to move ahead to thermonuclear weapons is broken out in David Alan Rosenberg, "American Atomic Strategy and the Hydrogen Bomb Decision," *Journal of American History* Vol. 66, No. 1 (June, 1979), pp. 62-88.

36.   See Richard Rhodes, *Dark Sun,* pp. 557-588.

37.   On the crucial role here of the vulnerability of Western Europe to Soviet conventional attack, see Fen Osler Hampson, "Groping for Technical Panaceas: The European Conventional Balance and Nuclear Stability," *International Security* Vol. 8, No. 3 (Winter 1983-1984), pp. 57-82.

38.   The American 1945 demobilization is described in Jack Stokes Ballard, *The Shock of Peace* (Washington, DC: University Press of America, 1983).

39.   See Harry R. Borowski, *A Hollow Threat* (Westport, CT: Greenwood Press, 1982), and Stephen M. Millet, "The Capabilities of the American Nuclear Deterrent: 1945-1950," *Aerospace Historian* Vol. 27, No. 1 Spring, 1980), pp. 27-32.

40. For an example of such an analysis, Matthew Evangelista, "Stalin's Postwar Army Reappraised," *International Security* Vol. 7, No. 3 (Winter, 1982-1983), pp. 110-138.

41. Robert S. McNamara, "The Military Role of Nuclear Weapons," *Foreign Affairs* Vol. 62, No. 1 (Fall, 1983), pp. 59-80.

42. On the anticipations of the missile gap, see James Gavin, *War and Peace in the Space Age* (New York: Harpers, 1958), John Medaris, *Countdown for Decision* (New York: Putnam, 1960) and Maxwell Taylor, *The Uncertain Trumpet* (New York: Harper, 1960).

43. On the logic of the Soviet Cuban Missile deployment, see Arnold F. Horelick and Myron Rush, *Strategic Power and Soviet Foreign Policy* (Chicago, University of Chicago Press, 1966).

44. The evolution of USAF bomber capabilities is spelled out in Michael Brown, *Flying Blind* (Ithaca, NY: Cornell University Press, 1992).

45. On the history of these bases, see Simon Duke, *U.S. Defense Bases in the United Kingdom* (London: Macmillan, 1987).

46. A most comprehensive coverage of these interactions can be found in Margaret Gowing, *Britain and Atomic Energy 1939-1945* (New York: St. Martin's Press, 1964) and *Independence and Deterrence* (New York: St. Martin's Press, 1974).

47. The McMahon statement is cited in Gowing, *Independence and Deterrence*, pp. 107-108.

48. On the consultation about Hiroshima, see Rhodes, *Making of the Atomic Bomb*, p. 655.

49. On the wrapping up of the war-time agreements, see John Simpson, *The Independent Nuclear State* (New York: St. Martin's Press, 1983), especially chapter 2.

50. These 1940 events are recounted in Denis Richards, *Royal Air Force 1939-1945* (London: H.M.S.O., 1953) Vol. I, p. 146.

51. On these trends of 1945, see P.M.S. Blackett, *Fear, War and the Bomb* (New York: McGraw-Hill, 1948), pp. 55-60, and Vannevar Bush, *Modern Arms and Free Men* (New York: Simon and Schuster, 1949), pp. 48-112.

52. The Korean air war is detailed in Robert F. Futrell, *The United States Air Force in Korea: 1950-1953* (Washington, DC: New York: Duell, Sloan and Pierce, 1961).

53. For details on the Hiroshima and Nagasaki attacks, see Robert Trumbull, *Nine Who Survived Hiroshima and Nagasaki* (New York: Dutton, 1957).

54. General Anderson argues this point very specifically in his Air War College lecture of September 26, 1950 (Air University Library, Maxwell Air Force Base, Montgomery, Alabama). See also his lecture of May 18, 1948.

55. This much-quoted statement of Baldwin can be found in *House of Commons Debates,* (Nov 10, 1932) cols. 631-638.

56. On the general American aversion to governing others against their will, see Philip S. Foner and Richard Winchester (eds.), *The Anti-Imperialist Reader* (New York: Holmes and Meier, 1984).

57. See John D. Montgomery, *Forced to be Free* (Chicago: University of Chicago Press, 1957).
58. The surprisingly liberal and nuanced record of MacArthur in Japan is recounted in William Manchester, *American Caesar* (Boston: Little Brown, 1978).

Chapter 6: Arguments Against: Procedural Questions

1.   For the wording of the Molotov speech, see David Holloway, *Stalin and the Bomb* (New Haven, CT: Yale University Press, 1994), p. 258.
2.   The actual process of the detection is described in Charles J.V. Murphy "The Hidden Struggle for the H-Bomb" *Fortune* Vol. X., No. 5 (My, 1953), p. 17, and James R. Shepley and Clay Blair, *The Hydrogen Bomb* (New York: David McKay, 1954), pp. 3-5.
3.   See Holloway, *Stalin and the Bomb,* chapter 10.
4.   On Iraq, see Ronald J. Bee, *Nuclear Proliferation: The Post-Cold War Challenge* (New York: Foreign Policy Association, 1995). On North Korea, Leon Sigal, *Disarming Strangers: Nuclear Diplomacy with North Korea* (Princeton, NJ: Princeton University Press, 1998).
5.   A picture of American smugness is in effect presented by Gregg Herken, *The Winning Weapon* (New York: Alfred A. Knopf, 1980), pp. 231-233.
6.   Truman quotation cited in Noell Pharr Davis, *Lawrence and Oppenheimer* (New York: Simon and Schuster, 1968), p. 260.
7.   Truman statements cited in Shepley and Blair, *op. cit.*, p. 18.
8.   See Samuel Goudsmit, *Alsos* (New York: A. Schuman, 1947).
9.   Bernard Brodie (ed.) *The Absolute Weapon*, pp. 72, 77, 84, 87.
10. On the assumptions of General Groves about uranium shortage, see Leslie Groves, *Now It Can Be Told* (New York: DaCapo, 1962), p. 176.
11. On the INFCE search for a way out of the bind caused by dual-use nuclear technology, see William C. Potter, *Nuclear Power and Nonproliferation* (Cambridge, MA: Oelgeschlager, Gunn and Hain, 1982), pp. 50-53.
12. On these estimates, John Prados, *The Soviet Estimate* (New York: Dial Press, 1982), chapter 2.
13. The on-going nuclear proliferation concern is analyzed in Leonard Spector, *Going Nuclear* (Cambridge, MA: Ballinger, 1987).
14. Capturing many of the concerns here was Albert Wohlstetter, "The Delicate Balance of Terror," *Foreign Affairs* Vol. 37, No. 2, (January, 1959), pp. 211-234.
15. For examples of such retrospective enthusiasm, see Marc Trachtenberg, "A Wasting Asset: American Strategy and the Shifting Nuclear Balance, 1949-1954," *International Security* Vol. 13, No. 3 (Winter 1988/1989), especially pp. 32-44.
16. Richard Betts, *Surprise Attack* (Washington, DC: Brookings, 1982).
17. Roberta Wohlstetter, *Pearl Harbor: Warning and Decision* (Stanford, CA: Stanford University Press, 1962).

18. On this point see Richard Ned Lebow, "Windows of Opportunity: Do States Jump Through Them?," *International Security* Vol. 9, No. 1 (Summer, 1984), pp. 147-180.

19. A valuable account is presented by Herbert Feis, *The Road to Pearl Harbor* (Princeton, NJ: Princeton University Press, 1950).

20. See Barton Whaley, *Operation Barbarossa* (Cambridge: MIT Press, 1973).

21. For evidence that Stalin planned to attack Hitler, see Edvard Radzinsky, *Stalin* (New York: Doubleday, 1996), pp. 452-456.

22. See William Langer and S. Everett Gleason, *The Undeclared War* (New York: Harper, 1953).

23. The nuclear factor in Roosevelt's actions before Pearl Harbor is discussed in Vannevar Bush, *Pieces of the Action* (New York: William Murrow, 1970).

24. Roosevelt's momentous commitment to the Manhattan Project is described in Richard G. Hewlett and Oscar E. Anderson, *The New World* (University Park: Pennsylvania State University Press, 1962).

25. On these issues, Richard Rhodes, *Dark Sun* chapters 1-10 and David Holloway, *Stalin and the Bomb*, chapters 6-10.

26. On the Bangla Desh liberation, see Richard Sisson and Leo Rose, *War and Secession* (Berkeley: University of California Press, 1990).

27. An inside account can be found in Bob Woodward, *The Commanders* (New York: Simon and Schuster, 1991).

28. On the interactions of Hitler and generals, see John Wheeler-Bennett, *The Nemesis of Power* (New York: St. Martin's, 1954).

29. Such theories of "bureaucratic politics" can be found in Graham Allison, *Essence of Decision* (Boston: Little Brown, 1971) and Morton Halperin, *Bureaucratic Politics and Foreign Policy* (Washington, DC: Brookings, 1974).

30. On the competing demands of preparations for alternative kinds of warfare here, see Glenn Snyder, *Deterrence and Defense* (Princeton, NJ: Princeton University press, 1961).

31. On such skepticism, see William W. Kaufmann (ed.), *Military Policy and National Security* (Princeton, NJ: Princeton University Press, 1956).

32. Pastoral Letter on *The Challenge of Peace: God's Promise and our Response* (Washington, DC: National Conference of Catholic Bishops, 1983).

33. On the justifications offered for the Allied blockade of Germany in World War I, see C. Paul Vincent, *The Politics of Hunger* (Athens: Ohio University Press, 1985).

34. The rationales for bombings or submarine warfare and blockades are discussed in Jeffrey Legro, *Cooperation Under Fire* (Ithaca, NY: Cornell University Press, 1995).

35. On the bombing of North Korea, see Robert F. Futrell, *The United States Air Force in Korea: 1950-1953* (New York: Duell, Sloan and Pearce, 1961).

36. The logic and effectiveness of bombings of North Vietnam are outlined in Robert Pape, *Bombing to Win* (Ithaca, NY: Cornell University Press, 1996).

37. See Robert Jervis, *The Illogic of American Nuclear Strategy* (Ithaca, NY: Cornell University Press, 1984).

38. See Colin Gray, *Nuclear Strategy and National Style* (Lanham, Maryland: Hamilton Press, 1980).

39. Such an argument about there being no cause for war is in effect presented by Richard Barnet and Marcus Raskin, *After Twenty Years* (New York: Random House, 1965).

40. Poll figures from Hadley Cantril, *Public Opinion 1935-1946* (Princeton, NJ: Princeton University Press, 1951), pp. 370-371, and "The Quarter's Polls," *Public Opinion Quarterly* Vol 13 No. 3 (Fall, 1949), p. 550.

41. Details on the interaction of German submarines and U.S. destroyers in the months before Pearl Harbor can be found in Langer and Gleason, *op. cit.*.

42. On these events, see Barry M. Blechman and Douglas M. Hart, "Afghanistan and the 1946 Iran Analogy," *Survival* Vol. 22 No. 6 (November/December, 1980), pp. 248-257.

43. The sequence of events in the 1946 Iran crisis is outlined in George Lenczowksi, *American Presidents and the Middle East* (Durham, North Carolina: Duke University press, 1990) and Bruce Kuniholm, *The Origins of the Cold War in the Middle East* (Princeton, NJ: Princeton University Press, 1980).

44. See C. P. Skrine, *World War in Iran* (London: Constable, 1962).

45. The pace of the Soviet seizure of political control in Eastern Europe is reviewed in Thomas I. Hammond (ed.) *The Anatomy of Communist Takeovers* (New Haven, CT: Yale University Press, 1975).

46. On the Communist take-over in Czechoslovakia, see Karel Kaplan, *The Short March* (New York: St. Martin's Press, 1987).

47. The Japanese expectations and grand strategy here are discussed in Edwin P. Hoyt, *Japan's War* (New York: McGraw-Hill, 1986).

48. For an example of a skepticism about the relevance of the Iran example, see Richard Betts, *Nuclear Blackmail and Nuclear Balance* (Washington, DC: Brookings, 1987), pp. 7-8.

49. The Berlin episode is dissected in W. Philips Davidson, *The Berlin Blockade* (Princeton, NJ: Princeton University Press, 1958).

50. Betts, *Nuclear Blackmail and Nuclear Balance*, pp. 23-31.

51. On the accusations of influence of Communists in Hollywood, see Bernard Dick, *Radical Innocence* (Lexington: University Press of Kentucky, 1989).

52. The general American mood about world affairs after 1945 is discussed in Stephen E. Ambrose, *Rise to Globalism* (New York: Penguin Books, 1971).

53. For an illustration of American interpretation of the bulk of Germans as Nazis, see John H. Waller, *The Unseen War in Europe* (New York: Random House, 1996), pp. 311-312.

54. American World War II attitudes about the Japanese people as a whole are discussed in John W. Dower, *War Without Mercy* (New York: Pantheon, 1986).

55. On the premises for the bombing of Dresden, see David Irving, *The Destruction of Dresden* (New York: Holt, Rinehart and Winston, 1964).

56. On these basic distinctions of nuclear strategy, a most useful analysis is again that of Glenn Snyder, *op. cit.*

57. For a possible exception, see Richard Pipes, *Russia Observed* (Boulder, CO: Westview, 1989).

58. On such speculation about ethnic targeting, see Richard B. Foster, *The Soviet Concept of National Entity Survival* (Arlington, VA: SRI International, 1978).

59. For examples of such an argument for finite deterrence, see Michael Mazarr and Alexander T. Lennon (eds.) *Toward a Nuclear Peace* (New York: St. Martin's Press, 1994).

60. The American memories of the League of Nations are reviewed in Eric Nordlinger, *Isolationism Reconfigured* (Princeton, NJ: Princeton University Press, 1995).

61. The basic logic of collective security is outlined in Inis Claude, *Power and International Relations* (New York: Random House, 1962).

62. Karl Von Clausewitz, *On War* (Princeton, NJ: Princeton University Press translation, 1984), p. 370.

63. See Richard Betts, "Collective Security, Arms Control and the New Europe," *International Security* Vol. 17, No. 1 (Summer, 1992), pp. 5-43.

64. The view that George Bush had finally activated the mechanism that was meant to work through the League of Nations and the United Nations is presented in the introductory chapter of T.V. Paul, Richard Harknett and James J. Wirtz (eds.), *The Absolute Weapon Revisited* (Ann Arbor: University of Michigan Press, 1998), pp. 1-18.

65. A valuable overview of these issues can be found in Cecil V. Crabb, *Invitation to Struggle* (Washington, DC: Congressional Quarterly Press, 1980).

66. On this aspect of the motivations for the McMahon Act, see Robert Gilpin, *American Scientists and Nuclear Weapons Policy* (Princeton, NJ: Princeton University Press, 1962).

67. The Congressional and American public reactions to the 1974 Indian detonation are discussed in Michael Brenner, *Nuclear Power and Non-Proliferation* (New York: Cambridge University Press, 1981).

68. On the JCAE aversions to sharing nuclear technology with France, see Lawrence Scheinman, *Atomic Energy Policy in France Under the Fourth Republic* (Princeton, NJ: Princeton University Press, 1965).

Chapter 7: American Morality

1. On the moral drives of American attitudes toward the world, see David Louis Cingranelli, *Ethics, American Foreign Policy and the Third World*

(New York: St. Martin's Press, 1993), and Robert Dallek, *The American Style of Foreign Policy* (New York: Alfred A. Knopf, 1983).

2.   For analyses debunking the role of American morality, see Gabriel Kolko, *Confronting the Third World* (New York: Pantheon, 1980), and Michael Parenti *The Sword and the Dollar* (New York: St. Martin's Press, 1989).

3.   *The New York Times* (August 5, 1966), p. 11, (August 6, 1966), p. 4.

4.   Bernard Brodie (ed.), *The Absolute Weapon* (New York: Harcourt Brace, 1946), William B. Borden, *There Will Be No Time* (New York: Macmillan, 1946).

5.   Brodie, *op.cit.* p. 72, Borden, *op.cit.* p. 223.

6.   Perry McCoy Smith, *The Air Force Plans for Peace* (Baltimore, MD: Johns Hopkins University Press, 1970).

7.   On the evolution of such involvements of extended nuclear deterrence, see Ivo Daalder, *The Nature and Practice of Flexible Response* (New York: Columbia University Press, 1991).

8.   Pierre Gallois, *The Balance of Terror* (Boston: Houghton Mifflin, 1961).

9.   See Michael Doyle, "Liberalism and World Politics," *American Political Science Review* Vol. 80, No. 4 (December, 1986), pp. 1151-1169, and Bruce Russett, *Grasping the Democratic Peace* (Princeton, NJ: Princeton University Press, 1993).

10.   Some good examples are Christopher Layne, "Kant or Cant: The Myth of the Democratic Peace," *International Security* Vol. 19, No. 2 (Fall, 1994), pp.5-49, and Edward D. Mansfield and Jack Snyder, "Democratization and the Danger of War," *International Security* Vol. 20, No. 1 (Summer, 1995), pp. 5-38.

Chapter 8: Preventive War After 1949?

1.   On these post-1949 speculations about a preventive war, see Anthony Cave Brown, *Dropshot: The American Plans for World War III with Russia in 1957* (New York: Dial Press, 1978, and Michael S. Sherry, *Preparing for the Next War* (New Haven, CT: Yale University Press, 1977), pp. 197-205.

2.   On the new media attention to nuclear attack scenarios, see Spencer Weart, *Nuclear Fear* (Cambridge, MA: Harvard University Press, 1988).

3.   The capabilities and limits of nuclear targeting intelligence are sorted out by John Prados, *The Soviet Estimate* (New York: Dial Press, 1982).

4.   On the reactions to Matthews and Anderson, see *The New York Times* (September 3, 1950), p. 8.

5.   The concepts here are elaborated by Morton Halperin, *Limited War in the Nuclear Age* (New York: Wiley, 1963).

6.   The arguments imputed to NSC-68 are discussed by Paul Y. Hammond in Warner Schilling, Paul Y. Hammond and Glenn Snyder, *Strategies, Politics and Defense Budgets* (New York: Columbia University Press, 1962), pp. 267-378.

7. The declassified text of NSC-68 was published in *Naval War College Review* Vol. 27, No. 6 (May/June, 1978), pp. 5-158.
8. See *The New York Times* (June 20, 1953), p. 1.
9. David Holloway, *Stalin and the Bomb* (New Haven, CT: Yale University Press, 1994), p. 218.
10. *Ibid.*, p. 267.
11. Richard Rhodes, *Dark Sun* (New York: Simon and Schuster, 1995), p. 353.

Chapter 9: Lessons, For the Future, and From the Future

1. For an example of such concerns, see Robert E. Osgood, *Limited War: The Challenge to American Strategy* (Chicago: University of Chicago Press, 1957).
2. A clear exposition of the importance of crisis stability can be found in Thomas C. Schelling and Morton Halperin, *Strategy and Arms Control* (New York: Twentieth-Century Fund, 1961).
3. For the McNamara testimony, see the *New York Times* (January 11, 1964), p. 1.
4. Oskar Morgenstern, *The Question of National Defense* (New York: Random House, 1958).
5. The assumption that the United States had passed the test so as to avoid any distrust is illustrated in Keith B. Payne, *Strategic Defense: "Star Wars" in Perspective* (Lanham, MD: Hamilton Press, 1985).
6. For an example from the 1980s, see Colin Gray, *Nuclear Strategy and National Style* (Lanham, MD: Hamilton Press, 1986).
7. Donald Brennan et. al., *Anti-Ballistic Missile, Yes or No?* (New York: Hill and Wang, 1968).
8. See Donald Brennan, "Commentary" *International Security* Vol. 3, No. 3 (Winter 1978-79), pp. 197-198.
9. The evolution of the nuclear proliferation problem is recounted in Leonard Beaton, *Must the Bomb Spread?* (Hammondsworth: Penguin Books, 1966).
10. Such alternative views of the Baruch Plan are outlined in McGeorge Bundy, *Danger and Survival* (New York: Random House, 1988), pp. 161-168.
11. Gregg Herken, *The Winning Weapon* (New York: Alfred A. Knopf, 1980) presents such a more skeptical view of the Plan.
12. On the supposed importance of the amendments here, see Larry Gerber, "The Baruch Plan and the Emergence of the Cold War," *Diplomatic History* Vol. 6, No. 1 (Spring, 1982), pp. 69-95.
13. On the veto issue, Richard G. Hewlett and Oscar E. Anderson, *The New World* (University Park: Pennsylvania State University Press, 1969), pp. 563-574.
14. For such an interpretation of this and many other Soviet proposals on arms reductions, see Joseph Nogee, *Soviet Policy Towards International*

Control of Atomic Energy (South Bend, IN: University of Notre Dame Press, 1961).

15. Stalin's domestic constraints here are discussed in John W. Spanier and Joseph Nogee, *The Politics of Disarmament* (New York: Praeger, 1962).

16. Dean Acheson's observations on this point are noted in Dean Acheson, *Present at the Creation* (New York: W.W. Norton, 1969), p. 155. See also Hewlett and Anderson, *The New World* p. 565.

17. For an example, see Bundy, *op. cit.*, chapters II and IV.

18. On the 1944 discussions, see Margaret Gowing, *Britain and Atomic Energy: 1939-1946* (New York: St. Martin's Press, 1964), pp. 347-360.

19. See Bundy, *op.cit.*, pp. 214-219.

20. The possibilities or impossibility of avoiding H-bomb development are outlined in Herbert York, *The Advisors* (San Francisco, CA: W.H. Freeman, 1976), and are reviewed by John Lewis Gaddis, *We Now Know* (Oxford: Clarendon Press, 1997), p. 101.

21. Richard Rhodes, *Dark Sun* (New York: Simon and Schuster, 1995), pp. 54, 74,107, 163.

22. An illustration of such pessimism about post-Cold War nuclear disarmament can be found in Michael Quinlan, "British Nuclear Weapons Policy: Past, Present and Future," in John C. Hopkins and Weixing Hu (eds.) *Strategic Views From the Second Tier* (San Diego: University of California Institute on Global Conflict and Cooperation, 1994), pp. 125-140.

23. On this point, see Gaddis, *op. cit.* pp. 96-98. See also David Holloway, *Stalin and the Bomb* (New Haven, CT: Yale University Press, 1994), pp. 127-132, and Richard Rhodes, *Dark Sun* pp. 177-178.

24. The accusation that such an assumption of the deterrability of Soviet leaders might be "ethnocentric" is made by John Ericson, "The Soviet View of Nuclear War," (Transcript of BBC radio broadcast, June 19, 1980).

25. For example, Richard Rhodes, *Dark Sun*, pp. 177-179.

26. Stephen D. Zaloga, *Target America* (Novato, CA: Presidio, 1993), pp. 50, 57, 68, Richard Rhodes, *Dark Sun,* p. 287, and Holloway, *Stalin and the Bomb*, p. 230.

27. *Ibid.* pp. 138-141.

28. On the TU-4, see Zaloga, *op. cit.*

29. Stalin quote cited in David Holloway, *The Soviet Union and the Arms Race* (New Haven, CT: Yale University Press, 1983), p. 20.

Chapter 10: Some Counter-Factual Speculations

1. Some possibilities of irritation being a part of nuclear deterrence are outlined in Martin Sherwin, *A World Destroyed* (New York: Alfred A. Knopf, 1975).

2. This would be the general analysis of the Cold War accepted by Herbert Feis, *From Trust to Terror* (New York: W.W. Norton, 1950).

3.   For an analysis by which the confrontation of nuclear weapons was actually a moderating factor in the Cold War, see John L. Gaddis, *The Long Peace* (New York: Oxford University Press, 1987).

4.   A more extended version of this author's analysis of this kind of question can be found in George H. Quester, "Nuclear Deterrence and Political Hostility" in Stephen J. Cimbala and Sidney R. Waldman (eds.), *Controlling and Ending Conflict* (New York: Greenwood Press, 1992), pp. 239-262.

5.   The French "all-azimuth" strategy was outlined and discussed by Charles Ailleret, "Defense Dirigee ou Defense Tous Azimuts?," *Revue de Defense Nationale* (December, 1967), pp. 1923-1932.

6.   On the U.S-.U.K. agreements as they were wound down, see John Simpson, *The Independent Nuclear State* (New York: St. Martin's Press, 1982), and Andrew Pierre, *Nuclear Politics* (London: Oxford University Press, 1972).

7.   The motives for British secrecy here are discussed in Margaret Gowing, *Independence and Deterrence* (London: Macmillan, 1974), pp. 179-185.

8.   On the Fuchs case and the American reactions, see Norman Moss, *Klaus Fuchs: The Man Who Stole the Atom Bomb* (London: Grafton, 1987).

9.   A useful analysis is provided in Kenneth Bourne, *The Balance of Power in North America* (Berkeley: University of California Press, 1967).

10.   On the post-1918 naval arms confrontation, see Harold and Margaret Sprout, *Toward a New Order of Sea Power* (London: Oxford University Press, 1943).

11.   See Ronald E. M. Irving, *The First Indo-China War* (London: Croon Helm, 1975).

12.   A very influential example has been Kenneth Waltz, *Theory of International Politics* (Reading, MA: Addison-Wesley, 1979).

13.   On the general Moscow endorsement of nuclear disarmament in the years of the American nuclear monopoly, see John W. Spanier and Joseph Nogee, *The Politics of Disarmament* (New York: Praeger, 1962).

14.   The logic of the "democratic peace" is broken out in Bruce M. Russett, *Grasping the Democratic Peace* (Princeton, NJ: Princeton University Press, 1993) and Michael Doyle "Kant, Liberal Legacies and Foreign Affairs," *Philosophy and Public Affairs* Vol. 1, Nos. 3,4 (Summer, Fall, 1983), pp. 205-235, 323-353.

15.   Samuel Huntington, "The Clash of Civilizations?," *Foreign Affairs* Vol. 72, No. 3 (Summer, 1993), pp. 22-49.

16.   For a variety of skeptical arguments about whether democratic countries are really so sure to stay at peace with each other, see Christopher Layne, "Kant or Cant: The Myth of the Democratic Peace," *International Security* Vol. 19, No. 2 (Fall, 1994), pp. 5-49, and David E. Spiro, "The Insignificance of the Liberal Peace," *International Security* Vol. 19, No. 2 (Fall, 1994), pp. 50-86.

17.   On Yeltsin's announcements, see Steven E. Miller, "Dismantling the Edifice: Strategic Nuclear Weapons in the Post-Soviet Era," in Charles

Hermann (ed.), *American Defense Annual 1994* (New York: Lexington Books, 1994), pp. 65-83.

18. ˙Conflicting views of the competence, and motivation, of the German nuclear physicists can be found in Robert Jungk, *Brighter Than a Thousand Suns* (New York: Harcourt Brace, 1958), and Samuel Goudsmit, *Alsos* (New York: A. Schuman, 1947).

19. On "Aryan physics," see Mark Walker, *Nazi Science* (New York: Plenum Press, 1995).

20. Conflicting views of who should get the credit for breaking the U.S. nuclear weapons monopoly are outlined in Richard Rhodes, *Dark Sun* (New York: Simon and Schuster, 1995), chapter 3.

21. An example of this kind of interpretation can be found in Frederick Schuman, *The Cold War: Retrospect and Prospect* (Baton Rouge: Louisiana State University Press, 1967).

22. On the necessity or non-necessity of these bombings, see Major General S. Woodburn Kirby, *The Surrender of Japan* Vol. 5 of *The War Against Japan* (London: H.M.S.O., 1969), and Stephen Harper, *Miracle of Deliverance* (London: Sidgwick and Jackson, 1985).

23. Japanese plans to resist amphibious landings are discussed in John Ray Skates, *The Invasion of Japan: Alternative to the Bomb* (Columbia: University of South Carolina Press, 1994. See also Robert C. Butow, *Japan's Decision to Surrender* (Stanford, CA: Stanford University Press, 1954). For a conflicting view, see Leon Sigal, *Fighting to a Finish* (Ithaca, NY: Cornell University Press, 1988).

24. Gar Alperovitz, *Atomic Diplomacy* (New York: Simon and Schuster, 1965).

25. On the reactions to the Bikini test, see David Bradley, *No Place to Hide* (Boston: Little Brown, 1948).

26. Stalin's investments in quantity production of the TU-4 copy of the B-29 are discussed in Steven J. Zaloga, *Target America* (Novato, CA: Presidio, 1993), pp. 72-79.

27. Albert Wohlstetter et. al., *Selection and Use of Strategic Air Bases* (Santa Monica, California: RAND Corporation R-266 April, 1954).

28. The post-1949 interactions of nuclear forces are covered well in Michael Sherry, *The Rise of American Air Power* (New Haven, CT: Yale University Press, 1987).

29. On the increase in U.S. nuclear weapons production, see David Alan Rosenberg, "The Origins of Overkill," *International Security,* Vol. 7, No. 4 (Spring, 1983), pp. 3-71.

30. Albert Wohlstetter, "The Delicate Balance of Terror," *Foreign Affairs* Vol. 37 No 2 (January, 1959), pp. 211-234.

31. Joel Larus, *Nuclear Weapons Safety and the Common Defense* (Columbus: Ohio State University Press, 1967), pp. 46-47.

32. See Avi Shlaim, *The United States and the Berlin Blockade* (Berkeley: University of California press, 1983).

33. David Holloway, *Stalin and the Bomb* (New Haven, CT: Yale University Press, 1994), chapters 7, 8, pp. 244-245.
34. The overall continuing Soviet air threat to the United States is surveyed in Zaloga, *op. cit.*
35. Rodney A. Burden (et. al.) *Falklands: The Air War* (New York: Sterling Publishing Co., 1986).
36. On the Japanese calculated gamble in attacking in 1941, see Herbert Feis, *The Road to Pearl Harbor* (Princeton, NJ: Princeton University Press, 1950).

Chapter 11: The Belated Non-Proliferation Barrier

1. Explanations for the purpose of British nuclear forces are discussed in Andrew Pierre, *Nuclear Politics* (London: Oxford University Press, 1970), and John Baylis, *Anglo-American Defense Relations* (New York: St. Martin's Press, 1981).
2. The French arguments for a separate nuclear force are outlined in David Yost, *France's Deterrent Posture and Security In Europe* (London: IISS Adelphi Papers #184-185, 1984-1985).
3. The texts of the Partial Test-Ban Treat and of the Nuclear Non-Proliferation Treaty can be found reprinted as appendices in William Epstein, *The Last Chance* (New York: Free Press, 1976), pp. 296-298, 316-321.
4. For reported inquiries to the USSR about the acceptability of an American preemption of Chinese nuclear weapons acquisition, see *The New York Times* (October 2, 1964), p. 3.
5. Fears of a Soviet attack on China's nuclear capability are noted in Litai Xue, "Evolution of China"s Nuclear Strategy," in John C. Hopkins and Weixing Hu (eds.), *Strategic Views From the Second Tier* (San Diego: University of California Institute on Global Conflict and Cooperation, 1994), p. 181.
6. Some additional discussion of this kind of suggestion can be found in James Mann, *About Face* (New York: Alfred A. Knopf, 1999), p. 20.
7. The Chinese "no-first-use" policy is discussed in Jonathan Pollack, "The Future of China's Nuclear Weapons Policy," in Hopkins and Hu, ibid., pp. 157-165.
8. On Soviet rumblings about severe reactions to any West German moves toward nuclear weapons, see Roman Kolkowicz et al., *The Soviet Union and Arms Control: A Superpower Dilemma* (Baltimore, MD: Johns Hopkins University press, 1970), pp. 70-115.
9. The evolution of the NPT is outlined in Lewis Dunn, *Controlling the Bomb* (New Haven, CT: Yale University Press, 1982).
10. The anti-nuclear thrust of the air war against Iraq is noted in Michael J. Mazarr, Don M. Snider, and James Blackwell, *Desert Storm: The Gulf War and What We Learned* (Boulder, CO: Westview, 1993).

11.   On the interactions here, see Margaret Gowing, *Independence and Deterrence* (London: Macmillan, 1974), pp. 210, 217, and McGeorge Bundy, *Danger and Survival* (New York: Random House, 1988), pp. 463-472.

Chapter 12: Some Conclusions

1.   For an illustration of such arguments, see Jonathan Schell, *The Abolition* (New York: Alfred A. Knopf, 1984).
2.   An elaborated statement of the case that deep cuts in nuclear force totals would increase crisis instability can be found in George Quester and Victor Utgoff, "U.S. Arms Reductions and Nuclear Proliferation; The Counterproductive Possibilities," in Brad Roberts (ed.), *U.S. Security in an Uncertain Era* (Cambridge, MA: MIT Press, 1993), pp. 291-307.
3.   Bernard Brodie, *War and Politics* (New York: Macmillan, 1973), p. 380.
4.   See Scott Sagan, *The Limits of Safety* (Princeton, NJ: Princeton University Press, 1993).
5.   Additional analyses of the ties between democracy and the initiation of war can be found in John M. Owen. "How Liberalism Produces Democratic Peace," *International Security* Vol. 19, No. 2 (Fall, 1994), pp. 87-125.
6.   For examples of a belief in such power of example, see William Epstein, *The Last Chance* (New York: Free Press, 1976).
7.   A very useful analysis of the interaction of Brazil and Argentina is provided by John Redick, *Military Potential of Latin American Nuclear Energy Programs* (Beverly Hills, CA: Sage, 1972).
8.   On India and Pakistan, see George Percovich, "A Nuclear Third Way in Asia," *Foreign Policy* No. 91 (Summer, 1993), pp. 85-104.
9.   The Iraqi nuclear threat is outlined in David Albright and Mark Hibbs, "Iraq's Quest for the Nuclear Grail: What Can We Learn?," *Arms Control Today* Vol. 22, No. 6 (July/August, 1992), pp. 3-11.
10.   On North Korean nuclear prospects, see Peter Hayes, *Pacific Powderkeg* (Lexington, MA: Lexington Books, 1991).
11.   John E. Mueller, *Retreat From Doomsday: The Obsolescence of Major War* (New York: Basic Books, 1989).
12.   See Robert Jervis, "The Political Effects of Nuclear Weapons," *International Security* Vol. 13, No. 2 (Fall, 1988), pp. 80-90, and Carl Kaysen, "Is War Obsolete?" *International Security* Vol. 14, No. 4 (Spring, 1990), pp. 42-64.
13.   Mueller, *op.cit.* pp. 64-71.
14.   For contending interpretations of the explanation for the end of the Cold War, see Ralph Summy and Michael E. Salla (eds.) *Why the Cold War Ended* (Westport, CT: Greenwood Press, 1995), and Godfried Van Benthem van den Bergh (ed.), *The Nuclear Revolution and the End of the Cold War* (London: Macmillan, 1992).

15. The possibilities of a greater "transparency" with the spread of democracy are discussed in John M. Owen, *op. cit.*

16. See, for example, Richard Betts, "Systems for Peace or Causes of War," *International Security* Vol. 17, No. 1 (Summer, 1992), pp. 5-43.

17. On the troublesome "dual-use" nature of nuclear technology, and other technologies, see William C. Potter, *Nuclear Power and Nonproliferation* (Cambridge, MA: Oelgeschlager, Gunn and Hain, 1982).

18. For speculation on the possibilities of a global nuclear force, see Richard Garwin, "Nuclear Weapons for the United Nations," and Vitalii Goldanskii and Stanislov Rodionov, "An International Nuclear Security Force," in Joseph Rotblat, Jack Steinberger and Bhalchandra Udgaonkar (eds.), *A Nuclear-Weapon-Free World: Desirable? Feasible?* (Boulder, CO: Westview, 1993), pp. 169-180, 181-190.

Bibliography

Acheson, Dean, *Present at the Creation* (New York: W.W. Norton, 1969).

Ailleret, Charles, "Defense Dirigee ou Defense Tous Azimuts?," *Revue de Defense Nationale* (December, 1967) pp. 1923-1932.

Albertini, Luigi, *The Origins of the War of 1914* (London: Oxford University Press, 1952).

Albright, David and Mark Hibbs, "Iraq's Quest for the Nuclear Grail: What Can We Learn?," *Arms Control Today* Vol. 22, No. 6 (July/August, 1992) pp. 3-11.

Allison, Roy, *Military Forces in the Soviet Successor States* (London: IISS Adelphi Papers No. 280, 1993).

Alperovitz, Gar, *Atomic Diplomacy* (New York: Vintage, 1965).

Alsop, Joseph and Stewart, *We Accuse! The Story of the Miscarriage of American Justice in the Case of J. Robert Oppenheimer* (New York: Simon and Schuster, 1954).

Ambrose, Stephen E., *Rise to Globalism* (New York: Penguin Books, 1971).

Amrine, Michael, *The Great Decision* (New York: Putnam, 1959.

Arnott, Peter, *The Romans and Their World* (New York: Macmillan, 1970).

Ballard, Jack Stokes, *The Shock of Peace* (Washington, DC: University Press of America, 1983).

Baucom, Donald R., *The Origins of SDI* (Lawrence: University Press of Kansas, 1992).

Baylis, John, *Anglo-American Defense Relations* (New York: St. Martin's Press, 1981).

Beaton, Leonard, *Must the Bomb Spread?* (Hammondsworth: Penguin Books, 1966).

Bee, Ronald J., *Nuclear Proliferation: The Post-Cold War Challenge* (New York: Foreign Policy Association, 1995).

Van Benthem van den Bergh, Godfried,(ed.), *The Nuclear Revolution and the End of the Cold War* (London: Macmillan, 1992).

Betts, Richard, "Collective Security, Arms Control and the New Europe," *International Security* Vol. 17, No. 1 (Summer, 1992) pp. 5-43.

Betts, Richard, *Nuclear Blackmail and Nuclear Balance* (Washington, DC: Brookings, 1987).

Betts, Richard, *Surprise Attack* (Washington: Brookings, 1982).

Betts, Richard, "Systems for Peace or Causes of War," *International Security* Vol. 17, No. 1 (Summer, 1992) pp. 5-43.

Beyerschin, Alan, *Scientists Under Hitler* (New Haven, CT: Yale University Press, 1977).

Blackett, P.M.S., *Fear, War and the Bomb* (New York: McGraw-Hill, 1948).

Blair, Bruce, *The Logic of Accidental Nuclear War* (Washington, DC: Brookings, 1993).

Blechman, Barry M., and Douglas M. Hart, "Afghanistan and the 1946 Iran Analogy," *Survival* Vol. 22 No. 6 (November/December, 1980) pp. 248-257.

Bourne, Kenneth, *The Balance of Power in North America* (Berkeley: University of California Press, 1967).

Borden, William B., *There Will Be No Time* (New York: Macmillan 1946).

Borowski, Harry R., *A Hollow Threat* (Westport, Conn.: Greenwood Press, 1982).

Bradley, David, *No Place to Hide* (Boston: Little Brown, 1948).

Brennan, Donald (et. al.), *Anti-Ballistic Missile, Yes or No?* (New York: Hill and Wang, 1968).

Brenner, Michael J., *Nuclear Power and Non-Proliferation* (New York: Cambridge University Press, 1981).

Brodie, Bernard (ed.), *The Absolute Weapon* (New York: Harcourt Brace, 1946).

Brodie, Bernard, *War and Politics* (New York: Macmillan, 1973).

Brown, Anthony Cave, *Dropshot: The American Plans for World War III with Russia in 1957* (New York: Dial Press, 1978).

Brown, Michael, *Flying Blind* (Ithaca: Cornell University Press, 1992).

Brooks, Lester, *Behind Japan's Surrender* (New York: McGraw-Hill, 1967).

Burden, Rodney A.(et. al.), *Falklands: The Air War* (New York: Sterling Publishing Co., 1986).

Bush, Vannevar, *Modern Arms and Free Men* (New York: Simon and Schuster, 1949).

Bush, Vannevar, *Pieces of the Action* (New York: William Morrow, 1970).

Butow, Robert, *Japan's Decision to Surrender* (Stanford, CA: Stanford University Press, 1954).

Bundy, McGeorge, *Danger and Survival* (New York: Random House, 1988).

Bushire, Russell D., and William Christopher Hamel, "War for Peace: The Question of American Preventive War Against the Soviet Union," *Diplomatic History* Vol. 14 No. 3 (Summer, 1990) pp. 367-389.

Cimbala, Stephen J., and Sidney R. Waldman (eds.), *Controlling and Ending Conflict* (New York: Greenwood Press, 1992).

Cingranelli, David Louis, *Ethics, American Foreign Policy and the Third World* (New York: St. Martin's, 1993).

Clark, Ronald William, *The Life of Bertrand Russell* (London: Jonathan Cape, 1975).

Claude,Inis, *Power and International Relations* (New York: Random House, 1962).

Von Clausewitz, Karl, *On War* (Princeton, NJ: Princeton University Press, 1984).

Clodfelter, Mark, *The Limits of Air Power* (New York: Free Press, 1989).

Coffey, Thomas, *Iron Eagle: The Turbulent Life of General Curtis LeMay* (New York: Crown, 1986).

Crabb, Cecil V., *Invitation to Struggle* (Washington, DC: Congressional Quarterly Press, 1980).

Craven, Wesley, and H. L. Cate, *The Army Air Force in World War II*, (Chicago: University of Chicago Press, 1948-1958).

Daalder,Ivo, *The Nature and Practice of Flexible Response* (New York: Columbia University Press, 1991).

Dallek, Robert, *The American Style of Foreign Policy* (New York: Alfred A. Alfred A. Knopf, 1983).

Davidson, W. Philips, *The Berlin Blockade* (Princeton, NJ: Princeton University Press, 1958).

Davis, Noell Pharr, *Lawrence and Oppenheimer* (New York: Simon and Schuster, 1968).

Dinerstein, Herbert, *War and the Soviet Union* (New York: Praeger, 1962).

Douhet,Giulio, *The Command of the Air* (New York: Coward-McCann, 1942).

Dower,John W., *War Without Mercy* (New York: Pantheon, 1986).

Doyle, Michael, "Kant, Liberal Legacies and Foreign Affairs," *Philosophy and Public Affairs* Vol. 1, Nos. 3,4 (Summer, Fall, 1983) pp. 205-235, 323-353.

Doyle, Michael, "Liberalism and World Politics," *American Political Science Review* Vol. 80, No. 4 (December, 1986) pp. 1151-1169.

Duke, Simon, *U.S. Defense Bases in the United Kingdom* (London: Macmillan, 1987).

Dunn, Lewis, *Controlling the Bomb* (New Haven, CT: Yale University Press, 1982).

Epstein, William, *The Last Chance* (New York: Free Press, 1976).

Evangelista, Matthew, "Stalin's Postwar Army Reappraised," *International Security* Vol. 7, No. 3 (Winter, 1982-1983) pp. 110-138.

Feinberg, Barry, *Bertrand Russell's America* (New York: Viking Press, 1974).

Feis, Herbert, *From Trust to Terror* (New York: W.W. Norton, 1950).

Feis, Herbert, *Japan Subdued* (Princeton, NJ: Princeton University Press).

Feis, Herbert, *The Road to Pearl Harbor* (Princeton, NJ: Princeton University Press, 1950).

Foner, Philip S., and Richard Winchester (eds.), *The Anti-Imperialist Reader* (New York: Holmes and Meier, 1984).

Foster,Richard B., "On Prolonged Nuclear war," *International Security Review* Vol. 6, No 4 (Winter 1981-82) pp. 497-518.

Foster, Richard B., *The Soviet Concept of National Entity Survival* (Arlington, VA: SRI International, 1978).

Futrell, Robert F., *The United States Air Force in Korea: 1950-1953* (Washington, DC/New York: Duell, Sloan and Pierce, 1961).

Gaddis, John Lewis, *The Long Peace* (New York: Oxford University Press, 1987).

Gaddis, John Lewis, *We Now Know* (Oxford: Clarendon Press, 1997).

Gallois, Pierre, *The Balance of Terror* (Boston: Houghton Mifflin, 1961).

Garthoff, Raymond, *Soviet Military Doctrine* (Glencoe, IL: Free Press, 1953).

Gavin, James, *War and Peace in the Space Age* (New York: Harpers, 1958).

Gerber, Larry G., "The Baruch Plan and the Emergence of the Cold War," *Diplomatic History* Vol. 6, No. 1 (Spring, 1982) pp. 69-95.

Gilpin, Robert, *American Scientists and Nuclear Weapons Policy* (Princeton, NJ: Princeton University Press, 1962).

Goudsmit, Samuel, *Alsos* (New York: A. Schuman, 1947).

Gowing, Margaret, *Britain and Atomic Energy* (London: Macmillan, 1964).

Gowing, Margaret, *Independence and Deterrence* (New York: St. Martin's Press, 1974).

Gray, Colin, *Nuclear Strategy and National Style* (Lanham, MD: Hamilton Press, 1980).

Graybar, Lloyd J., "Bikini Revisited," *Military Affairs* Vol. 4, No. 3 (October, 1980) pp. 118-123.

Groves, Leslie, *Now It Can Be Told* (New York: DaCapo, 1962).

Halperin, Morton, *Limited War in the Nuclear Age* (New York: Wiley, 1963).

Hammond, Thomas I. (ed.) *The Anatomy of Communist Takeovers* (New Haven, CT: Yale University Press, 1975).

Hampson, Fen Osler, "Groping for Technical Panaceas: The European Conventional Balance and Nuclear Stability," *International Security* Vol. 8, No. 3 (Winter 1983-1984) pp. 57-82.

Harbutt, Fraser, *The Iron Curtain: Churchill, America, and the Origins of the Cold War* (New York: Oxford University Press, 1986).

Harper, Stephen, *Miracle of Deliverance* (London: Sidgwick and Jackson, 1985).

Hayes, Peter, *Pacific Powderkeg* (Lexington, MA: Lexington Books, 1991).

Hein, Laura, and Mark Selden (eds.), *Living With the Bomb* (Armonk, NY: M.E. Sharpe, 1997).

Helmreich, Jonathan, *Gathering Rare Ores* (Princeton, NJ: Princeton University Press, 1986).

Herken, Gregg, *The Winning Weapon* (New York: Alfred A. Alfred A. Knopf, 1980).

Hewlett, Richard C., and Oscar E. Anderson, *The New World 1939-1946* (University Park: Pennsylvania State University Press, 1962).

Hinsley, F. J., *Power and the Pursuit of Peace* (New York: Cambridge University Press, 1963).

Holloway, David, *The Soviet Union and the Arms Race* (New Haven, CT: Yale University Press, 1983).

Holloway, David, *Stalin and the Bomb* (New Haven, CT: Yale University Press, 1994).

Hopkins, John C., and Weixing Hu (eds.) *Strategic Views From the Second Tier* (San Diego: University of California Institute on Global Conflict and Cooperation, 1994).

Horelick, Arnold F., and Myron Rush, *Strategic Power and Soviet Foreign Policy* (Chicago, University of Chicago Press, 1966).

Horowitz, Irving Louis, *The Idea of War and Peace in Contemporary Philosophy* (New York: Paine Whitman, 1957).

Hoyt, Edwin P., *Japan's War* (New York: McGraw-Hill, 1986).

Huntington, Samuel, "The Clash of Civilizations?," *Foreign Affairs* Vol. 72, No. 3 (Summer, 1993) pp. 22-49.

Huntington, Samuel, *The Common Defense* (New York: Columbia University Press, 1961).

Hyde, H. M., *The Atom Bomb Spies* (New York: Ballantine, 1981).

Irving, David, *The Destruction of Dresden* (New York: Holt, Rinehart and Winston, 1964).

Irving, David, *The German Atomic Bomb* (New York: Simon and Schuster, 1968).

Irving, Ronald E. M., *The First Indo-China War* (London: Croom Helm, 1975).

Jervis, Robert, *The Illogic of American Nuclear Strategy* (Ithaca, NY: Cornell University Press, 1984).

Jervis, Robert, *The Meaning of the Nuclear Revolution* (Ithaca, NY: Cornell University Press, 1989).

Jervis, Robert, "The Political Effects of Nuclear Weapons," *International Security* Vol. 13, No. 2 (Fall, 1988) pp. 80-90.

Jungk, Robert, *Brighter Than a Thousand Suns* (New York: Harcourt Brace, 1958).

Kaplan, Karel, *The Short March* (New York: St. Martin's Press, 1987).

Kaysen, Carl, "Is War Obsolete?," *International Security* Vol. 14, No. 4 (Spring, 1990) pp. 42-64.

Kaufmann, William W. (ed.), *Military Policy and National Security* (Princeton, NJ: Princeton University Press, 1956).

Kennan, George F. ("X"), "The Sources of Soviet Conduct," *Foreign Affairs* Vol. 25, No. 4 (July, 1947) pp. 566-582.

Kennedy, Paul, *The Rise and Fall of British Naval Power* (New York: Charles Scribner's Sons, 1976).

Kirby, Major General S. Woodburn, *The Surrender of Japan* Vol. 5 of *The War Against Japan* (London: H.M.S.O., 1969).

Kolko, Gabriel, *Confronting the Third World* (New York: Pantheon, 1980).

Kolkowicz, Roman et al., *The Soviet Union and Arms Control: A Superpower Dilemma* (Baltimore, MD: Johns Hopkins University Press, 1970).

Kuniholm, Bruce, *The Origins of the Cold War in the Middle East* (Princeton, NJ: Princeton University Press, 1980).

Langer, William, and S. Everett Gleason, *The Undeclared War* (New York: Harper, 1953).

Larus, Joel, *Nuclear Weapons Safety and the Common Defense* (Columbus: Ohio State University Press, 1967).

Layne, Christopher, "Kant or Cant: The Myth of the Democratic Peace," *International Security* Vol. 19, No. 2 (Fall, 1994) pp.5-49.

Lebow, Richard Ned, "Windows of Opportunity: Do States Jump Through Them?," *International Security* Vol. 9, No. 1 (Summer, 1984) pp. 147-180.

Legro, Jeffrey, *Cooperation Under Fire* (Ithaca, NY: Cornell University Press, 1995).

Lenczowksi, George, *American Presidents and the Middle East* (Durham, NC: Duke University Press, 1990).

Lilienthal, David E., *The Atomic Energy Years* (New York: Harper and Row, 1965).

Mahan, Alfred Thayer, *The Influence of Sea Power Upon History* (Boston: Little Brown, 1890).

Manchester, William, *American Caesar* (Boston: Little Brown, 1978).

Mann, James, *About Face* (New York: Alfred A. Alfred A. Knopf, 1999).

Mansfield, Edward D., and Jack Snyder, "Democratization and the Danger of War," *International Security* Vol. 20, No. 1 (Summer, 1995) pp. 5-38.

Mazarr, Michael M., *North Korea and the Bomb* (New York: St. Martins Press, 1995).

Mazarr, Michael, and Alexander T. Lennon (eds.) *Toward a Nuclear Peace* (New York: St. Martin's Press, 1994).

Mazarr, Michael J., Don M. Snider, and James Blackwell, *Desert Storm: The Gulf War and What We Learned* (Boulder, CO: Westview, 1993).

McCormick, James M., *American Foreign Policy and American Values* (Itasca, IL: F. E. Peacock Publishers, 1985).

McNamara, Robert S., "The Military Role of Nuclear Weapons," *Foreign Affairs* Vol. 62, No. 1 (Fall, 1983) pp. 57-80.

Medaris, John, *Countdown for Decision* (New York: Putnam, 1960).

Meyer, Stephen M., "How the Threat (and the Coup) Collapsed," *International Security* Vol. 16 No. 3 (Winter 1991-1992) pp. 5-38.

Mikheev, Dimitri, *The Soviet Perspective on the Strategic Defense Initiative* (Washington, DC: Pergamon-Brassey's, 1987).

Miller, Steven E., "Dismantling the Edifice: Strategic Nuclear Weapons in the Post-Soviet Era," in Charles Hermann (ed.), *American Defense Annual 1994* (New York: Lexington Books, 1994) pp. 65-83.

Millet, Stephen M., "The Capabilities of the American Nuclear Deterrent: 1945-1950," *Aerospace Historian* Vol. 27, No. 1 Spring, 1980) pp. 27-32.

Montgomery, John D., *Forced to be Free* (Chicago: University of Chicago Press, 1957).

Morgan, Thomas, *Atomic Energy and Congress* (Ann Arbor: University of Michigan Press, 1956).

Morgenthau, Hans, *Politics Among Nations* (New York: Alfred A. Knopf, 1967).

Morgenstern, Oskar, *The Question of National Defense* (New York: Random House, 1958).

Moss, Norman, *Klaus Fuchs: The Man Who Stole the Atom Bomb* (London: Grafton, 1987).

Moss, Norman, *Men Who Play God* (New York: Harper and Row, 1968).

Mueller, John E., *Retreat From Doomsday: The Obsolescence of Major War* (New York: Basic Books, 1989).

Murphy, Charles J.V., "The Hidden Struggle for the H-Bomb" *Fortune* Vol. X., No. 5 (May, 1953).

Nogee, Joseph, *Soviet Policy Towards International Control of Atomic Energy* (Notre Dame, IN: University of Notre Dame Press, 1961).

Nordlinger, Eric, *Isolationism Reconfigured* (Princeton, NJ: Princeton University Press, 1995).

Osgood, Robert E., *Limited War: The Challenge to American Strategy* (Chicago: University of Chicago Press, 1957).

Owen, John M., "How Liberalism Produces Democratic Peace," *International Security* Vol. 19, No. 2 (Fall, 1994) pp. 87-125.

Pape, Robert, *Bombing to Win* (Ithaca, NY: Cornell University Press, 1996).

Parenti, Michael, *The Sword and the Dollar* (New York: St. Martin's Press, 1989).

Paul, T. V., Richard Harknett and James J. Wirtz (eds.), *The Absolute Weapon Revisited* (Ann Arbor: University of Michigan Press, 1998).

Payne, Keith B., *Strategic Defense: "Star Wars" in Perspective* (Lanham, MD: Hamilton Press, 1985).

Percovich, George, "A Nuclear Third Way in Asia," *Foreign Policy* No. 91 (Summer, 1993) pp. 85-104.

Pierre, Andrew, *Nuclear Politics* (London: Oxford University Press, 1972).

Pipes, Richard, *Russia Observed* (Boulder, CO: Westview, 1989).

Pipes, Richard, *Russia Under the Bolshevik Regime* (New York: Charles Scribner's Sons, 1974).

Pipes, Richard, "Why the Soviet Union Thinks It Could Fight and Win a Nuclear War," *Commentary* Vol. 64, No. 1 (July, 1977) pp. 21-34.

Potter, William C., *Nuclear Power and Nonproliferation* (Cambridge, MA: Oelgeschlager, Gunn and Hain, 1982).

Poundstone, William, *Prisoner's Dilemma* (New York: Doubleday, 1993).

Powers, Thomas, *Heisenberg's War* (New York: Alfred A. Knopf, 1993).

Prados, John, *The Soviet Estimate* (New York: Dial Press, 1982).

Quester, George, "On the Identification of Real and Pretended Communist Military Doctrine," *Journal of Conflict Resolution* Vol. X, No. 2 (June, 1966) pp. 172-179.

Quigg, Philip, *America the Dutiful* (New York: Simon and Schuster, 1971).

Radosh, Ronald, and Joyce Milton, *The Rosenberg File* (New York: Vintage Books, 1984).

Radzinsky, Edvard *Stalin* (New York: Doubleday, 1996).

Redick, John *Military Potential of Latin American Nuclear Energy Programs* (Beverly Hills, CA: Sage, 1972).

Reiners, Ludwig, *The Lamps Went Out in Europe* (New York: Pantheon, 1955).

Rhodes, Richard, *Dark Sun* (New York: Simon and Schuster, 1995).

Rhodes, Richard, *The Making of the Atomic Bomb* (New York: Simon and Schuster, 1988).

Richards, Denis, *Royal Air Force 1939-1945* (London: H.M.S.O., 1953).

Roberts, Brad (ed.), *U.S. Security in an Uncertain Era* (Cambridge, MA: MIT Press, 1993).

Rosenberg, David Alan, "American Atomic Strategy and the Hydrogen Bomb Decision," *Journal of American History* Vol. 66, No. 1 (June, 1979) pp. 62-88.

Rosenberg, David Alan, "The Origins of Overkill," *International Security* Vol. 7, No. 4 (Spring, 1983) pp. 3-71.

Rosenberg, David Alan, "U.S. Nuclear Stockpile, 1945 to 1950," *Bulletin of the Atomic Scientists* Vol. 38, No. 5 (May, 1982) pp. 25-30.

Rotblat, Joseph, Jack Steinberger, and Bhalchandra Udgaonkar (eds.), *A Nuclear Weapons-Free World: Desirable?, Feasible?* (Boulder, CO: Westview, 1993).

Russett, Bruce, *Grasping the Democratic Peace* (Princeton, NJ: Princeton University Press, 1993).

Sagan, Scott, *The Limits of Safety* (Princeton, NJ: Princeton University Press, 1993).

Scheinman, Lawrence, *Atomic Energy Policy in France Under the Fourth Republic* (Princeton, NJ: Princeton University Press, 1965).

Schell, Jonathan, *The Abolition* (New York: Alfred A. Knopf, 1984).

Schelling, Thomas C., *Arms and Influence* (New Haven, CT: Yale University Press, 1966).

Schelling, Thomas C., and Morton Halperin, *Strategy and Arms Control* (New York: Twentieth-Century Fund, 1961).

Schilling, Warner, Paul Y. Hammond and Glenn Snyder, *Strategies, Politics and Defense Budgets* (New York: Columbia University Press, 1962).

Schmitt, Berndadotte, *The Coming of the War: 1914* (New York: Scribners, 1930).

Schuman, Frederick, *The Cold War: Retrospect and Prospect* (Baton Rouge: Louisiana State University Press, 1967).

Semmel, Bernard, *Liberalism and Naval Strategy* (Boston: Allen and Unwin, 1986).

Shepley, James R. and Clay B. Blair, *The Hydrogen Bomb* (New York: David McKay, 1954).

Sherry, Michael S., *Preparing for the Next War* (New Haven, CT: Yale University Press, 1977).

Sherry, Michael S., *The Rise of American Air Power* (New Haven, CT: Yale University Press, 1987).

Sherwin, Martin, *A World Destroyed* (New York: Alfred A. Knopf, 1975).

Shlaim, Avi, *The United States and the Berlin Blockade* (Berkeley: University of California Press, 1983).

Sigal, Leon, *Disarming Strangers: Nuclear Diplomacy with North Korea* (Princeton, NJ: Princeton University Press, 1998).

Sigal, Leon, *Fighting to a Finish* (Ithaca, NY: Cornell University Press, 1988).

Simpson, John, *The Independent Nuclear State* (New York: St. Martin's Press, 1983).

Skates, John Ray, *The Invasion of Japan: Alternative to the Bomb* (Columbia: University of South Carolina Press, 1994).

Skrine, C. P., *World War II in Iran* (London: Constable, 1962).

Smith, Perry McCoy, *The Air Force Plans for Peace* (Baltimore, MD: Johns Hopkins University Press, 1970).

Smyth, Henry Dewolf, *Atomic Energy for Military Purposes* (Princeton, NJ: Princeton University Press, 1946).

Snyder, Glenn, *Deterrence and Defense* (Princeton, NJ: Princeton University Press, 1961).

Spanier, John W. and Joseph Nogee, *The Politics of Disarmament* (New York: Praeger, 1962).

Spector, Leonard, *Going Nuclear* (Cambridge, MA: Ballinger, 1987).

Spiro, David E., "The Insignificance of the Liberal Peace," *International Security* Vol. 19, No. 2 (Fall, 1994) pp. 50-86.

Sprout, Harold and Margaret, *Toward a New Order of Sea Power* (London: Oxford University Press, 1943).

Steinberg, Jonathan, *Yesterday's Deterrent: Tirpitz and the Birth of the German Battle Fleet* (New York: Macmillan, 1965).

Summy, Ralph and Michael E. Salla (eds.) *Why the Cold War Ended* (Westport, CT: Greenwood Press, 1995).

Szilard, Leo, *Leo Szilard: His Version of the Facts* (Cambridge, MA: MIT Press, 1962).

Taylor, Maxwell, *The Uncertain Trumpet* (New York: Harper, 1960).

Trachtenberg, Marc, "A Wasting Asset: American Strategy and the Shifting Nuclear Balance 1949-1954," *International Security* Vol. 13, No. 3 (Winter 1988-1989).

Truman, Harry S., *Years of Trial and Hope* (Garden City, NY: Doubleday, 1965).

Trumbull, Robert, *Nine Who Survived Hiroshima and Nagasaki* (New York: Dutton, 1957).

Ulam, Adam B., *Dangerous Relations* (New York: Oxford University Press, 1983).

Ulam, Adam B., *Stalin: the Man and His Era* (New York: Viking, 1973).

Vincent, C. Paul, *The Politics of Hunger* (Athens: Ohio University Press, 1985).

Walker, Mark, *Nazi Science* (New York: Plenum Press, 1991).

Waltz, Kenneth, *Theory of International Politics* (Reading, MA: Addison-Wesley, 1979).

Weart, Spencer, *Nuclear Fear* (Cambridge, MA: Harvard University Press, 1988).

Webster, Charles and Noble Frankland, *The Strategic Air Offensive Against Germany* Vol. III. (London: H.M.S.O., 1961).

Wells, Samuel F., "Sounding the Tocsin: NSC-68 and the Soviet Threat," *International Security* Vol. 4, No. 2 (Fall, 1979) pp. 116-138.

Whaley, Barton, *Operation Barbarossa* (Cambridge, MA: MIT Press, 1973).

Wohlstetter, Albert, "The Delicate Balance of Terror," *Foreign Affairs* Vol. 37, No. 2, (January, 1959) pp. 211-234.

Wohlstetter, Albert (et. al.), *Selection and Use of Strategic Air Bases* (Santa Monica, CA: RAND Corporation R-266, April, 1954).

Wohlstetter, Roberta, *Pearl Harbor: Warning and Decision* (Stanford, CA: Stanford University Press, 1962).

York, Herbert, *The Advisors* (San Francisco, CA: W.H. Freeman, 1976).

Yost, David, *France's Deterrent Posture and Security in Europe* (London: IISS Adelphi Papers #184-185, 1984-1985).

Zaloga, Stephen D., *Target America* (Novato, CA: Presidio, 1993).

Index